Diary of a
Shy Backpacker

ii. Eye on the Prize

Bruce Spydar

Bruce Spydar

In my late 40s I began a journey of re-invention. A health scare, coupled with career-detonating regime change at work, forced me into a major life re-think.

Perhaps I had entered a fully blown mid-life crisis. I wasn't sure ... so I started writing about it, partly to re-engage with my long-lost creative side. Reflection was in itself cathartic for me, as I created my first publication *Crossing the Wilderness: Stepping through the midlife crisis.* As I wrote and searched for my own greater meaning and happiness, I immersed myself amongst the nature to be found close to my home. This inspired me, and led to the creation of a new mind model for happiness, as published in *Spydar's Web: How to Capture Happiness.*

Turning 50 passed by me almost unnoticed. Then, during a period of several months spent in hospital wards visiting my mother, often struggling for new topics of conversation, I realised that I had evolved over time into a really dull person. Half-a-life ago I was moderately interesting ... I played sport, I travelled, I was a romantic failure. But then I had settled down to a reasonably normal working life ... a settled job, a mortgage, a marriage and offspring, a timetable of responsibilities and absence of freedom.

This spurred me on to begin writing about those earlier days, re-imagining some of my previous adventures, albeit with a fading and selective memory. They begin with the *Diary of a Shy Backpacker: Awakening Down Under,* and continue here with *Diary of a Shy Backpacker: ii. Eye on the Prize.* I hope you enjoy reading them.

Diary of a Shy Backpacker:
i. Awakening Down Under

Review snippets ...

"*A saucy, fun, entertaining read which perfectly captures the backpacking experience.*"

"*Laugh-out-loud hilarious and an absolute must read!*"

"*From the opening question: "Will my life all be downhill from here?" I knew I was going to connect with this book.*"

"*Very entertaining ... I really enjoyed this book! Traveling with BJ on his journey down under had me Googling sites he'd seen and laughing with amusement as he shyly made his way through Australia.*"

"*I also thoroughly enjoyed the arguments he had with himself regarding his sexual frustrations which had me dying with laughter.*"

"*This book was not only extremely entertaining, it was insightful, heart-warming, and brilliantly written*"

"*I felt like I was there ...*"

"*I have never had a desire to visit Australia, but thanks to Bruce and his incredibly talented way with words, I have to say I see the appeal.*"

To my wife and daughter for their love and support, and for allowing me the freedom to re-explore all the baggage of my past.

Diary of a
Shy Backpacker
ii. Eye on the Prize

Bruce Spydar

Diary of a Shy Backpacker: ii. Eye on the Prize
© 2020 by Bruce Spydar.
All Rights Reserved.

Cover designed by Bruce Spydar.

ISBN-9798695220902

Roadmap

Introduction – The journey so far

[From Diary of a Shy Backpacker: Awakening Down Under]

After six weeks Down Under, I had just become as happy as I could ever remember. Back in England I had been isolated from friends, had no semblance of a love-life, was without employment and drifting with no sense of purpose. Today, life was so much brighter. It was a beautiful sunny day, and I had just rediscovered Suzanne, a wonderful girl, who I had first discovered and then lost over a month ago.

When I had set out from home on January 10th 1992, I was seeking adventure; searching for something new and exciting. Most exciting of all, my losing-streak with the fairer-sex seemed to be changing. Five sexually-charged liaisons with five different girls in five weeks ... all of which came out of the blue. This never happened to me ... this was more than my quota for the last five years.

Apart from this, in my six weeks in Australia, I had really had some tremendous experiences. In Darwin, I had experienced what heat exhaustion felt like, and had witnessed an old cowboy-style bar fight. I had observed life-and-death struggles of lizards vs. cockroaches, while my mind began to drift to erotic visions featuring two really hot, and rather kinky girls. And one of these dream-girls was now holding my hand, and we were kissing, while half-watching World Cup cricket at the MCG.

I saw a luxuriant oasis of green-and-blue suddenly turn to black-and-grey in a Kakadu storm. I had surprised a dingo at dawn, and feasted on goanna and green ants. I had suffered vertigo in a bubble-copter above the spectacular Katherine Gorge, and had seen the changing sunset hues at Uluru. I had found Uluru to be the perfect place to say 'Ding Dong!' and discovered that playing tonsil-hockey was a more than pleasant way of passing the time on a night bus across the desert.

In Townsville, I had encountered South America's answer to David Livingstone, while on Magnetic Island I discovered that a possum vs. a kookaburra is an even-money match. I had also found that the Superbowl was best served by a busty barmaid with a good hands-on grasp of Catholic doctrine and family values.

In Queensland, I had swum in crocodile-infested waters, and snorkelled amongst blue-stars on the Great Barrier Reef. I was still terrified of bungee-jumping, and also of inebriated, athletic, well-built German girls. In a Brisbane cinema, a Tassie-girl taught me a lesson or two about the pleasures of giving, while at Byron Bay I was uninspired by its lack of poetry.

Sydney proved to be a good place for an unexpected bar crawl with mates from back home, and its harbour-backdrop was truly a great scene, which lived up to its celebrity status ... unlike Canberra which lived up to its own billing for clinical dullness. It seems that despite Paul Keating and the republican movement, The Queen and Brits are, for now, still popular in Oz. Perhaps that will change if we win the Cricket World Cup.

And now I am in Melbourne. I am on the far side of the world and have just unexpectedly caught myself a Geordie-girl. It seems that when I dangle my rod Down Under there is a reasonable chance of a bite. I have no real insight yet as to where to dangle it ... but something REALLY is different out here.

A few more days in Melbourne, then next stop New Zealand.

Part I: Melbourne, Australia

Melbourne

Chapter 1: Bowled over ... Melbourne

Sunday 23 February – Melbourne

[First part of the day ... began in **Awakening Down Under**]

At last it was the day I had been waiting for. I had known for a while that the first day's matches were in Auckland and Perth, and that these were not on my itinerary, but finally I could now get to see the World Cup for real.

I was relaxed about not having bought a ticket. There was no way that the largest cricket stadium in the world, the Melbourne Cricket Ground, with a capacity in the order of 90,000 seats, was going to be a sell-out. Although this was the World Cup, this was Pakistan against the West Indies in the first group match ... it was not Australia in the final.

I grabbed a couple of croissants and a coffee for breakfast at the hostel, and then, at around 9:30am, full of excitement and expectation, I set off on foot in the direction of the MCG.

Although it was not England playing, for me this was the next best thing. In football there is a saying that everyone's second favourite team is Brazil. Over many years the Brazilian style of play was so attractive, attacking and laid-back ... and they also won a lot. In cricket the equivalent was the West Indies. They had won the first two World Cups and, for a decade or more, they were arguably the best team in the world. Despite having fallen a little from those dizzy-heights, they still had the swashbuckling, cavalier style of play, that would see them play brilliantly one day, and diabolically the next. The 1992 squad contained a few big stars and match-winners such as Richardson, Haynes, Ambrose and Lara, but they rather lacked strength in depth.

By around 10:00am I stood outside the MCG, queueing to get in. There were not huge numbers of people, low-thousands probably, but certainly a few hundred maroon shirts of the West Indies, and similar numbers of the lime-green shirts of Pakistan.

As I expected, it was no problem acquiring a ticket, and only paying face value for it, rather than the inflated prices that some re-sellers and touts get away with. Alongside the ticket, I purchased a programme, and then entered the ground.

My ticket gave me a seat with a fine view from the western end of the Southern Stand. I was in the bottom tier, on the end of a row, about twenty rows back from the pitch. It was a pretty good spot, with a good view of the pitch and scoreboard, and a lovely trap for the warmth of the morning sun.

It was at about 10:45am that Richie Richardson and Imran Khan, the two captains, came out for the coin toss. Richardson won and then elected to field.

By around 11:30, Richardson's decision to field first looked as though it might have been a poor one. Rameez Raja and Aamer Sohail, the Pakistan openers, had seen off the new-ball blitz from Marshall and Ambrose, and were getting into their stride. The crowd, thinly-spread around the massive ground, politely applauded the odd boundary, and also at each change of over ... but everyone was anticipating a greater adrenalin rush as the game really got going.

Suddenly, I felt a tap on my shoulder. I turned around.

"Hi BJ! ... Do we still have a date?"

Adrenalin rush. *Fuck me! ...*

The feelings that shot through me within the next two seconds were an indescribable mix of heart-stopping shock, elation and adrenalin. It was Suzanne ... wide-eyed, smiling, and looking drop-dead gorgeous.

"Well BJ, do we still have a date?" she repeated.

I was stunned ... shocked ... totally lost for words. I had been dreaming of her so much over the last few weeks.

Was this a dream?

I couldn't speak ... and my legs had turned to jelly. Somehow, I rose to my feet and stumbled forward. I flung my arms around Suzanne, and, without a thought, I kissed her firmly on the lips.

Whether this had been what she had expected, I may never know, but she did not pull back. Far from it, her lips pursued my kiss for all it was worth.

In this one moment, all the electricity, the emotional tension ... no other kiss I had ever experienced felt like this. My mind was blank, and there was nothing else in the world, just Suzanne and I ... and *fuck* ... I had a hard on.

"Hey fella! Sit down!"

There was a friendly, but irritated shout from a couple of guys sitting behind. This was probably fair enough, as I am sure we were obscuring their view ... and our kiss must have lasted forever. Well, it wasn't forever, but it was long enough that I hadn't noticed that the West Indies had struck with their first wicket, and that Inzamam was already walking out to replace Sohail, who was more than half way back towards the pavilion.

"Sorry," I replied to the guys behind, while taking Suzanne by the hand, and guiding her to a pair of seats just across the aisle.

So many thoughts came flooding through my mind. *Why had I kissed Suzanne like this? This isn't me ... I am always too shy ... I never do this. But fuck, it felt fantastic. ... But, when I last saw her, I had just been tongue-wrestling with her best friend Megan. Oh fuck! ... But Suzanne came ... Suzanne REALLY came.*

"Oh Suzanne, please forgive my language ... and my behaviour ... but bloody-hell, is this for real? It is just so wonderful to see you."

"I didn't know what to expect coming here today BJ. I wanted to see the cricket, but more than that I really wanted to see you again. I haven't stopped thinking about you since Townsville."

Wow! Am I dreaming?

"You're kidding, right? It has been the same for me," I responded. This wasn't far from the truth, despite one or two lustful deviations along the way. "I hope you didn't mind me kissing you like that. I sort of ... wasn't thinking."

"Did I mind? ... What do you think BJ? ... Try me again and see."

My God! My crotch felt tight. There was a real awakening down-under. I leaned over and engaged her lips again ... this time with a gentler, more lingering connection. *Wow, her lips feel amazing ... so soft, moist, and eager.* After remaining locked together as long as my lungs would allow, I drew breath.

"Is Megan here with you?"

Suzanne smiled.

"No, thankfully I have you all to myself today. I hope you are not disappointed."

I kissed Suzanne again ... *Was I disappointed?... I think not.*

"Does this seem disappointed?" I kissed her again. "... Not at all Suzanne. But what would Megan think of this?" I enquired, not wanting to ruin the moment.

"I am sure she would be pleased for me ... well, perhaps for us. She's been behaving herself in the last few weeks, and also feeling very guilty about her boyfriend at home. Anyway, she knew how much I liked you. But enough of her for now. It's just the two of us today."

We began to kiss again. This time it prompted some cheers and encouraging comments from the rows behind ... "Get in there mate!" ... "Get a room!" ... "Hey mate, give her one from me!" Perhaps our own excitement had enhanced theirs ... the action on the pitch had been a little slow.

"Well, today there's just the two of us, and the other few thousand in the crowd," added Suzanne.

Normally so self-conscious, today I didn't care about the crowd, nor now about the cricket match. I was at the MCG, with the girl of my dreams in my arms. *Had all my Christmases just arrived at once?* I was in a zone ... in a different world.

Maybe my time had come at last. Today, at least, it was REALLY, REALLY going to be my day.

♦ ♦ ♦

Eye on the Prize

So, here I was, late morning at the Melbourne Cricket Ground with West Indies having just taken their first wicket against Pakistan in the Cricket World Cup. I had just been re-acquainted in the best possible way with Suzanne, a wonderful young lass from near Newcastle (UK not NSW) whom I had first met, and indeed last met, over a month ago. Suzanne was travelling with her best friend, Megan, a slightly less reserved character. I had become quite well acquainted with both of them (especially Megan) on a lengthy bus journey across the outback. After that bus journey, we went our separate ways, but had planned to meet up again in Cairns. Well, that never happened. But I had been so captivated by both of them, and had been thinking of them ever since. And now, today at the MCG, Suzanne and I had just exchanged electrifying first kisses and we were being further encouraged by some of the more boisterous cricket supporters.

♦ ♦ ♦

"I am so glad that you came Suzanne. After I got your note in Cairns, I thought that I'd never see you again."

"Likewise," responded Suzanne, "but I also didn't really know whether you liked me. It was, after all, Megan who got to you first. She then got cold feet, and was confused about James; it seemed as though she didn't really want to see you again. But anyway, here we are."

"Yes, here we are. Wow! Here we are. It doesn't seem real to me yet."

"No ... nor for me," agreed Suzanne. Her eyes were sparkling as she smiled at me. I kept hold of her hand.

"Where are you staying? I am at the Carlton hostel ... just like we said. How about you?"

"That's great. Megan and I are there too."

I glanced up at the scoreboard, to see that Pakistan were steadily moving their innings forward, and were now past 80, with only one wicket down.

"So, I guess Megan didn't want to watch the cricket then?"

"Are you kidding?" replied Suzanne, amused at the question. "If it was Neighbours or Home and Away, then perhaps ... but sport? No, it's really not her thing. I think she might be doing a bit of clothes shopping in one of the downtown malls this morning."

"To be fair, Suzanne, apart from you, I have only ever known one girl who liked cricket ... and she was ... (I hesitated) ... well, she was a bit weird."

"Perhaps I am weird too," Suzanne responded, while at the same time trying to screw her face up into a gurning expression. This prompted a giggle that sent a warm tingling sensation through my heart. It is such a wonderful feeling you get when you discover that someone really hot is both attracted to you, and enjoys your company.

"You don't seem overly weird to me," I said, "but I suppose if you fancy me, you must have some sort of screw loose."

This prompted a playful punch to my ribs. I caught her hand in mine, allowing me to pull her close for another kiss.

"You know ... you punching me reminds me that perhaps I do only seem to attract weird girls, or ones who appear to enjoy hitting me. One girl at college only went out with me after she nearly broke her wrist by punching me in the ribs ... she needed a sling, and was in bandages for months. So, Suzanne ... please ... no punching me in the ribs ... for your own sake." I smiled.

We heard a polite roar and a ripple of applause from the crowd. Cricket crowds, especially when sparsely populated, cannot usually bring themselves towards fever-pitch levels of excitement.

"Oh, someone's out," remarked Suzanne.

"It looks like Inzamam," I responded. "You know, since you came, I haven't noticed how the cricket has been progressing ... you are somewhat distracting."

It was now 97 for 2, and it was indeed Inzamam who had just lost his wicket. This resulted in one of Pakistan's all-time greats, Javed Miandad, arriving at the crease.

"OK BJ. Let's watch some of the cricket," suggested Suzanne. "No more kisses until the next wicket."

"So, do you like playing games too then? What other ones do you play?"

"Perhaps you might find out later," she replied, aiming another mock punch to my ribs.

I was soon to discover that Suzanne could be a stickler for adhering to rules. Lunchtime came and went, and Rameez Raja and Javed Miandad were methodically building the Pakistan total. In fact, they carried their bats right through to the end of the Pakistan innings, which ended with Pakistan on 220 for 2 after their 50 overs.

Suzanne's game had not been a good game for me to play. The good form of Rameez and Javed ensured that I had been made to wait a couple of hours without any further kiss ... not so great when I had just experienced some of the most passionate kisses ever, and was hungry for more. I was really frustrated that the West Indies bowlers had let me down, and was especially disappointed in Curtly Ambrose and Malcolm Marshall. These two always took wickets, but there had been none for them today. So, having just begun to get deliciously re-acquainted with Suzanne, her moreish lips had been taken off the menu.

"How about a kiss for the end of the innings?" I enquired, as we stood to applaud the teams coming off the field.

"Rules are rules BJ. Only after each wicket." Suzanne grinned, and then stuck her tongue out.

"Blimey Suzanne ... you really are playing hard to get."

"Perhaps, BJ, but you just need to play by my rules."

I pondered the rules, considering whether there might be some bending to do.

"OK, fair enough Suzanne. So, what are your other rules?" I put my arm back around Suzanne's waist as we sat back in our seats.

"OK BJ ... well, let me see." She flicked her hair away from her face and moved her hand to pretend to scratch her chin. "Hmm ... let me see. Perhaps the first one is that you stop calling me Suzanne ... you sound just like my dad telling me off. Sue or Suzi if you don't mind."

"OK, Sue or Suzi ... which do you prefer? Megan calls you Suzi ... so ... Suzi ... I like that."

"Yeah, that's fine Mr Bruce."

"OK Suzi ... so what other rules do you have?"

"Well, you know, I am not like Megan ... I am a good Christian girl, so I don't go sleeping around."

Fuck ... this sounds familiar, I thought. *Where had I heard that before? Shit ... yes ... the last time it was Elaine on Magnetic Island ... although I really did have some fun with her. Yum ... great kisser... and fantastic hands ... my loins still seem to remember. Look BJ, forget about Elaine now. And not sleeping around is really a good thing ... maybe Suzi might just be a long-term prospect. Maybe she is THE ONE.*

"OK Suzi." I continued. "So, do you have any rules on this?" As I asked, I slowly moved my hand up under her blouse and gently caressed the skin around her waist.

"Hmm ... not so far," she giggled. "I like that."

"So, how about now?" I began moving my hand, up her side and tummy until my fingers were caressing just below her bra.

"Any further is a restricted zone," Suzi instructed.

I stopped immediately.

"Restricted to what?" I enquired.

"I'll have to think," replied Suzi, with a brief chuckle. "But definitely not allowed in public, for a start."

"OK Suzi, we'll have to return to that one later then."

I then removed my hand from under her blouse and placed it on her lovely smooth bare leg, just below her cut-off denim shorts. This was exciting.

"How about now Suzi?" ... I playfully teased her with my fingers as I slowly moved them further up her thigh, sliding them under her shorts around to feel the soft skin of her bottom.

"Any further and you get a smack," she giggled again.

"Just so that I get to know the boundaries," I said, looking into her eyes, trying to put an angelic innocence on my face. "There weren't so many boundaries to see out there in the first innings."

Sitting in these seats, my arm was not long enough to enable me to stretch my wandering fingers across to her inner thigh, but knew in any case that it was far too soon to even politely explore, so my hand returned to her waist. I wanted Suzi to feel relaxed with me, not to scare her off. I was more than happy for her to set the pace for exploration, but it was helpful to get an early indication of what she expected from me.

For a few moments my mind drifted back to that night with Jeannie in the Brisbane cinema, when she had kidnapped my hand and led my fingers into her forbidden zone ... *That was so amazing,* I thought, as I imagined a similar vision with Suzi. *Wow! Maybe one day I might be able to provide Suzi with similar pleasure.*

♦ ♦ ♦

As the West Indian openers Haynes and Lara came out to bat, I felt conflict inside. I wanted the West Indies to win, but I also wanted further mouth-to-mouth engagement, which was only to be forthcoming at the loss of wickets.

I had faced many conflicting scenarios in my life, but this was definitely a new one for me. Not that I had any influence over the outcome, I just had to wait and see. People often say that romance is all about the chase ... the waiting, the anticipation, that adds to the pleasure and excitement. Perhaps so, but it certainly adds to the frustration.

Frustration was a subject that I knew more than a little about. My years at university had promised so much, but delivered only a barren wasteland in the arena of sex and romance. I had spent most of my three years searching, but I had discovered that kisses were like needles in haystacks ... not to mention the rarity of finding any chance of a shag. My shyness and introversion in no way helped me to overcome the hurdles. I was too reserved to put myself out there much, and when I had tried to, I always seemed too tongue-tied and awkward to ever have much success. I was hardly ever brave enough to introduce myself to any new girls on the scene that I liked the look of. I had to get to know them first ... and that took time, and lots of patience. Then, when I did finally get to know them ... if I was still attracted to them at that point, they had usually become friends, which meant I then had something to lose. While I played several sports quite proficiently, I was just so inept at the dating game.

My luck had certainly improved in Australia, with four different intimate encounters over the last few weeks. Suzi was now number five. I had never experienced such a purple patch before. It was akin to the cliché of waiting three hours for a bus, only to find three coming along at once. It was just that here my bus stop was located on the other side of the world. As I sat with my arm around Suzi, taking in the cricket, I quietly reflected on how my fortunes seemed to have changed.

Suzi and I chatted about what we had seen and done around Cairns, and about where we had both been since. Suzi and Megan had bypassed Townsville and gone for a few days to the Whitsundays before heading on to Brisbane, Canberra and Sydney, and arriving in Melbourne a couple of days before me.

As we were talking, I took out my Lonely Planet guide from my day-pack. A bit crumpled now, but still being used as my bookmark, I took out the note from Cairns ...

> "Dear BJ,
> If you get to read this ... so sorry, we've gone to the Whitsundays. Diving was fab ... so gone to do some more. REALLY, REALLY hope to see you in Sydney (Glebe) + Melbourne (Carlton) ... Really sorry again.
>   Love Suzi (+Megan) XXXX."

"Look! I still have it." I showed the note to Suzi. "I wrote notes for you in Sydney, but weren't too hopeful that you would show up."

Suzi reached for her day-pack.

"Close your eyes BJ."

I did as I was told, suddenly thinking that perhaps she had kept one of my notes? *She couldn't have ... I ...*

A long warm moist kiss on the lips was my reward.

"Not a wicket, but an apology BJ. I am really sorry about Cairns, and also sorry that we didn't come to the Glebe hostel. Megan wanted to go to the Jolly Swagman in Kings Cross."

"No worries. It's all in the past. But Suzi, I only wish I had known."

"Well, here we are today ... all the best things are worth waiting for. But you'll still have to wait until the next wicket for another kiss."

◆ ◆ ◆

As Suzi mentioned The Jolly Swagman hostel, I began to tell her about Jason and Colin, my two school friends who were working there, and whom I had bumped into in Pizza Hut. In that context, I also told Suzi about the German girls, and especially about Brigit, who had unexpectedly pounced on me in a nightclub in Cairns, and then later had similarly ambushed Jason in Sydney.

"By chance, Brigit and her two friends Vanessa and Kirsten are also staying at the Carlton hostel. Maybe you've seen them? I am sure they'd be interested to meet you. They were with me when I was depressed after reading your note when I arrived in Cairns. They teased me about it."

"Interesting," mused Suzi. "But now that I have found you again, I don't want to be fighting others off. I don't know what Megan will really think either. I know she still likes you, but she's also still confused about James."

"Well, I will try to fight them off," I said smiling, "but that might depend a little on your rules. If I have to wait for a wicket every time that I want a kiss ..."

"Well, we might have to rethink that one," Suzi responded, leaning over to kiss me again. "You know, I am also rather disappointed at the lack of wickets; that wasn't in my plan. You would normally expect several more ... so, OK ... for the rest of the game we will say three kisses for every wicket that falls."

I suddenly burst into song ... while trying to do a little dance in my seat ...

[1]*"... I say I don't like cricket ... uh ... oh no.*
I love it. ..."

"I can't remember whose song that is, but it seems rather appropriate right now ... or it would do, if only I could sing reggae."

"Yeah BJ, I remember the tune ... even with you trying to sing it. But I have no idea who sang it either."

Anyway, what appeared like an improvement to the rules did have a major flaw ... wickets were still required. As Suzi talked of rule changes, West Indies had been shaping a solid run chase, with both Haynes and Lara taking the score past 100, and then past 150 without a wicket. This had been several hours of kiss-deprivation. However, during this time, Suzi and I did start to get to know each other better, as we relaxed in the sunshine, sipping beer and buying the occasional snack from vendors who drifted past us.

In the end, Lara retired hurt on 88, when the score had moved to 175. Following this, Haynes together with his captain, Richie Richardson, comfortably closed out the match, defeating Pakistan with around four overs to spare. My first taste of international cricket at the MCG had been an exceptional experience. The West Indies had won the match, I had re-discovered Suzanne, who I was now calling Suzi ... and the moratorium on kisses had formally ended.

♦ ♦ ♦

Suzi and I made our way out from the MCG and ambled, hand-in-hand, back in the rough direction of the hostel. It was early evening, the sky was still blue, the sun still shining, and the air still comfortably warm. Such a balmy evening was perfect for a detour through Fitzroy Gardens on the way back.

I remembered being back in Townsville, when I first had romantic visions of walking hand-in-hand with Suzi. I had imagined us pausing for the occasional kisses in the shade underneath the arches or balconies of Townsville's Victorian buildings. Today, my dream was becoming reality ... only here it was amongst the tree-lined avenues and vibrant herbaceous borders of Fitzroy Gardens. In this moment, it felt like I was the luckiest guy alive.

As I revealed this to Suzi, she teased me about my romantic daydreaming. I also told her about my visions of us walking through St James's Park in London, feeding the ducks and pelicans on the lake, and walking along Horse Guards Parade. However, now was still too soon to divulge my visions of us together, shopping for clothes in Marks and Spencer with a baby-buggy in tow. It was also not the appropriate time to disclose how Suzi had appeared in my more erotic visions, nor indeed those featuring Megan, complete with bondage gear ... the full works. I was not too sure what Suzi would make of this, or the many variations on this theme that had appeared in my mind over the last month or so. Suzi would probably run a mile from such a deviant.

There are some experiences in life, although perhaps only a few over a lifetime, that you never want to end. This walk was one of them. I was experiencing the feeling of new-found love ... yes, it really did feel like I was falling in love. This wasn't just a crush, or the exciting extension from burning fires of lust, such as I had felt with my other recent romantic encounters in Australia. No, this time it was the glow of a smouldering log fire, that sense of warmth running through every muscle of every limb ... not only through the groin area.

With Megan on the bus from Tennant Creek, Elaine on Magnetic Island, and then Jeannie in Brisbane ... all these encounters had been sprung on me without warning. All three of them had been wonderful in their own different ways. All three girls had a definite, but different sexual attraction each time ... *Hmm ... yes, they had been really rather good ...* But this time, although it had been a surprise to be re-acquainted with Suzi so suddenly at the MCG, after my month of visualising her in my head, it all seemed to feel as if it was meant to happen. It seemed to fit together ... it just felt right. Holding Suzi in my arms felt warm and cosy but not quite relaxing. I still had butterflies in my stomach. Each kiss felt electrically charged ... or perhaps more magnetically charged, as every lip to lip encounter tended to linger before separation.

Inevitably, our walk had to end, and at just after 8:30pm, we arrived back at our hostel in Carlton. As we walked through reception, I glanced through to the common room, and caught sight of Kirsten, Vanessa and Brigit. I waved.

"Suzi, let's go over and see my German friends ... I'd love you to meet them."

We walked over to a cluster of arm chairs where they were seated.

"Oh! Hi Bruce!" The girls greeted me almost in sync.

"Hi ladies! Have you had a good day? Do you see this smile on my face? I have finally found my *REALLY-REALLY* girl. This is Suzi."

"Wow Bruce!" responded Kirsten ... I am so pleased for you. Nice to meet you Suzi. Bruce has told us so much about you."

"Oh, really?" replied Suzi. "Nothing bad, I hope? ... Look, I must just go and check whether Megan is around. I'll be back in a few minutes."

Suzi then walked out of the common room and disappeared up the staircase by reception. I remained there to catch up with Kirsten, Brigit and Vanessa.

"So," said Kirsten, "finally you've found your *REALLY-REALLY* girl. That's so wonderful."

"Aahh ... so romantic," teased Vanessa. "And which one of the two is this one?"

"Ah-ha ... yes. This is not the one who I snogged on the bus from Tennant Creek. No, that was Megan. No, Suzi is the other one."

"Wow – Stud! You really are quite something," added Brigit.

"You're quite something yourself Brigit," I replied ... "Oh ... and I did tell her briefly about our ... how would you say it ..."

"Drunken grope?" said Brigit, offering to finish my sentence.

"Hmm ... yes ... that's a ... fair way of putting it."

Kirsten and Vanessa laughed, as indeed did Brigit.

"So, how was the cricket Bruce?" asked Vanessa.

"It was great," I explained. "Although, as you might imagine, I was somewhat distracted. It was soon after the start when Suzi found me, and from then on I rather had my mind on other things."

"And your hands too perhaps?" Brigit added with a smile.

"Hey Bruce," Kirsten interjected. "We went to see the penguins today. Oh, they were so cute. You really should go to see them."

A more detailed and enthusiastic account of their day trip to Phillip Island followed, and it was clear that it would be an interesting place to visit: a seal colony, and lots of waddling penguins ... it sounded great.

As we then started to talk about places we might like to see, Suzi returned to the common room accompanied by Megan. I stood up, and rushed to give Megan a hug.

"Hey Megan, it's so great to see you," I said.

"And you too BJ. It really is."

"You are looking well." *Hot might have been a more accurate description,* I thought, as Megan was wearing a figure-hugging T-shirt and tight denim shorts. Her dark brown eyes sparkled just as I had remembered.

"Suzi told me that you and her ... well, you know. I am really so pleased for you both. Oh my gosh BJ, she's been cursing me ever since Cairns for us not sticking around." Megan then pulled close and whispered in my ear. "I still think you're hot BJ, and I am a bit jealous ... but Suzi's my best friend, and she deserves to be happy. So, don't you dare hurt her."

"What are you two whispering about?" asked Suzi.

"Oh, nothing," replied Megan. "I was just telling BJ how happy I am for you both. You just seem so sickeningly well-suited."

The German girls laughed, while Suzi and I smiled at each other, and then held hands again.

"So ... which of you girls is Brigit then?" asked Megan.

I cringed. *Oh no ... what is she going to say?*

"Me," replied Brigit. "Why?"

"Well, it seems as though both you and I let this boy get away," said Megan. "What a shame ... because he's quite handsome, and he seems like a good catch. He's all yours now Suzi."

I felt a flush to my cheeks. This was a bit like going to a consultation evening when I was back at school. It was like when a teacher had said positive things about me to my parents ... it shouldn't have felt embarrassing, it just did. It was also like an interview or an audition; here I was with five girls, three of whom I had now snogged, and it seemed as though I was standing in front of them, waiting to be marked out of ten.

As they continued discussing me amongst themselves, I happened to catch sight of the result of the other World Cup match on the TV, in which Sri Lanka had overcome Zimbabwe in a close match. Neither of these teams were expected to progress to the last stages, but you just never know.

We all stayed chatting in the common room for another hour or so, discussing what things were worth seeing in and around Melbourne. We then enquired about one or two interesting trip options at the reception. One excursion that we all wanted to do was to travel along part of The Great Ocean Road, which is one of the world's most spectacular stretches of coastal scenery. The hostel manager recommended one particular tour, which he said still had some spaces for Tuesday. So, figuring that we expected still to all be on good terms when Tuesday came around, all six of us decided to sign up for this trip.

I must admit, now that I had found Suzi again, I didn't really care what we did ... I just wanted to spend time with her. I also knew that it would be difficult to get much of her undivided attention, as she was travelling with her best friend Megan, and Suzi was hardly going to abandon her, and nor should she.

Kirsten, Vanessa and Brigit were planning to leave Melbourne for Adelaide on Wednesday, while Suzi and Megan had planned to go in a similar direction on Friday. I had my own flight for

Christchurch confirmed for Thursday, so Suzi and I were not going to have much time together.

During the afternoon I had discovered from Suzi, that she and Megan were going to Adelaide and then on to Perth, where they were going to stay with some friends of Megan's family. Although I desperately wanted to spend more time with Suzi, it was not realistic to tag along and travel with them. After Perth they planned to fly over to Auckland, to see a bit of New Zealand. At least that meant it might be possible to catch up with them again for a few days. I would just have to hope that Suzi still liked me after spending another month apart.

Perhaps I should just take it day by day, I thought. *Let's begin with Suzi still liking me tomorrow. That would be a good start.*

Having heard from the three German girls about the Phillip Island excursion, Suzi, Megan and I were quite keen to go on this one too, but there were no spaces until Thursday. Not an option for me, but still a possibility for Suzi and Megan.

"So sorry that we can't go tomorrow," said Suzi. "Is there anything you'd like to do instead BJ?"

"I'm happy just to go with the flow," I replied. "We could wander around bits of Melbourne, or go out to the zoo, or ..."

"The zoo could be fun," suggested Megan enthusiastically. "I still haven't seen any koalas in Australia, and I hear the zoo here is pretty good and easy to get to. Anyone fancy that?"

Suzi and I agreed that the zoo could be a good option ... it would keep Megan on-side, while we could enjoy spending more time together. Kirsten, Brigit and Vanessa decided that shopping was going to be more their scene. They also decided to call an end to the night and head off to their dorm. It was now just after 11:30pm.

"I shall call it a day too," said Megan, "and leave you two lovebirds alone. Shall we meet for breakfast around 8:00am?"

Suzi and I agreed, and then sat down again on a sofa in the common room ... both of us letting out a huge sigh as we did so.

"I have you to myself at last," said Suzi. "But I won't stay long, I am so tired."

"Me too Suzi ... meeting you again is so exhausting," I joked. As I did so, I received a deserved poke in the ribs. "And I warned you about poking me in the ribs," I said, as I wrestled with her, eventually tickling her into submission, and then pulling Suzi close for a kiss.

"You know the rules BJ," Suzi giggled. "No kiss unless there's a wicket."

"I think that you elbowing me in my middle stump just now counts," I retorted, as Suzi puckered her lips and closed her eyes in anticipation.

I gratefully accepted the invitation and planted a gentle kiss on her lips, while running my fingers through her hair. The first gentle connection became firmer, as we both hungered for more, and then turned in to a full-on snog, with our tongues getting mutually acquainted.

"Now we will just need to re-negotiate the kissing rules," I suggested. "Some days there is no cricket at all ... so we can't have that."

"Well, perhaps so BJ, but I'll think about that tomorrow."

After sprawling on the sofa, cuddling each other and kissing for several more minutes, oblivious to other people coming and going, we then decided it was time to turn in. I kissed Suzi goodnight at the foot of the stairs by reception. I hugged her tightly one more time and then watched as she headed up the stairs. Naturally, I stayed to admire her rear view, before I went along a ground floor corridor to my own dorm.

Monday 24 February – Melbourne

I didn't get much sleep during the night. There were three other guys in my dorm, all snoring from time to time … but it was more my thoughts about Suzi that kept me awake.

Was this thing real with Suzi? It had been such an amazing day. Could it be the real thing this time, after so long? Could it really be true that she had been wanting to meet up again ever since I got off the bus in Townsville? Well, she did come to find me at the cricket. But what did she see in me? What could she actually see in me? It can't be my looks … I am not exactly a male model, and I am certainly not wealthy. I do have a decent sense of humour, or rather an indecent sense of humour. But I am an introvert, and so often I am not great company. Who knows? I only hope that I don't fuck it up again this time.

I often drifted into the territory of negative thoughts. Deep down I definitely had relationship insecurities, but I couldn't really figure out what they were, or why. And those insecurities started with the relationship I had with myself. I often had a pretty low self-opinion; I rarely felt that I was good enough. Whatever I was doing, I usually expected more of myself, but failed to deliver. I was never really comfortable with my looks; I hated the large gap between my front teeth, and hated that I had begun to lose my hair at such a young age. I also disliked aspects of my personality. My shyness and introversion seemed to hinder me from getting really close to anyone … others just didn't seem to understand why I didn't always feel like being sociable.

I didn't hate my religion, or in my case the lack of it … although I did recognise that it could possibly be a hindrance to my happiness. I had no God to turn to, and other people who were believers often seemed to treat me as an outcast who had lower moral standards. My sometimes-coarse language, I suppose, did nothing to help my cause. I was searching for some sort of purpose or calling in life, but after 23 years there was still no sign of any answers.

Bruce Spydar

I had known precious little in the way of romantic relationships or sex life, and desperately wanted it ... but at the same time I was scared. A couple of weeks was about the longest any romantic relationship of mine had lasted, and I had not experienced many fantastic moments of intimacy. My time in Australia had been something of an awakening, and the romantic encounters that I had experienced with Megan, Elaine, Brigit and Jeannie had been a wonderful tonic for me, had restored my optimism and boosted my mojo. But these encounters had all been so brief. The longest was less than 24 hours, and on each occasion, I had not done any chasing, and therefore had no expectations for what might transpire.

This time, however ... with Suzi it was different. I had first met her in the second week of January, in Darwin, and then saw her again while climbing Uluru (Ayers Rock). We had then spent long hours together on the overnight bus from Alice Springs via Tennant Creek to Townsville ... which is where I lost her. I had of course been playing tonsil hockey with her best friend Megan on that journey, but despite that, I had also sensed a slight spark with Suzi during a short cuddle over an early morning coffee.

When I reached Brisbane, I met up again with Neil, a chap who I had spent some time with in Darwin. He was well acquainted with Megan and Suzi (in a hot, steamy sex-romp kind of way), and Neil had told me over a beer in Brisbane, that Suzi really liked me. This had just made me want to see her again even more. And then yesterday, Suzi appeared suddenly at the MCG ... and it seemed like we were destined to be together. It felt so right, it felt natural ... *which is why it's so scary, I just don't want to fuck things up.*

♦ ♦ ♦

I got up at about 7:30am. I shaved, showered and shat, and then went along to the breakfast area to where Suzi and Megan were already tucking into some cereal and yoghurt. As I walked across to their table, I suddenly felt uneasy ...

Do we start where we left things last night? I pondered. *Or do I need to retreat a little and restart?* Thankfully, I didn't have to wait long for an answer to this question.

"Oh, hi BJ!" said Suzi, getting to her feet. "Did you sleep well?" Suzi then reached across to me with her hand, and pulled me close for a good morning kiss.

Oh, thank God. We are not back at square one.

"Well, I have slept better," I responded. "The other guys in my room were all snoring quite loudly. How about you girls?"

"Like a log," replied Megan.

"Not so much either," added Suzi. "I was just thinking about things."

"Oh, not bad thoughts I hope," I responded.

"No, no ... just the opposite. Just thinking about yesterday."

"Oh bluurgh!" interjected Megan. "The two of you seem so sickeningly happy. So, shall we go to find the zoo today? I don't mind being the gooseberry."

"Yes," said Suzi. "Let's do that. I think there is a tram that we can catch from just around the corner."

"Always the fountain of knowledge," responded Megan. "It's a good job I am travelling with you. On my own I am useless."

"I am sure that's not true," I countered.

"Yes, it really is," continued Megan. "I have no sense of direction, and I can never remember any details. After looking something up in a guide book, it takes about two minutes before I have forgotten the answer again."

"Well, I think I must be quite similar to you then, Megan. My memory is hopeless. I think after my finals last summer, my brain must have decided that it had overstretched its capacity. Let this be a warning to you Suzi ... although, at least this morning, I did remember not to call you Suzanne."

I proceeded to get myself a bowl of muesli from the breakfast bar, and then managed to spray half a cup of coffee all over the floor, due to my incompetence with the coffee machine.

"You say you are useless Megan ... perhaps I need Suzi to help me with my coffee. I can never get the hang of these damned machines." I wiped up the mess, and returned to the girls to finish my breakfast.

♦ ♦ ♦

Just along the road from the hostel, we caught a tram that took us up towards the zoo. The tram was painted in Aussie colours of green and gold, and looked as though it had been in operation for several decades. The paint that was peeling off the outside, together with the decaying red-rust of the ironwork underneath, indicated that it was in need of some renovation.

We were dropped off close to the entrance of the zoo, which was in the leafy Parkville area just north of the city centre. The zoo itself was the oldest in Australia, and had opened back in 1862.

As Suzi, Megan and I paid for our admission, and then walked through the gates, I remembered the last occasion that I had visited a zoo on a date. It was back in my second year at college, and I had been staying up through part of the Easter holidays to do some project work for my degree. I was actually doing some research in which I was training starlings to fly through obstacles ... another story entirely. During this time, I had started dating a physicist in my year. Incidentally, this was the same girl who had nearly broken her wrist by punching me in the ribs. Anyway, that day out at London Zoo turned out to be the nail in the coffin of our relationship. I really liked her; she had a good sense of humour, and she was quite sexy, but she just seemed on a different planet sometimes. With the benefit of hindsight, I can see that our brief romance was pretty weird. We were both too relationship-naïve and nervous around each other to relax, and once we started kissing, neither of us seemed to know what to do next. All along it just felt like the wrong chemistry; not chalk and cheese, more like chalk and Lancashire Hotpot?

Today, I did not feel totally relaxed with Suzi and Megan either. It was difficult for me to feel completely at ease with what I hoped was the start of a wonderful relationship with Suzi, when I considered that Megan still knew far more about me than Suzi did. Megan and I had shared a long heart-to-heart on the bus from Alice Springs to Townsville. Oh, yeah ... and we had also engaged in some rather fantastic snogging on that bus journey too, which might have gone further if I had agreed to her indecent demands.

After Suzi's kissing rules had been abandoned, I had more than made up the ground on the snogging front, having now exchanged multiple mouth-to-mouth encounters. But here was I with these two wonderfully attractive, witty, warm-hearted girls ... and I just didn't want to blow it.

After we made it through the entrance, we stood for a few minutes in front of a large pictorial map of the zoo. We tried to work out which route we ought to take, so as to ensure that we didn't miss any of the A-list animals. Not that there really are any A-listers, as different creatures do appeal to different people. However, few people visit a zoo for a day out to see salamanders or leaf-cutter ants, whereas lots are attracted to koalas and lions. As we stood together in front of this large map, Suzi and I found it the right moment for another spot of lip-to-lip catching up.

"Oh, you two ... behave!" said Megan. "Am I just going to be playing gooseberry all day?"

"Sorry Megan," I replied. "I am not so sure that Suzi would want me making out with you today instead. And anyway, yesterday she would only allow me to kiss her when somebody got a wicket. Suzi made these unfair rules, so now I just have to take my chances whenever I can."

"Oh really?" asked Megan. "So, Suzi has rules, does she? Suzi, you didn't mention that to me."

"I always have rules," Suzi replied, "but some of them are not really so relevant to you, Megan."

"You've made me curious now," said Megan. "So, tell me all about these rules?"

"I'd kind of like to know about them too," I added.

"Well," said Suzi, now blushing a little. "I kind of make them up as I go along."

"Ah-ha, I see," said Megan, "... those kinds of rules."

"Yes," replied Suzi, winking and giggling with Megan, "... those kinds of rules."

I was now starting to feel more like the odd one out again. Best friends always seem to have their own language and understanding which baffles other people around them. You can be a gooseberry when you are with two best friends just as much as you can when you are the extra person to a romantic couple. 'Two's company, three is a crowd' so often holds true.

"So then Suzi," said Megan, with a smile on her face indicative of mischievous intent, "... for Bruce's benefit, what are your rules for kissing today?"

"Well, I think I am now happy to remove the kissing rules ... I enjoy BJ's kissing." Suzi giggled. "You were right Megan all those weeks ago. BJ is a pretty hot kisser." They both laughed.

It's great when others are discussing my aptitudes, I thought. *It looks like I am also one of the zoo's exhibits today.*

"OK," continued Megan. "That's base one covered. So, let's think, what are the rules for base two?"

"Sorry?" asked Suzi, perhaps hoping that she had deflected this line of questioning.

"So, Suzi, we also need to know ... what are the rules for BJ caressing your bum and your titties?"

"Megan, please," said Suzi. "You are so embarrassing."

I had to agree with Suzi here, particularly when a middle-aged couple looked around at us. They were grinning, evidently having just overheard this part of the conversation. However, I was also desperate to know the answer; some boundary guidance here would be extremely useful.

"OK then Suzi," continued Megan. She was clearly relishing the chance to make her best friend feel uncomfortable. "Let us work back in stages. Now, you told me that you thought you wanted to sleep with BJ sometime, didn't you?"

I half-choked in surprise. *Well, this is cutting to the chase.*

"Oh, Megan. Why did you have to say that?" Suzi protested. "I should never talk to you again." Suzi was, at this point, flushed pink with embarrassment.

"Oh Suzi," I interjected. "You really don't have to answer that one. If that is true, I am sure that would be just wonderful, but we have all the time in the world to get to know each other first."

"Oh BJ," said Megan, "don't shoot yourself in the foot. I am just trying to help, babe. You are both clearly crazy about each other." She started giggling. "And you did tell me a month ago that you were gagging for a shagging. Didn't you, BJ? Don't deny it."

"Ssshhh. What are you saying?" I said, realising that the embarrassment was far from finished.

"Come on you both," continued Megan. "Stop pretending. You are both up for it, aren't you?"

"OK Megan," Suzi now intervened. "Just zip it! Please. And, OK look ... yes BJ, I think that I probably do want to sleep with you sometime. Just not quite yet. I want to get to know you better first."

"There. Thankyou Suzi," Megan continued. "That wasn't so hard was it? Now we are getting there. So ..."

"Look BJ ... before Megan says any more. Look, we only have a couple more days together now, and then I won't see you for at least three weeks, but I really hope that we can meet up again in Auckland. If we still want to be together then ... well, let's see then."

Both Suzi and Megan seemed oblivious to the other people passing by and overhearing.

"OK! We are almost there," pushed Megan. "So, how about you sleep with BJ to celebrate England winning the World Cup?" Megan looked over to catch my gaze of amazement, her chestnut eyes sparkling with mischief.

"I'm not making promises like that," Suzi replied. "And besides, who says BJ would want to sleep with me?"

"Of course, he does," said Megan. "Don't you BJ?"

"I am actually here you know," I reminded them. It felt like I was a small child again, back at nursery school, with my parents talking to the teacher about how I was getting on (albeit with rather different conversation topics). "Look ... if we still feel hot for each other in Auckland, then let's see. But England might have to wait another 50 years before they win the World Cup, so I am not so sure I like this rule either."

"Hmm ... well," continued Megan, refusing to be silenced. "Games are fun ... and games need rules. So, why don't we say ..." Megan hesitated. "Yes ... why don't we say that first prize is a fuck for the trophy? Yes, if England win the World Cup. A fuck for the cup ... sounds good. Then this means second prize is oral ... for England reaching the final. And then the third prize must be a hand-job for the semi. That'd give you a bit more than a semi, BJ."

"Alright," said Suzi, who was now really quite annoyed. "Alright, fine ... something like that then, Megan. Now just shut-the-fuck-up."

Compared to Megan's mischievous eyes, Suzi's eyes were also dark brown, but, at this point, they were fixed on Megan's and betraying real annoyance. This was the first time that I had seen Suzi even slightly mad, but she was really sexy with it too ... as long as the anger wasn't heading in my direction.

"Sorry BJ," continued Suzi. "Anything to shut her up. And it's none of her business what happens between the two of us."

"No, of course not," I agreed. "Nor the business of these dozens of visitors in the zoo. I am sure they don't want to know about us."

"But on the other hand ..." continued Suzi, displaying a wicked grin and raising her eyebrows ... "it would give us a really special date to look forward to in Auckland."

"Ah-ha! You know I am right." Megan chuckled. "You know that you both want to do it. You just need the step-by-step rules towards your sexual MOT ... manual, oral, and total service." Megan giggled, which also set me off, and Suzi too.

"OK then," I concluded. "Now that you girls have got that all settled, let's go over there to see the wombats.

♦ ♦ ♦

What the heck have I landed myself in? I thought, as we made our way over to the Australian marsupial enclosures. It was both exciting and unnerving to be the centre of other people's plans, especially when those other people had appeared in my dreams, and when they were as hot as Suzi and Megan.

The first enclosure that we came to was one housing a delightful pair of common wombats. The two of them were shuffling about, in and out of a partially-decayed, hollowed-out tree stump.

"Oh, so cute," said Suzi, giving me a tight cuddle. "Oh, I want one; they're so gorgeous."

While taking a few moments to enjoy these cute fluffy bundles, my mind drifted back to Magnetic Island, and my brief time with Elaine. I wondered what she was doing right now. She was a lovely girl, and I was sure that I would always have fond memories of her.

"You know Suzi, when I was on Magnetic Island, I said to someone that I was searching for blue wombats; those things you look for in your dreams but don't really exist. Well, right now, being with you ... I keep wondering if I will soon wake up and find that this was just a dream."

"You don't need to worry BJ ... I'm very real," replied Suzi.

"I've had so many weird dreams since Townsville," I said, before immediately regretting it.

"Oh, did you really?" asked Megan. "Do tell us, BJ? Please enlighten us about your wicked fantasies?"

"Oh fuck! Why did I say that? No, I can't say ... really."

"Come on BJ," insisted Megan.

"No, really. You wouldn't like it."

"That's it, BJ," said Suzi, removing her arms from my waist and stepping back. "No more kisses or cuddles until you tell us."

"Oh, bloody hell! Me and my big mouth." *This could prove tricky.*

"Come on BJ," said both Megan and Suzi in unison, "please?"

"Well OK, but don't say I didn't warn you." There was no way that I was going to reveal all of my visions with them, but I had to tell them something. I then began. "OK, well I suppose it began in Darwin, just after I first met you."

"When you were with Neil, by the pool in Frogshollow," remembered Suzi. (Neil was a Welsh lad that we had all befriended several weeks earlier).

"Yes," I continued. "And, Megan, I know I have told you some of this before, but ..."

"Oh, about me and Neil," Megan nodded.

"Well, continuing for Suzi's benefit ... Neil had told me about your night of passion in Broome. He told me of the sex, and tying him to the bed, and then how you gave him oral, and Suzi stripping off in front of him ..."

"I was only getting into bed," Suzi protested, "I was definitely NOT part of their shenanigans."

"Hmm ... well," I continued, "... it was a vision that stuck in my head, regardless of the reality. After first seeing you both in your sexy swimming costumes, and then picturing Neil's story, I just kept seeing you in my visions. Sometimes you were clothed, other times naked, or in a bondage-type situation. When I was in Kakadu, at Nourlangie Rock, I imagined you cavorting naked with the Rainbow Serpent."

"Wow BJ!" said Suzi. "You really have a vivid imagination ... and a very dirty mind." She laughed, and then gave me a forgiving kiss.

Phew, I thought.

"Yes, wow indeed, BJ," responded Megan. "I should never have let Suzi get her hands on you ... you really are a dark horse."

Having only told them about a small sample of my visions, it had appeared to satisfy their curiosity, so I decided to quit while I was ahead. I had, of course, several other imaginary plotlines featuring Suzi and Megan in the cast.

While in Kakadu, I had daydreamed about them, dressed in skin-tight, shiny black leather; they were trying to tie me up ... I was a small crocodile that had jumped into their rowing boat. And then in Brisbane, I had visions of being up in the tallest office tower at Waterfront Place, chained naked to an office desk, while Megan had her tortuous way with me. And following that one, another similar vision, but with Suzi setting me free. And once more, in Sydney, the three of us were cavorting together on a motor launch, travelling up and down the harbour ... an extravagant picture of excess wine and insufficient clothing. And lastly there were the even seedier visions of us appearing in a remake of an old porn video which I had seen in a friend's house in London. All of these were definitely best kept to myself ... at least for now.

♦ ♦ ♦

From the wombat enclosure, we moved on past dingbats and possums, and then into a walk-through grassy paddock containing wallabies and grey kangaroos. This was seemingly the equivalent of a petting zoo, and some of the animals, especially the wallabies, were extremely tame and seemed to enjoy small children stroking them in exchange for food pellets.

This was such a cute sight. My daydreaming drifted me towards Suzi and I holding the hands of our two children (one boy, one girl, both around 3 years old) while we all petted the wallabies. *Don't get carried away BJ,* I told myself. *It's a big step from going out together for two days, to settling down and having kids. And my few previous relationships had hardly made it past two weeks.* But I could really imagine it. It just seemed to feel right. With Suzi, it was far more than just about lust, and far more than the exciting new possibility of a World Cup double celebration. No. Here, this time, I really felt that I was falling in love. I cherished every moment of Suzi's touch: when we held hands, her fingers would stroke my palms; when we cuddled there was always an additional caressing touch; and when we kissed there was always that extra little bit of lingering exploration. Being with Suzi just felt so good, and it was also beginning to feel so natural.

After the kangaroos and wallabies, we then moved on to the butterfly enclosure, which was one of the zoo's star exhibits. It was a walk-through greenhouse-type structure, with dozens if not hundreds of different species of tropical and sub-tropical butterflies. It was a photographer's dream, with spectacular colours everywhere you could look. My camera was a Pentax SLR, to which I attached a 35mm to 200mm zoom lens. The long lens was hardly necessary in here, as the butterflies were so close. One after another, different butterflies, painted with rainbow-arrays of colour, would land on our heads, shoulders and arms, or indeed on top of my zoom lens.

The butterflies were indeed stunning, but I probably spent as much time watching Suzi and Megan. For me, they were such a thrill to observe, as butterflies would land on their hands only a few inches from their noses. I could see such joy in their faces, and occasionally even see the reflection of a butterfly wing in the pupils of their eyes ... and both Suzi and Megan did have such alluring brown eyes. I had first noticed Megan's dark chestnut eyes when I sat next to her on the bus from Alice, and over the last couple of days I had been so deeply entranced by Suzi. It is definitely a girl's eyes that captivate my desires; it's the eyes that ensnare me.

After the butterfly house, we walked past an enclosure containing red Kangaroos. These were somewhat larger than the grey ones we had seen before, and these were not allowed to mingle with the visitors. Reds had a reputation for being aggressive at times, and when they stood up tall, they were taller than the average man. Today however, they were all lying down on the dirt, stretched out and yawning, as though it was their afternoon siesta.

It was just before noon, and we decided to stop at a picnic area where there was a kiosk selling coffees and snacks. Suzi secured a picnic bench, while Megan and I went up to queue at the kiosk.

"I'm so glad that you and Suzi got together BJ," said Megan. "You know, you seem so good together."

"Thanks Megan. You know I was gutted when I got to Cairns to find you had gone, but at that point, after that bus ride, I suppose it was probably more you that I had the hots for. I was attracted to you both, but it was you who got to me first."

"Well, I've also been thinking about you a lot too," continued Megan. "But I am still mixed up in my head with James. I really can't work out whether I want to stay with him. So, rather than screwing you around, what better thing could I do than let my best friend have you? So, babe, while I still think you are quite hot too, you are now off limits." As she said this, she pinched my bottom. "But that doesn't mean I can't have a bit of fun with you from time to time."

"Well, maybe so Megan, but I really do want things to work out with me and Suzi. So, you'll have to behave."

"OK BJ, I'll be a good girl. You won't have to spank me."

"Oh Megan, please don't put such teasing thoughts into my mind. You know how dirty it is."

"Yes babe, indeed I do."

"Babe?"

"Oh, you don't mind me calling you babe, do you? I don't think about it; I just say it sometimes with friends."

"No, not at all. But I thought all Geordies said 'pet.'"

"Not all of us do, pet! That's a bit of a stereotype. But, actually, I do use it sometimes. Anyway, what shall we get for lunch? There doesn't look to be a lot of choice."

"What have they got? Looks like burgers, hotdogs, sausage rolls, chips, ice cream, chocolate ..."

"Not great if you are vegetarian," said Megan.

"It's lucky that you aren't then, isn't it? And yes, I do remember from our bus journey, your classic words ... 'I am too fond of my meat.'"

Megan laughed. "Yes, that does sound like me."

"So, what shall we get? Coffees, sausage rolls and chocolate? How does that grab you?"

"Why not? A very balanced meal. Well, perhaps we could get something healthier tonight."

As we reached the front of the queue, we realised that the confectionary choices were dominated by Mars, Nestlé and Cadbury, just as they were in most places back in the UK. Together with our sausage rolls and coffees, we also bought Twix, Kit Kat and Dairy Milk to share between us.

We then re-joined Suzi at her picnic table which was situated right next to an old wooden horse-drawn cart. The cart had been propped up, and beautifully planted with several different varieties of fuchsia, which drew the attention of dozens of bees.

As we sat down and chatted over our snack lunch, we watched a pair of kookaburras in a nearby cage, which were hopping around and making whistling noises from time to time, as if to attract our attention. I told the girls about the kookaburra and possum at the hostel on Magnetic Island; I fondly recalled throwing small pieces of barbecued meat in their direction to try to induce a quarrel.

As I was re-telling the story, I was also remembering Elaine, the lovely girl who took me off to see her gran. I told Suzi and Megan a bit about Elaine and her gran, but felt it wise not to reveal anything about Elaine's handywork on the beach. I felt a twitch in my groin just thinking about it again. I had certainly enjoyed some great hours with Elaine, and did genuinely hope that her own life journey would work out well for her. We seemed to have really connected with each other, but I think we both felt it was only going to be a quick holiday romance, never more than a brief encounter, but a wonderful one all the same.

From having spent many hours together on the bus from Alice Springs to Townsville, Suzi and I also seemed to have developed a real connection. It was not perhaps as swift and lustful as with Megan, but Suzi and I clicked, and we had more interests in common. It really did feel that there might be the potential for something special.

After finishing our snack lunch, and having taken a comfort break in some washrooms, I had a moment's reflection. This then prompted me into another question when Suzi and Megan returned.

"You know girls … I met you for the first time back in Darwin, something like 6 weeks ago. We have spent quite a few hours together, and I still don't know your surnames. It would be rather helpful, if I ever have to write another note to you."

"Yes, that's true BJ," agreed Suzi. "And we don't know yours either."

"OK … just wait a minute you two," interjected Megan. "Wait, we can play a game. BJ, you have to guess our names, and we will try to guess yours. And we will give each other silent clues … a bit like playing charades."

"OK then, but I am bloody useless at charades," I confessed.

"Alright. We'll go first," continued Megan enthusiastically. "I'll give you clues for Suzi's name."

Megan then looked around the immediate area, prospecting for ideas for her clues. After only about 15 seconds, she had begun pointing and gesticulating back towards the picnic table where we had consumed our lunch.

"Table? Bench? … Picnic?" I began. "Suzi Picnic-table … how about that?"

Megan started swirling her arms around in circles.

"Waving? … Arms? … Round? … Circles … Suzi Circles?"

Megan gesticulated further, pointing again back over towards the table and cart with the fuchsias.

"Oh, am I getting closer? … Suzi Cart? … Suzi Carter? … Suzi Fuchsia-bushes? … Suzi Horse-and-carriage? … I told you I was rubbish at this."

Megan began to rotate her arms again, then pointed back in the same direction.

"Suzi Round? … Suzi Wheel?"

Megan jumped up and down, crazily waving her arms round and round.

"Suzi demented-chimpanzee? … No … Wheels? … No … Suzi Wheeler?"

"Got it!" screamed Megan, now releasing all her pent-up frustration at my slowness to guess correctly. "Demented chimpanzee? I'll give you a slap BJ. Anyway, yes, it's Suzi Wheeler. OK Suzi, now it's your turn to give clues for me."

My guesswork was once again rather laboured before finally succeeding with guessing Megan Turner. Many of the gesticulations, this time from Suzi, were not terribly dissimilar from those of Megan. Both Turner and Wheeler can be described by various revolving motions. I was just a bit dim. This time, I did at least restrain myself from likening Suzi to a demented chimpanzee.

"So, Megan Turner and Suzanne Wheeler. I guess it must be my go then."

I thought for a moment. "Do either of you know any Spanish?" My thinking was that the name 'Spydar' could be split into the English word 'spy' together with the Spanish word 'dar', which is the verb 'to give.' Pointing out or pretending to be a spider appeared rather too easy.

"No, sorry BJ, not a word."

"OK, a slight rule change then." I looked over about 50 yards away to where I saw the entrance to the nocturnal house. "OK, we will find the clue in there."

"Oh ... Bruce Bat? ... No ... Batman ... Bruce Batty? Bruce Owl?"

As we walked slowly through the double-door entrance and into the darkness of the nocturnal house, I found an opportune moment for a surprise snog with Suzi.

"Mm-hmm ... Bruce Kisses?" she guessed. "I like that."

"No, but I might have had to change my name if it was. Can you imagine?"

Megan continued on in front of us. "Mouse? ... Snake? ... Oh, yes, Bruce Snake ... that describes you well." Megan giggled.

"How about Rat?" asked Suzi. "I hope you aren't a love rat BJ," she continued as she stole another kiss.

After moving on through gerbil, flying fox, viper, tree-boa, python, cockroach and gecko ... the girls finally guessed spider.

"Wow! Bruce Spider. That's very different," said Megan.

"Yes, with a 'Y' and an 'A', so 'Spy', as in observe, and 'dar', as in the Spanish word to give. So, I see and I give," I explained. I then clasped Suzi's hand and pulled her close. "I see you need a kiss ... so, I give you a kiss." I followed up with a gentle, long, lingering smacker.

"Shocking BJ," exclaimed Megan in a disapproving tone which then turned into a laugh. "So, how many times have you used that corny line?"

"Well, not half as often as I wanted to over the years. But it's a real corker, isn't it? It certainly deserves an outing or two, once in a while."

♦ ♦ ♦

On exiting the nocturnal house and re-emerging into the bright sunny afternoon, it suddenly occurred to me that Megan already knew quite a lot about my love life over the years (or rather, the barrenness of it), and that I also knew quite a bit about Megan. This is what had kept us entertained for several hours on the bus from Alice Springs to Townsville. But I didn't know how much of this Megan would have told Suzi, and I still knew hardly anything about Suzi's love history.

As we walked past the next few enclosures, including emus and cassowaries, Megan began singing the theme to Spiderman.

"Spiderman, Spiderman ... does whatever a spider can."

Meanwhile, I gradually probed Suzi to tell me a little more about her love-life, while also downloading some of my own past. While I think it may be a good thing to keep some aspects of one's past deeply buried, there are other aspects which allow someone who is close to you to get a better understanding of you as a person. It helps to be aware of sensitive subjects and possible trigger points.

Relationship-wise, it appeared that Suzi was several levels more experienced than me. Although she had not been seeing anyone for more than a year, she had been with the same boyfriend for most of her first two years at university. Before that, she had a couple of other shorter-term flings during sixth form. So, she was streets ahead of me in terms of the amount of time spent in any romantic relationship. Suzi was not so forthcoming about sexual intimacy, perhaps not surprisingly. I was also not so forthcoming with any of the intimate details about Elaine or Jeannie. They were best left in the past, as perhaps were my liaisons with Megan and Brigit, both of which Suzi knew about anyway.

My own sexual experiences were still rather limited, but I had certainly been rediscovering my mojo since I had been out in Australia. Although none of the recent romantic encounters had involved sleeping together, this was probably a good thing. In each case, I had only known these girls for a few hours, and although the physical attraction may have been there, I was not even close to being emotionally ready. *What am I talking about? I know I'd have gone to bed with any of them given half a chance. Well, maybe not Brigit, but definitely the others ... and especially Megan.*

These counter-thoughts probably confirmed how emotionally immature I still was. I was also undoubtedly not yet ready for things to advance too far sexually with Suzi, despite me really aching for it. It was perhaps a good thing that the prospect of sex had been moved off the table for now. But, would I be any more ready in a few weeks' time if England won the World Cup? While I didn't really care for one-night stands, I just didn't know whether I would ever be long-term relationship material? My experiences so far provided no supporting evidence.

When one cuts through all the emotional side, and looks at the facts and logic (which, being an overthinker, I frequently do), there was a good case for optimism of something longer-term with Suzi. We were at a similar stage in life, both just out of university, both in Australia to discover a bit more of the world, and both lined up with career-starting jobs in London when we returned to England. That all seemed to align quite well. Suzi had not already been put off by my looks, so it was only going to fall apart if she started to see through my rubbish personality.

While Suzi and I had been talking relationships, Megan had been chatting to one of the zookeepers who had been bringing food to the cassowaries.

"Hey Suzi, BJ," called Megan. "Did you hear just now about how dangerous these cassowaries are?"

"Sorry, no," I responded. "We were just talking."

"Well, you see those sharp claws ... they have been known to kick men in the balls, disembowelling them with one strike."

"No kidding? Well, I am glad that there is this wire fence between us then," I replied.

"Hmm," continued Megan, looking at me with an evil grin. "I think I like cassowaries. They are fast becoming my favourite bird."

As she was saying this, another zookeeper appeared behind us, carrying a couple of sleepy-looking koalas, which were holding on tight, one to each shoulder.

"Oh, they're so cute," said Megan.

"Do you want to hold him?" asked the keeper, a sturdy girl, about 5 ft 6, with short-cropped light brown hair and a broad smile.

"Oh, I'd love to," replied Megan.

The keeper then introduced us to her koalas.

"This one here is Olly. Olly's a male, just over three years old. And the sleepy one here is Meg, and she is just over two years old ... aren't you?"

"Oh, that's so cool. I'm called Meg too." Megan began stroking her namesake on the back of the head.

"Here. I think Olly is good for a cuddle, but Meg has been a bit reluctant today. She seems to be much the shyer one of the two."

"Not like you, hey Megan?" quipped Suzi.

The keeper then carefully lifted Olly onto Megan's shoulder, which he seemed to take to happily. Olly hardly opened his eyes, but just sat there and held on tight.

"They never really do a lot more than that," the keeper explained. "Well, in the wild they tend to just sit high up in the gum trees, munching away, but they don't usually move terribly far."

Suzi and I gave Olly a stroke on the back of his head, while Megan supported Olly under his bottom.

"He's not going to poop on me, is he?" asked Megan.

"Who knows?" replied the keeper. "They are just like human babies; something could come out of either end at any time."

On hearing this, Megan became a little more circumspect, and Suzi rather less maternal, declining to take over cuddling duties for Olly. It was probably just as well, as by now there were several other visitors gathered round, all eager for their turn.

"I'd better put on hold my visions of the two of us in Marks & Spencer with a baby buggy," I commented to Suzi.

"You didn't mention that particular dream, BJ," Suzi responded. "You are now going to have to tell me all about it. And you should tell me about any other dreams you haven't yet revealed."

With my arm around Suzi's shoulder, and her arm around my waist, we followed Megan in the direction of the big cats, as I tried to describe how I had imagined the scene.

"It was winter, and we both had typical heavy winter jumpers on ... not quite the garish Christmas jumper type, but not too far off. We were in the M&S store beside the market place in central Cambridge. (It was a store I knew well.) We were travelling up the escalator from the food section on the ground floor, up to menswear on the first floor. We were struggling with this buggy, one of those light-weight Maclaren-stroller types, probably containing a 12 to 18-month-old baby. I had never really pictured what the baby looked like in the dream. Maybe it wasn't a baby at all. Perhaps it was just a koala, or even a sack of potatoes. Whether it was a baby seemed unimportant in the dream, but I had seen us in a typical young parents' situation, seemingly living normal lives together. And we appeared to be very happy."

"What else was I wearing?" asked Suzi.

"Sorry?"

"What other clothes was I wearing? I want to know more about how you saw me."

"Well Suzi, it wasn't black figure-hugging leather, like in those other visions I told you about." I laughed. "No, this time, if my memory doesn't deceive me, you were wearing this blue and white patterned woolly sweater, and you had a thick padded winter coat ... a black one. And you also had black ankle-length boots and light blue jeans ... which were hugging your wonderful bottom." I gave Suzi an appreciative pat on her bum.

"Oh, OK ... I seem fairly normal then." At least Suzi wasn't offended by my imagination this time.

"Did you have any such visions of me?" asked Megan, having been eavesdropping on what I had thought was just between me and Suzi.

"Ah-ha, Megan, you were listening?"

"Yes. Naturally."

"Well," I started. I looked first into Suzi's eyes to sense her mood which appeared relaxed and happy, and then to Megan who always appeared to have that mischievous glint in her eye. "Well, I can't say that my visions of you ever really moved past the tight-black leather." I laughed, and thankfully, so did the girls. "And wonderfully attractive images they were too," I added as I smiled and closed my eyes pretending to be drifting towards those visions again. This prompted a playful smack from Suzi.

♦ ♦ ♦

As we reached the leopard enclosure, I had suddenly become a bit wheezy, and reached into my pocket for a puff of Ventolin.

"I didn't know you suffered from asthma," said Suzi, with concern. "Are you OK BJ? Do you need to sit down for a bit?"

"I'm sure that I'll be fine in a few minutes," I replied, slightly breathless. "It was possibly the koala's fur that set me off. I used to get asthma a lot as a kid, but through university, thankfully, I largely got rid of it. They do say that many people grow out of it. But I do still get set off sometimes by pollens, pet fur, farm animals and so on." I coughed, and spluttered a little as I explained.

"Oh, you poor thing," said Suzi. "Here, let's sit down on that bench for a moment, while you catch your breath."

"Thanks." I sat down.

"I suppose that means that in addition to the woolly jumpers and baby buggy, we won't be getting a cat or dog when we are married." Suzi kissed the top of my head.

This, perhaps throwaway comment immediately sent a warm feeling to my heart.

Wow! Did she say that just in jest, or does she really think we might have a future? But talking marriage? Pets? Kids? Is that all too soon? ... I suppose I was the one who brought all this up.

After a few moments the effects of the Ventolin had enabled my breathing to return to near normal again, and we continued to meander around the other big cats. As we walked and viewed the ocelot, jungle cats and lynx, I told Suzi and Megan more about how my asthma had impacted me during my school years.

"The family moved to Cambridge in the winter of 1974, when I was just turning six. Before that, I think I had suffered some bronchitis when I was four or five, but I cannot remember anything of that. But in the spring and summer, as I was trying to fit in at my new primary school, I started to suffer from asthma. We had a wheat-field at the back of our house, which was always being sprayed, and there were also so many trees and grasses around. I think the asthma might have been linked with that. Anyway, I got dosed up with medicines of different types, but throughout the summer months I had to avoid going onto the school playing fields at breaktimes and during lunchtime. That was a bit shitty. It meant I didn't get to play with many friends, just one or two kind souls who sometimes stayed with me indoors or on the tarmac playground. With hindsight, probably the worst part of it, was that I never really got to play with any girls. I missed out on games like kiss-chase, which I remember well from back then. Did you two ever play that? Perhaps kids aren't allowed to play it these days. But I was always the outcast, which may be why for as long as I can remember, I have been shy with girls."

"Wow!" said Megan. "You just don't really think about how things like this can impact you in such different ways. I am so lucky I have always been healthy. Oh, and yes, I do remember kiss-chase. I was always running after one particular boy when I was six or seven. His name was Shawn. I never caught him. I guess he must have been my very first crush."

"Yep, and you are hardly shy," added Suzi. "At my primary school we never really had enough outside space for such games. So, no, I never played kiss-chase. I have no idea what shaped my own reserved character, but I have never really given it too much thought."

"Well," I continued, "there must be a lot that is genetic. My grandad is quite shy too, but like so many things, it's a mix of nature and nurture."

Megan then began to sing as we continued walking around the big cats.

"[2]*...Every breath you take ...*"

It seemed that Megan's singing habit was a bit like mine, except that I always sung in my head when other people were around. Megan was also far more tuneful. I didn't find out, but it was probably my asthma that triggered this particular Police song to pop into her head. However, I did wonder if it might have been a subtle, and perhaps subconscious, warning to that she would be keeping a watch over me, making sure I treated Suzi well. Maybe it was a bit of both, and Megan never appeared to be focussing on the words that she was singing.

We continued to meander past the other enclosures and cages, and then, towards the end of our route, we reached the sealions and then the penguins. There were several species of penguin on display, ranging from the largest emperor penguins, to the smallest little penguins.

"Oh, cute," said Megan, on seeing a group of little penguins scuttling along a small sandy beach at the edge of their swimming pond.

"I think they are the same type that you'll see out at Phillip Island," I commented.

Suzi also thought so. "Yes, it's such a shame you can't come and see them too."

"Well, we've still got all day tomorrow before I have to lose you again. This time, at least I know your names. Hey, you should also give me your home phone numbers, just in case something happens and I don't see you in Auckland. Oh, it would be so bad not to see you again in three weeks or so, but even more disastrous if I could never find you again."

Without hesitation, the girls thought this was a good idea, and there was no time like the present. I found a pen and my travel diary, and wrote their numbers down. I also ripped off a corner of a page and wrote my number for them.

"Ah-ha! So, you are keeping a travel diary, are you?" asked Megan, with excited curiosity. "What do you write about? Are Suzi and I in there?"

Before responding to this question Suzi interrupted.

"A person's diary is their own business. Isn't it, BJ?"

"Indeed, it is. Thank you, Suzi."

"My pleasure darling. I'll make you show me it later." Suzi laughed.

♦ ♦ ♦

We took a tram back to the city centre, ending up close to Flinders Street station, where we alighted. After just a short walk, we discovered a riverside bar where we stopped to take in a few drinks and some pizza.

During a moment when Suzi had gone to use a washroom, Megan commented ... "I hope you don't mind that it is not just you and Suzi. I know I am a bit of a gooseberry."

"I don't mind one little bit," I said honestly. "Don't even think it Megan. You are such a joy to be around. I am no longer allowed to say that I also think you are sexy ... so I won't."

"No, you aren't, babe ... but I don't mind." She laughed.

"So, what do you think you are going to do with James when you get back home? Suzi told me that you have really been beating yourself up over the situation."

"Oh BJ, I really don't know. I keep thinking about it. I do still love him, I guess, but I just cannot see that being my life any longer. I have a new job in London, and there's no way he is going to move down there from Newcastle. Perhaps I could get a transfer up there with the firm in a couple of years, but it's a long time to be apart. We were apart for many weeks while I was at York, and sometimes it was hard. But James also wants to settle down, have kids and so on ... and I just don't think that's for me for a few years yet. I want, at least, to try to do something with a career first."

"I don't envy you that decision, but there are certainly many guys out there who'd date you like a shot. I know I would, if I wasn't now with Suzi. And there was Neil ... and ..."

"Yeah, Neil," Megan giggled then whispered. "That sex was so lush. But I wasn't so keen on his personality; he did seem a bit full of himself, and he was a bit insensitive. And then there was you babe. You were quite exciting ... but you got away."

"I don't think anyone has ever called me exciting ... thanks."

"You're welcome. But, anyway, you opened my eyes in many ways beyond what I had with James."

"Well Megan, there are certainly other people. Heck! You might even go for one or two of my friends. Most of them were as sex starved as I was in college; really sound blokes, but there was a real lack of available females."

"Do you think of me as just being about sex BJ?"

"No, no Megan, of course not. That's not what I meant."

"No babe, I know you didn't ... you are so sweet. Well, if we all live in London, and I am on the lookout, who knows? I'd love to meet your friends anyway."

"Lookout for what?" asked Suzi on her return from the washroom.

"We were talking about Megan's love life," I replied.

"About James?" asked Suzi.

"Yes ... James again," replied Megan. "I don't know Suzi. You know I just keep going over it in my head. I guess we are at a crossroads where we just want different things."

"Do you really know what it is you do want though?" I asked.

"Well, I think I do, and ..." Megan whispered again, "... and really great sex is definitely a part of it."

"Oh, dear Megan," said Suzi with a look of disappointment. "Life isn't all about sex."

"What?" said Megan, a bit taken aback. "Excuse me BJ, but you may wish to close your ears. Look Suzi ... although you slept with Matt a few times while in York, you never said that it was ever wonderful, did you?"

Suzi paused for a moment before responding. "So ... where is this heading?"

"So, Suzi. Well, with me and James it was never electrifying, even at the start. But then, with Neil it was just SO lush. It was REALLY amazing ... just so different."

"But Megan," said Suzi, "Neil was just a one-night stand. I am sure you would have found that the excitement would have tailed off pretty quickly, if you had slept with him a few more times."

"Well maybe Suzi, but I would have loved to have found out. Well, the sex bit anyway ... I wasn't into the rest of him so much. Oh, sorry BJ. Neil was your mate. I didn't mean ..."

"No worries Megan," I said. "Please say what you think."

"So, what do you think BJ?" asked Megan. "Perhaps you are the modern-day Casanova? Are you shit-hot in bed?"

At this point, Megan suddenly realised she may have gone too far. "Oh, I'm so sorry BJ ... and sorry Suzi ... I didn't mean to ..."

"Hey, no worries Megan," I said, thankfully not having to think of a witty response to her question.

"Me and my potty mouth. I am really sorry."

"Don't worry Megan," added Suzi. "I am quite certain that BJ is more than satisfactory in the bedroom." She winked at me. "And,

I'll tell you all about it after England win the World Cup." Suzi and Megan both laughed.

I excused myself from the table, and went to find the toilets. I thought they could continue their discussion without me. Now, however, I was less than sure that I was going to live up to Suzi's bedroom expectations. I was hardly God's gift to women, and I wasn't so sure that Suzi would find me 'more than satisfactory'.

Just inside the entrance to the men's toilets there was a condom machine. As I looked at it, I remembered when Megan had caught me standing next to one at the roadhouse at Tennant Creek. As I stood at the urinal, I considered the situation. I still hadn't replaced the two old condoms in my wallet. I would definitely need to do so before I could engage in any après World Cup Final action ... although an England win was still no more than a long shot. *But, if Suzi does really like me, it might not be totally out of the question.*

After I washed my hands, I checked to see whether I had any dollar coins in my pocket. I had a couple. I then made my way back towards the door to check how much was required for the vending machine.

"Oh! Wrong turn. This is not the ladies!" exclaimed Megan, appearing at the door. "Ah-ha, BJ! Are you getting prepared for later?"

"Fuck Megan! Why do you always come along when I am at a condom machine?" I immediately felt myself starting to blush.

"Well, I am glad you at least think about protection, and don't just leave it to the girl."

"Perhaps, but I have probably got fuck all chance of ever using them."

"Don't be silly babe. Look, how much have you got? Here ... let me give you a couple of dollars ... I wouldn't want you disappointing Suzi when the time comes." Megan smiled, clearly enjoying seeing me floundering.

"Oh, ookaay mom," I replied. *Man, this was embarrassing.*

It was 3 dollars for a pack of 3 condoms, so I took a dollar off Megan to add to the two I already had.

"So, which are you going to choose BJ?" Megan teased me further, as another man walked through into the washrooms, and just smiled.

I had never really considered different options, the few times I had bought condoms before; I had just taken what was in the machine. But here the vending machine offered a choice. By this time, Megan was enjoying it even more.

"So, babe, do you like standard ones, or super-sensitive? Or ribbed ones? Or even cherry flavour perhaps?"

"OK Megan, as you appear to be the expert, what do you prefer?"

"Well, they aren't for me, are they? OK, well, go for the ribbed ones ... Suzi might enjoy those more."

I put the coins in, and pulled the handle of the machine. Nothing happened.

"Fuck!" I tried the handle again. Nothing. And then a third time. Still nothing. "Shit! Why does this always happen?"

"Shall I tell the man behind the bar?" asked Megan.

"No Megan, please ... just wait a minute."

I then hit the side of the machine quite hard, and then hit it again. The second time, it was hard enough that I knocked the cover off the front of the machine, making it fall down in front of us to be suspended only on its hinges. At the same time, about twenty packs of assorted condoms dropped out of the machine and onto the floor.

"Coffee machines, condom machines ... you've got a real knack BJ."

Hastily, Megan and I picked up the condoms from the floor, and put them back in the machine. I took hold of a pack of ribbed ones, and put them in my pocket, before replacing the front of the machine as best I could.

With the vending machine now looking as though it was fixed, we left the gents toilets.

"I'd better go and find the ladies now," said Megan.

"It's over there." I pointed across to the other side of the bar.

"OK BJ, I won't say anything to Suzi. Just our secret," whispered Megan, while at the same time opening her purse to show me two extra packs of condoms which she hadn't returned to the machine. "It's just in case you needed some more, lover-boy." She smiled and disappeared over to the washroom, while I re-joined Suzi.

♦ ♦ ♦

After our meal, we walked along a path beside the Yarra River before making our way back to the hostel. On arriving back, we discovered Kirsten, Vanessa and Brigit in the common room, and joined them for a few minutes to chat. We didn't stay too long, as we were all booked on the Great Ocean Road excursion in the morning, which required a 6:00am pick up from the hostel. After a brief snog with Suzi at the foot of the stairs by reception, I kissed her goodnight, and we all returned to our rooms.

Tuesday 25 February - Melbourne

After a pretty decent night's sleep, I got up, got myself showered and dressed, and then met the girls in the breakfast area at 5:45am. Vending machine coffee (spurting half on the floor as usual) and some slices of toast were all I could muster before Jake, our guide for the day, appeared. At around 6 ft 4, athletic build, six-pack and designer stubble, Jake appeared to make the girls go weak at the knees. This appeared especially true for Brigit, who quickly latched onto him, and was busily conversing.

There were two other people on the excursion out to the Great Ocean Road: a Dutch couple in their early thirties, who were perhaps a little overwhelmed by the sudden influx of six more exuberant youngsters. We packed ourselves into Jake's 12-seater people carrier. Brigit quickly hopped into the front seat next to Jake. Then in the back, the Dutch couple were furthest forward, then the Germans (Kirsten, and Vanessa), then Megan on the next row, leaving Suzi and I together on the back seat.

"Behave yourselves back there you two," said Megan, with her customary teasing smile.

"I will try to live up to your impeccably high standards," I replied with a grin. My mind drifted back briefly to the bus journey from Tennant Creek, when Megan had tried to slide her hands into my shorts. Although back then I had cursed myself afterwards for stopping her, now that I was becoming more intimate with her best friend Suzi, I was glad that things with Megan hadn't gone any further. Well, probably.

"May I remind you two lovebirds of the rules," Megan countered. "There are to be no HJs until the semi-finals."

Suzi and I both laughed, as we cuddled up close. It had been so long since I had felt such a relaxed closeness to anyone, or at least it seemed so, but perhaps with each new experience our brains make us forget the past. Today, I didn't feel like I had to be on my best behaviour, and I also didn't feel like I needed to pretend to be someone else. Suzi really made me feel at ease with myself.

As Suzi and I chatted on the back seat, I could hear snippets of the conversations in front, including the odd reference that Megan was making to the Cricket World Cup, as she talked with Kirsten. They were also laughing quite a bit, and as neither had much interest in cricket, I was sure that Megan was telling Kirsten about 'Megan's rules' in respect of my relationship with Suzi.

Although rather silly, and although Suzi and I could certainly take or leave them, 'Megan's rules' did add a bit of fun and spice to our own conversations. They would also ensure that Suzi and I were both paying attention to all the World Cup matches, and probably Megan too, even though she had no interest in cricket. Today's match up was pitting Sri Lanka against New Zealand. This early in the competition, such games didn't really hold a great deal of fascination. Both teams, I suppose, were potential semi- finalists, but one suspected neither would be capable enough to go all the way. *Possibly a bit like me.*

While Suzi and I were both reserved in character, and dressed in relatively sober cut-off denim shorts and light-coloured pastel tops (mine was a mint-green polo shirt, and Suzi's a sky-blue sleeveless denim blouse), Megan and Kirsten were far more flamboyant, both in character and in dress sense. From my limited experience of both girls, it seemed that Megan was keen on figure-hugging black tops (not just in my dreams), while Kirsten seemed to go for brighter reds and oranges (today crimson was her colour). I must admit, I didn't even notice what Brigit and Vanessa were wearing. Probably as a typical young male, I only really took notice of the individuals who I found sexy. I was forever being dragged around by my libido.

Jake was in his mid-to-late thirties, and had been conducting tours for about ten years. He lived in central Melbourne, and alternated his excursions between The Great Ocean Road and Phillip Island, doing each of them twice a week in high season when the demand was there. Three years ago, he had set up a small company, with four other like-minded people, to specialise in these particular backpacker-oriented trips.

He drove us for just over an hour, to the south west of Melbourne, through Geelong towards our first stop of the day, where we were to be provided with a light breakfast and some much-needed coffee. The stopping point was Anglesea golf course, and there were two specific reasons for stopping here. First was that there was a café with decent food and reasonable toilet facilities, and second was that the golf course was well known as the home to hundreds of grey kangaroos, which were sufficiently relaxed around people to provide a great photo opportunity. The kangaroos were still wild, but were habituated to a life of grazing the greens and fairways of the golf course, in addition to receiving lots of human-provided food treats, which probably did them little good.

From the golf course we then travelled along some beautifully rugged coastline, past Cape Patton, Apollo Bay and Cape Ottway, before the road headed north west up towards Princetown and Port Campbell. The coastal views were magnificent. It was much like the mix of cliffs, sandy beaches and rocky shores that you find in Cornwall, or Pembrokeshire. Following this, we then got our first sight of The Twelve Apostles ... and these views were off the scale.

The Twelve Apostles is a stretch of coastline which contains vast sea-stacks, many of them over a hundred feet high, comprising bright yellowy-white sandstone, which had eroded from the main cliffs over millions of years. On a sunny day, with just a few cotton-wool clouds overhead, the beauty of these sentinel rocks rising up from the azure-blue sea, with intermittent frothy breakers crashing onto the beaches of golden sand ... it was simply breathtaking. And it was so fantastic for me to be sharing the experience, rather than just savouring the majesty of it all by myself.

We walked along the beach for about twenty minutes to get the sea-level view, before returning to the road along the cliff top, where we took in several further viewpoints. These clifftops, just like many others I had walked along in my lifetime, were sufficiently high and sheer to give me vertigo. Of course, none of the girls suffered from vertigo; it was just me, lumbered with my own afflictions. Yesterday it had been asthma, today it was the stupidly-irritating phobia that turned my legs to jelly, and led to voices of 'don't jump' appearing for no logical reason in my mind. At least today, unlike in the past with my family and friends, these girls were all sympathetic, rather than making fun of my discomfort. Well, mostly. They did still all have a bit of fun at my expense.

♦ ♦ ♦

A little way further on from The Twelve Apostles, we saw Island Arch, which was a sizable chunk of headland that had become separated off and eroded. The erosion was both around the rock and right through the middle of it, creating an archway. This coast was heaven for any landscape photographer.

Following on from Island Arch, we stopped for a cliff-top view of Pudding Bowl Rock.

"That's no pudding bowl," declared Megan. "No, that's two Penises! Look! ... Or is it penii? ... Suzi, what is the plural of penis?"

"I don't think I have ever needed to use the plural," said Suzi. "One cock is usually more than enough."

"One cock, two cocks. One dick, two dicks. One phallus, two phalluses ... isn't it? One penis, two penises?" Megan was still trying to work out what sounded correct. None of the rest of us were any the wiser.

Megan did have a valid point, however, that Pudding Bowl Rock did carry quite a resemblance to two male members standing proud next to each other.

"Two cocks and no balls," said Megan, continuing the theme.

"Yes ... two cocks being sucked off by the sea over millions of years," I added, unable to resist adding to the crudeness. "Strewth! I wonder what that would feel like."

"You'll have to wait until at least the final," responded Megan, laughing again at her own cricket rules.

"Oh, you guys ..." interrupted Kirsten. "Always with sex on the brain."

The six of us (Megan, Suzi, Kirsten, Vanessa, Brigit and I) then had a conversation justifying what other possible non-sexual imagery you could see in relation to Pudding Bowl Rock. It sure as hell looked nothing like a pudding bowl. The only other likeness we could think of was the twin rockets which launched the Space Shuttle, but all agreed that the male member was the closest match.

Our next stop was at Loch Ard Gorge, where we took a picnic lunch down onto the beach. The gorge was a narrow chasm which had eroded out of high sea cliffs, leaving a wonderful sheltered cove, and a large smugglers cave at the end. This was another beautiful spot along a coastline which was truly idyllic. I could have easily spent days here just relaxing, taking in the beauty of it all. It was all quite rushed for just one day, but it was so wonderful to be sharing the experience with these girls, and especially with Suzi whose hand or waist I was holding for much of the time. I had certainly fallen for Suzi in a big way.

At each place we stopped, on a beach or at a clifftop, I had the visions of feminine beauty to accompany the magnificence of the seascapes. And at each of the picturesque viewpoints, I had the additional experience of breathtaking kisses to supplement the spectacular views. Could life really get any better than this?

From Loch Ard Gorge, we then passed through Port Campbell and along to the Old London Bridge. I recalled that just a few years earlier, my brother had been here too, and in his photos the Old London Bridge had contained two arches and was still connected to the mainland. Back then the eroded cliffs had still been a real bridge. However, the arch that was closest to the headland had collapsed, and there was now just one isolated arch, but no bridge. Despite this, it was still ruggedly spectacular.

Our final stop-off for the day was at a small inlet with a sea cave which was known as The Grotto. Here, I found some lovely reflections in the calm waters of the rock pools, and I also discovered one or two smooth rocks which were perfect for a short rest and surreptitious snog with Suzi. *Yeah ... I could go back to visit this place again.*

♦ ♦ ♦

As we returned by road to Melbourne, Suzi and I cuddled each other on the back seat, with our bare legs entwined. I had never really given much thought as to why girls went to such great efforts to shave their legs. Like most of what I understood about female beautification activities, leg waxing and shaving all seemed a bit unnecessary ... and certainly doubted whether it was worth the enormous amount of time that it took. However, I couldn't complain as I was savouring the feel of Suzi's silky-smooth skin against my own weather-worn hairy legs.

This had been such a perfect day out, and I really didn't want it to end. I knew that I only had one more day with Suzi before heading off to Christchurch, and then I wouldn't get to see her until near the end of March. It also crossed my mind that it was quite possible I might never see Suzi again. It was far from guaranteed even if that's what we were now planning. Maybe her feelings for me would turn cold again after a few days apart. My stomach started to churn with anxiety, as I felt in my gut that the perfection of today was about to be wrenched away from me, perhaps never to return.

As Suzi and I chatted on the way back, and then continued over an intimate dinner together when we got back to Melbourne (Megan had decided to give us space), I was perhaps experiencing what true love felt like for the first time. But love was hard. It was not just about those fulfilling warm feelings inside, but love also went hand-in-hand with both fear and pain. I felt afraid that something would tear us apart, and worry that something would hurt the one I had become so close to. I feared never holding Suzi's hand again, or receiving the warmth of her cuddle or the softness of her kiss.

Walking back from the restaurant to the hostel, I began to hum, and also sing a little...

"[3]... Is this love that I'm feeling ..."

I was never really into Whitesnake as a youngster nor indeed into much that might be described as heavy rock, but 'Is this love' was one song that I'd found more catchy and tuneful ... at least before I began to sing it.

"It's lucky that I didn't fall for you thinking that you were a great singer," said Suzi laughing. "Even my dad is more tuneful than you, BJ."

"Well, thanks a lot," I responded. "That hurts. But hey, Whitesnake are not exactly great singers either. Perhaps I can serenade you with something else when I see you again in Auckland."

"Oh, I just can't wait, BJ." I detected more than a bit of sarcasm in her tone.

Once we got back to the hostel, we spent a little time in the common room with Kirsten, Vanessa, and Brigit, before I said my farewells to them. It was probably the last time that I would ever see these three, as they were departing Melbourne for Adelaide in the morning. As I hugged Kirsten for the last time, she whispered in my ear ...

"Hey BJ, I really hope that England win the World Cup now. I'll certainly be supporting them for you. And I really hope everything works out for you."

"Thanks Kirsten ... it's not often that a German gets to support England."

After hugging and saying our last goodbyes, I then gave another goodnight hug to Megan, before giving Suzi a much longer, more special goodnight cuddle and kiss.

Wednesday 26 February - Melbourne

The night had been long and sleepless. I had experienced a full range of emotions, from the elation and excitement of new-found love, to the sadness and despair of sensing that I might be about to lose it all. I had been so buoyant during the last couple of days, I just wanted the floating feeling to last forever. At least I still had one last day with Suzi before we parted.

I met the girls in the breakfast area at around 9:00am. I prepared some breakfast, and managed to squirt my coffee on the floor yet again. Why was I just so incompetent with coffee machines? After wiping it up, and struggling to pour a second cup, I joined them at their table.

We agreed on quite a leisurely day, walking around some of the central city area, taking in the botanical gardens, walking by the river, visiting both St Paul's and St Patrick's cathedrals, and wandering around some of the shopping centres.

The girls went into a travel centre to confirm their flights from Adelaide to Perth for a few days' time. They were taking another long bus journey from Melbourne to Adelaide, but felt they didn't also want to do Adelaide to Perth by bus. I couldn't blame them.

Today was really just a day of drifting. For most of the time I was hand-in-hand with Suzi, just trying to savour the moment, indulging in her company for the remaining few hours that I could. The three of us had a light lunch in a café by the river, and we must have walked many miles before ending up back at the hostel early in the evening. The time seemed to pass by so quickly, despite not really doing anything, and just talking a lot about everything and nothing.

I so enjoyed being with Suzi and Megan; they were both such genuine, kind-hearted, witty, caring and beautiful people. I was going to miss them so much, even if it was only going to be for just over three weeks.

Back at the hostel in the evening, we watched extended highlights of the Australia vs. South Africa game on the TV in the common room. Suzi and I were entwined on the sofa, while Megan occasionally made fun of us. We didn't pay too much attention to the cricket, but it was interesting for me to see that Australia were quite comfortably beaten, and, as the pre-tournament favourites, they had lost both of their first two games of the competition.

Perhaps England really could win it, I thought quietly to myself, as I imagined what such a result might mean for England's sense of national pride, and also what such a result might mean for me personally under 'Megan's rules'.

I forced myself to halt my daydreaming. I did not want to tempt fate. I knew it was highly improbable for England to win. And, in any case, I was so enjoying how Suzi and I were in this moment, with her soft caring touches and her tender kisses … I didn't need any further distracting thoughts in my head.

The clock eventually ran out for us. Megan signalled her intention of going to bed, and came over to give me a big hug and kiss. She pulled me close and whispered in my ear.

"I can sense that you are anxious BJ. But don't worry, we will see you in Auckland. I promise."

"Thanks Megan, I really do want to see you both again. And I do mean both, coz you also mean the world to me. These last few days I have been on cloud nine."

"I have noticed," continued Megan. "And so too has Suzi. You mean the world to her. And, you know BJ, I am pretty fond of you too. So please take care of yourself, and I will see you in Auckland."

After another big hug, Megan then left Suzi and I to say our farewells.

Suzi and I agreed that it was better that she didn't get up early just to see me off to the airport, before they later went off on their excursion out to Phillip Island. We both felt that it would just make us sad all over again. Saying goodbye was so hard, even if it was just for the few days that we hoped it would be. It was all tears, kisses, and telling each other how much we wanted our relationship to continue. We truly did not want this to be the end. In Churchill's words, we hoped that we had only just reached 'the end of the beginning.'

As I held Suzi tight, and then kissed her one last time, I even said a little prayer to God that this would not be the end for us. Well, even as an atheist, I wanted to cover all bases, in case I was wrong. I hoped that this would not turn out to be a curse.

♦ ♦ ♦

Part II:
South Island,
New Zealand

Chapter 2: Wizards and wedding tackle ... Christchurch

Thursday 27 February – Melbourne to Christchurch

After an early morning start, a long wait in an airport departure lounge, approximately four hours in the air, a long queue through immigration, and then a shuttle bus in from the airport ... at just before 5:00pm, I finally arrived at the Christchurch YHA hostel. Throughout the day, I had generally felt quite low. Leaving Suzi and Megan behind in Melbourne was gut-wrenching, as I knew that it would be at least three weeks until I would see them again. I was also feeling a bit apprehensive arriving in a new country without anywhere to stay, just like I had done when I arrived in Darwin in the second week of January. I was not in the most positive of moods as I arrived in Christchurch.

"Sorry mate, the hostel's full tonight," said the chap at the YHA reception.

"Bugger!" I said, both surprised and disappointed.

After finding it so easy to get backpacker accommodation in Australia, was I about to find New Zealand much more of a challenge? Thankfully the reception staff at the YHA were extremely helpful; they called around other nearby accommodation to help me find a bed for the night.

It was a bit of a trek away from the YHA hostel and a little out of the centre, but they had found me a bed for the night at the

Ambassador Hotel, which was close to the railway station. After a quick read in my Lonely Planet, I thought that this should be fine, as the guide described it as 'quite a flash old hotel, with leaded cut-glass windows, a lovely lounge area, and deep velvety carpets.' When I actually arrived at the hotel, I thought that the latter part of the description might have described it better in its heyday, well before it had become 'old' as well as flash. It was in reality a dark, dreary place, with threadbare carpets, but it was certainly adequate for me, at least for my first night. After so many recent nights sleeping in dormitory rooms, it was a welcome change to have my own room again.

What wasn't so good, was that after the first part of the week when I had felt on top of the world being with Suzi, I was now all alone again, in a new country, and feeling quite downbeat. In Melbourne everything was warm and sunny … in Christchurch, my world was now grey and cold.

From feeling so alive yesterday, all I now felt like doing was to snuggle up under a duvet and hibernate. But I was hungry. I hadn't had much more than a standard in-flight lunch on my Air New Zealand flight, and by now, I was naturally feeling quite peckish. Unfortunately, the Ambassador Hotel did not serve dinner. Tea and coffee facilities, and light buffet breakfasts were its limit, so I had to venture outside to find sustenance.

I set out from the hotel and walked northwards up Manchester Street and continued along High Street up to Cathedral Square, where I stopped to have a brief look around. It was now nearly 7:00pm, and most businesses appeared to be closed. The architecture and grey-masonry of the cathedral reminded me a bit of Aberdeen … as did the overcast skies and chilly temperature. On one side of Cathedral Square was the central post office, a substantial two-storey building, built with red-brick and white 'trim', complete with a rather attractive four-faced clock tower. This part of Christchurch was certainly pleasing to the eye.

As food was my primary purpose of being out, I didn't spend much time sightseeing; I was more on the lookout for cheap takeaways. Close to the square, I found a cheap burger-type diner, from which I bought a takeaway burger and fries, to be consumed on my walk back to the hotel.

On returning to my room, I flicked through the channels on my TV set. This was a welcome feature of the room. For the last month or so, if I had wanted to watch TV, I was forced to go into a hostel common room, which meant that I had to fit in with what other backpackers had wanted to watch. It had also meant mingling with other people, which, as a natural introvert, I did not always feel like doing. I wouldn't go quite so far as to categorize myself as a reclusive person, but I am certainly much less sociable than many, and do value having time to myself.

Although I was alone now, I didn't really wish to be with other people. Well, with the exception of Suzi, but she was now hundreds of miles away. I wondered how she and Megan had enjoyed their excursion to see the Phillip Island penguins. It was such a shame I wasn't still with them.

After flicking through the TV channels, I finally found some cricket coverage. I wasn't quite sure whether the game was live, but it was in the final few overs of the match between West Indies and England from Melbourne. I thought back to that game just a few days ago. How I wished I was back in Melbourne, watching the cricket with Suzi. Even if she had reinstated her 'no kiss until a wicket' rule, that wouldn't have mattered. I just wanted to hold her tight, to smell the coconut oil shampoo in her hair, to caress and feel the warmth of her skin and to lose myself gazing into her eyes.

I thought back to last night, when I had told Suzi how much I wanted to see her again, and how much she meant to me. *I didn't tell her that I love her. I'm pretty sure that I felt it though. Yes, I certainly felt it … and I feel it now. Does Suzi feel the same way? She didn't tell me either. Perhaps I should have told her. But the words 'I love you' are so strong … and once said, you cannot go back. Was it too soon? How would*

I know when the right time was? Maybe I have already blown it. Well, there was nothing I could do about that now. The next chance I might get wouldn't be for another three weeks.

In the cricket, England were cruising to victory. West Indies had been bowled out for a relatively poor total of 157. Chris Lewis, with 3 wickets, was the pick of England's bowlers, and then Graham Gooch struck an assured 65 with the bat, to steer them towards victory with 10 overs to spare. England had now beaten India and West Indies in their first two matches. These were two of the top-tier teams, and on this form, England would certainly be on course to finish in the top 4 of the group table and qualify for the semi-finals. As I thought about this, I laughed to myself, thinking about Megan's rules ... *That would qualify me for a hand-job.*

As this thought passed across my mind, I suddenly drifted back to the last week of January, and the brief time I had spent with Elaine on Magnetic Island. She was exactly what I had needed right then. Elaine was friendly, caring, and pretty hot ... a real breath of fresh air (despite her smoking). And thinking back to that evening on the beach ... *Mm-hmm ... she really did let her hands do some work. I could feel it now. I was getting aroused just thinking of it ... the mischievous look in Elaine's eyes, her face so alight with anticipation as she worked me towards a climax.* My wedding tackle had felt pretty sore for a day or two afterwards mind you.

I then tried to imagine what the MOT might be like with Suzi, but as I did so, it was Megan rather than Suzi who appeared in my thoughts. *Why did I see Megan?* Perhaps it was the difference between lust and love. I had fallen big-time for Suzi, and with her my feelings were much deeper than just physical attraction. There was definitely lust there, but my heart had melted too. However, with Megan, my mind still couldn't shake off visions that had begun back in Darwin six weeks ago, and there was also our snog on the bus from Tennant Creek, and her naughty proposal. I couldn't help but still feel attracted to her, even though it was Suzi that I wanted to be with.

After coverage of the England game had finished, I watched some highlights of Pakistan vs. Zimbabwe. Not surprisingly, Pakistan won the match quite comfortably. This game hadn't held too much interest for me; so little interest in fact, that I fell asleep with the TV on.

Friday 28 February - Christchurch

It was Friday again, and now 7 weeks since I left Britain ... I was still counting. Was I missing anything? Yes, I was, but not from back home. It had only been just over a day, but I was missing Suzi dreadfully. In distance, she was now well over a thousand miles away, and in time it would be at least 3 weeks before I would see her again.

My insides were churning with emotions. My heart held onto the feelings of warmth and excitement of new-found love, but this was all locked away beneath a wrapping of anxiety: the worry that I might never get to see her again. I was here in Christchurch, alone in time and space, but a part of my heart was many miles away and heading towards Adelaide.

After some fresh melon and grapefruit, and a bowl of muesli to accompany my coffee for breakfast, I set out from the hotel towards the town centre. Although the YHA hostel did have beds available for that night, I decided to remain at the Ambassador, as it was little different in price from the hostels, and here I had a private room where I could be miserable on my own when I so felt ... and today, I did feel pretty gloomy.

I had never been one for seeking the company of other people when I felt low. I always preferred to keep to myself and work my way through it. If I was with other people, I would have to bottle up my feelings, but they would still be there eating away at me. By myself, I could let my emotions out. I could let them have their say, and then hopefully let the bad feelings run their course before getting back on a more positive footing.

Anyway, although I was a bit down, I wasn't despondent. I was frustrated that I couldn't see Suzi, but I was still buoyed up by the fact that Suzi had liked me in the first place. Although she wasn't physically here with me, for the first time in a year or two, I did consider myself attached, and that felt good. I could visualise going to see one of my grannies (both departed now), and, at last, having a response to shut them up when they asked "have you got a girlfriend yet?" This time, yes, I fucking-well had got a girlfriend, it's just that she was thousands of miles away.

And Suzi was just the type of girl who both my grannies would have approved of; not that it mattered now. She was well educated, polite, attractive, friendly, and a good conversationalist ... this would have ticked most of their boxes. *Hmm now ... I still don't know whether she can cook.* For my grannies, and that generation, how a girl performed in the kitchen was of great importance. To me, not so much ... I loved my food, and so I was beginning to get reasonably proficient in the kitchen myself. If you are single and enjoy your food, there is really no sensible alternative, unless you are stinking rich and can afford to eat out all the time.

◆ ◆ ◆

I walked along Manchester Street, retracing my steps from last night, but this time continued further up and returned to the YHA hostel. It occurred to me that they had a massive amount of information about different backpacker excursions and also bus routes, and might be a better place than the Ambassador to advise me on any trips which I might wish to take.

I had read in my Lonely Planet about a few places to go within shooting distance of Christchurch, and there were two excursions which were of particular interest. One was to go whale-watching from Kaikoura, and the other was to visit the spectacular scenery of Mount Cook National Park. I was not planning to be in New Zealand for more than a month, and did have to be selective. Perhaps my plans would change after meeting Suzi and Megan again in Auckland, but who knows? I also had to be selective as I didn't have an infinite supply of money.

A friendly chap at the YHA reception showed me several different options, and then helped me to book up a couple of trips. Saturday would be whale-watching, and Monday to the mountains, with both trips picking me up at 8:00am from the Ambassador Hotel. Having got Saturday and Monday settled, I would then have today and Sunday to see what Christchurch itself had to offer.

I picked up several excursion leaflets, bus timetables and also a timetable for the Picton-Wellington ferry which I would need to take later to cross the Cook Straight, to get from South Island to North Island. Before I left the YHA, the final recommendation I was given was to go to Cathedral Square at 1:00pm to see The Wizard. I was told he was a character whom I would never forget. I had a couple of hours to explore before I would get to see him for myself, but Cathedral Square was where I headed next.

Even more so than I had found in Australia, the little bit that I had seen of Christchurch definitely felt considerably British. It is on record that Christchurch was given its name in 1848, but apparently, to this day, people were still debating the association of the name. While there were suggestions that it might have been named after Christchurch in Dorset, or after the cathedral at Canterbury, the more widely accepted version is that it was named after Christ Church College in Oxford. One of the city's 'founding fathers,' J R Godley, had studied there, and the early pilgrim settlers had described visions of building a city around a cathedral and university based on the model of the Oxford college.

I decided, as I so often do, to find a vantage point with a good view of the city in order to get my bearings and start to plan what I wanted to see. So, I walked into the cathedral and paid my $1 to climb the tower. The cathedral tower was a tall spire construction, but about half way up, at around 30 metres above the ground, there were viewing platforms that were built around the cathedral bells. The views were pretty good, if unspectacular. Although I was not too high up, most of the central buildings were not high-rise, and there was a good sense of space. I was able to get a reasonable mental picture of the layout of the city, as well as taking some photos over Cathedral Square and the surrounding area. Despite it not being too high up, it was still high enough for my legs to tremble with a mild dose of vertigo.

I soon found out that vertigo was not the only thing to cause trembles here. When I read some of the information boards next to the bells, I discovered that the tower had suffered mild earthquake damage a few times in the past. It was also perhaps an indication as to why there were so few high-rise buildings. [*What nobody was to know back here in 1992, was that between 2010 and 2012, Christchurch was to suffer several earthquakes and aftershocks that would devastate the city. The most severe was in February 2011, when thousands of buildings across the city collapsed or were severely damaged (including the cathedral) and 185 people lost their lives.*]

After descending the tower, I meandered around the interior of the cathedral. It seemed unremarkable, but when you have been into as many cathedrals and churches as I had, it really didn't appear to possess anything terribly special. Once outside again, I walked across the square to ANZ bank to change some travellers' cheques to top up my cash supply. Although I did have a credit card with me, it had been my experience in Australia that VISA wasn't universally accepted, and for buying food and small items, cash was still king. It was just after 1:00pm that I emerged from the bank. I picked up a couple of filled rolls from an adjacent delicatessen, and then walked back into the square.

As I did so, I soon spotted a crowd of people, who were all gathered around a tall red step-ladder. Then, a moment or two later, there he was ... the famous Wizard. He was a middle-aged man, perhaps late fifties to early sixties, medium height with a long grey beard. He was certainly distinctive. He was dressed in a long white velvety gown, with bright red and green trim. He also wore a matching tall white hat in the shape of a sink-plunger. He climbed up a couple of rungs on his ladder and then began to speak.

Today's subject seemed to be the 'New World Order', or something similar, as he ranted on about ineffective government, corporate greed and other such matters. He was known to talk on all sorts of topics, from local and global politics to human rights and feminism. The Wizard was a man who had an opinion about everything. He was quite an impressive and eloquent speaker, and his patter went on for around twenty minutes. He was interrupted several times by hecklers, which I thought might have been planted, as he had an amusing riposte ready and waiting each time.

After he had finished, I had a few words with him, while I purchased a copy of the Wizard's Map of the World. This was a South-North view, with New Zealand placed near the top, and the poles reversed … an interestingly different perspective from what old conventions had established over hundreds of years.

♦ ♦ ♦

After listening to the Wizard, I headed a few blocks west of Cathedral Square and wandered into the botanical garden, and Hagley Park. I had found when in Melbourne, Sydney and Brisbane, that the botanical gardens had been lovely places to spend time away from the bustle of people, while also seeing not only botanical specimens, but a bit of local nature, such as birds and butterflies. In this regard, today I was a little disappointed, as I spotted little wildlife of note as I walked around. However, with the park being on a hill, there were at least great panoramic views westwards across the plains and towards the foothills of the Southern Alps.

As I walked around by myself, perhaps my mind was inspired by the Wizard, as I started singing Queen's 'A kind of magic'. I then seemed to be stuck in a Queen mood as I began to think again of Suzi. I became more melancholic, as the songs moved to 'Love of my life' and 'Save me'. I was feeling downbeat being by myself again after having had such a wonderful time in Melbourne. I so looked forward to meeting up with the girls again in Auckland, so much so that I was almost wishing my life away. I had to snap out of it. I still had lots to see and do in the intervening weeks, and I hadn't come to the other side of the world just to be miserable.

I walked back into the city centre along perhaps the most British bit of the city: the part of the River Avon, which was flanked by Cambridge Terrace to the north and Oxford Terrace to the south. Before turning to walk alongside the river, I stopped to look at the Scott statue on the corner of Oxford Terrace and Worcester Street. Robert Falcon Scott and his expedition parties had used Christchurch as a base before setting off for the Antarctic (a little more adventurous than I was). The statue itself had been carved by the explorer's widow who, judging by the quality of carving, must have been quite an artist.

The whole feeling of this area of town was quite similar to that of the River Cherwell as it flows through Christ Church Meadow in Oxford, and also similar to parts of the Backs in Cambridge. The Avon was quite narrow, and it was lined with grassy banks on which visitors were sitting or lying down enjoying the afternoon sun. On one of the manicured lawns there was an art class. A teacher and a dozen mature students sat in front of their easels, trying to capture the distinctive architecture of Christ's College. Intermittently, as I walked alongside the river, I was passed by tourists paddling along the river by canoe, or zigzagging along in punts.

The whole scene reminded me of many a sunny afternoon in the lead-up to taking my Finals, sitting by the River Cherwell with my study notes, trying to find the motivation to revise. I remembered that I was always pretty hopeless at revising in the sunshine. As I sat by the river, I could rarely focus on my study. My mind was almost always preoccupied by the paucity of my love-life. Finding love, to me, had always seemed of far greater importance than what class of degree I achieved, but it was always so elusive. And yet now, in Melbourne, just a few days ago, after travelling to the other side of the world, perhaps I had finally found what I had been searching for. Well, maybe I had found who I had been searching for, but the girl in question was still eluding me, now being a thousand or more miles away across the Tasman Sea.

Despite feeling somewhat melancholic, I still enjoyed meandering around this 'little Oxbridge'. With Christ's College, the Victoria Clock Tower, the Cathedral of the Blessed Sacrament, Antigua Boat Houses, and the pastel-coloured art deco buildings of New Regent Street, Christchurch was a delightfully relaxing city to wander around. As late afternoon turned into evening, I popped into a mini-supermarket, and purchased some bread, cold meats, tomatoes and so on ... and by so on, of course I meant plenty of chocolate. These groceries were both for an evening snack, and to enable me to make myself a packed lunch for tomorrow's trip to Kaikoura. I also found the latest copy of the International Express newspaper, which I thought was worth a look, to catch up on what had been going on back home in the UK.

When I got back to my room in the Ambassador Hotel, I switched on the TV, and was disappointed to discover that there was no cricket showing. Today's game from MacKay in Queensland, between India and Sri Lanka, had been abandoned in the first over due to rain. *And people say that rain only ruins the cricket in England.*

So, for the remainder of the evening, I skipped though the TV channels and tuned and retuned my radio, trying and failing to find something mildly entertaining. I also flicked through my newspaper but, disappointingly, this didn't contain much of interest either.

Saturday 29 February – Christchurch to Kaikoura

As I got up and put my watch on, I noticed that it was February 29th. ... Or was it? Perhaps it was March 1st? I always get caught out by leap years, just like I usually do when the clocks change forward to British Summertime and then back again to Greenwich Meantime. I switched the TV on to find a news channel to try to confirm dates, and then checked on my excursion booking slip. Both appeared to confirm it was February 29th, and that it was indeed a leap year. So, today was the one day in every four-year cycle in which it was all good and proper for your girlfriend to ask you to marry her.

Well, that wasn't going to happen for me today, was it? However, at least I might be a bit closer this time. I do, at least, have a girlfriend. Well, I think so ... I did three days ago anyway. I hope that Suzi is missing me, and wants to get back together when we reach Auckland. Quite pointlessly, my mind then got immersed in hypotheticals. *But what if she had been here today, and what if she had asked me to marry her? Highly unlikely, but let's just say ... what if she had? Would I have said yes or no?*

This question now bothered me. How ready was I for any long-term relationship? How about commitments? Deep down, I did feel like I was falling in love with Suzi, but was I actually ready for commitment? And if so, how much? Was Suzi really the one? I had never really been in any position where I could even contemplate such a thing before.

Perhaps it's a good thing Suzi isn't here. I just don't know what I would do. I sure don't want to lose her, but how do I know if she is really THE ONE? Shit! ... I really don't know. But how will I ever know? Will I ever be ready for lifelong commitment, and what does that feel like? And if I did get married, the next thing is kids ... Wow! ... And then your life, your freedom totally disappears. Shit! ... I really need to get my head together before Auckland.

I consoled myself that the possibility of any marriage proposal really was a long way off. *I had after all only been seeing Suzi for a few days. Why was I even thinking about this? I should just count myself exceedingly lucky if I actually get to see Suzi again in Auckland. This is by no means certain, and any number of things could still prevent that from happening.*

♦ ♦ ♦

After all this strange and largely irrelevant thinking, I was pleased when the minibus for Kaikoura pulled up in front of the hotel at 8:00am. I could now focus my attention on other matters. A handful of other backpackers were already on board the bus, but apart from a polite nod or hello from a couple of them, nobody was especially keen to engage in any conversation. I settled into a double seat towards the back, and then we were off.

The plan for the day was to drive from Christchurch, northwards for just over a hundred miles to Kaikoura. We would then have a bit of time to wander around the small town, then at 1:00pm we were scheduled to take a boat out whale-watching. I couldn't wait.

I had never been whale-watching before, and the prospect was exciting. Kaikoura was considered to be the best place in the world for nature lovers to come to see sperm whales. According to the promotional leaflets, sightings were almost guaranteed. Kaikoura had a rare and special geography. Just over half a mile out from the shore, there is a sudden drop where the continental shelf comes closest to the land. From a depth of less than 100 metres, the sea bottom suddenly falls off to nearer 800 metres. Warm and cold currents converge, and an upswelling is created which brings nutrients up from the ocean floor. These nutrients pull in all the small marine creatures, which then entice the bigger fish and squid, which in turn attract the sperm whales.

The bus journey of around two and a half hours was quite tedious, although we did get a few decent views of the coastline on the way. However, arriving in Kaikoura, the scenery became spectacular, windswept and wild. The small town was set beachside on its own small quasi-peninsular, while inland the backdrop comprised snow-capped mountains. Until a few years ago Kaikoura was just a small fishing village, well known for its crayfish, but otherwise quite an obscure backwater. Then, in 1987, the first of the whale-watching tours began, and since then the town was rapidly transforming into an ecotourism hotspot.

There were two companies running whale-watching tours from Kaikoura, and they cooperated with each other with regard to sightings. It made sense for them to do so, because the success of one contributed to the success of both. The more tourists who saw whales and went away happy, the more this would attract others. Both operations used boats equipped with hydrophones to locate the whales, and boats which could move quickly enough to where a whale surfaced for air, before the whale dived again. The tour leaders maintained that, at this small scale, the boats did not seem to affect the whale behaviour, and appeared to have no negative impact. I don't think any research had actually been done to verify this, but with only a couple of boats operating, it was unlikely to be too intrusive to the whales. However, if the nature-tourism continued its exponential growth, I could envisage this might soon become a problem. Even if there were five or six boats operating in the same area, it would be a substantially different picture, and it might lead to the whales choosing to go somewhere else. It was a difficult balance.

The boat which I boarded seated about twenty people, and had a high-powered engine which sped us along towards the area where sightings were most frequent. Our guide, Billy, appeared knowledgeable about the area and its wildlife, and was bubbling with enthusiasm. He explained much about the ocean currents, the food chains, and different species to be found in the area. Whales were his particular favourite.

"I'll tell you a few facts about sperm whales," Billy declared. "They are present in all the oceans of the world, and we are lucky that Kaikoura is a fantastic place to see them. They migrate up to warmer waters for breeding ... I think this is true across the globe, but certainly is for the whales that we see here. The only real predator that a sperm whale has, other than humans of course, are packs of Orcas (or killer whales). We don't know how frequent such attacks are, and my guess is that Orcas might attack the calves, but not so often the adults. Sperm whales are best known for eating squid, but will eat other cephalopods (octopus and cuttlefish) as well as fish. They are known to live up to 70 years, and maybe more, by which time a fully grown male might be 15 to 16 metres in length and 35 to 45 tonnes. Yeah, they get pretty big! The females are much smaller, perhaps 10 to 12 metres, and 15 to 16 tonnes. Females reach maturity between 7 and 14 years, while males become mature at around 18 years. Yeah, a bit like humans ... males are always slower, aren't they?"

Billy paused for a moment while he spoke to his counterpart on the other boat. This had also set off from Kaikoura at the same time, but was heading in a different direction. The other boat confirmed that they had still picked up no signs on their sonar.

"Does anybody know why they are called sperm whales?" continued Billy. "No? ... OK, well, they were called sperm whales because of a special organ that they have inside the head ... the spermaceti organ. It produces a white waxy substance, which people initially confused with semen."

Billy, at this point, paused and looked around as if to check on his audience. He smiled. "Anyway, as we are talking sperm ... sorry to the ladies by the way ... but can anyone guess how big a whale's penis is?"

Always good to get down to base humour.

Together with a couple of my fellow boat companions, we made gestures with our hands and arms to suggest that we thought the answer might be close to a metre. I couldn't remember having seen any whale-dick footage on David Attenborough programmes ... they were more family-friendly viewing. But it seemed to me that the answer had to be at least a metre ... minimum.

"Well," continued Billy, "the sperm whale penis is a little smaller than the largest whale penises, which are thought to be the blue whales. Now those ones can reach more than 3 metres in length. Real whoppers, yeah? How about that?" He winked at one of the young ladies on board, who quickly looked away, blushing.

"Unlike many other mammals, not too much is known about whale mating behaviour. It is not so easy to study. However, with technology and study techniques getting better, our knowledge is improving all the time." Billy paused for a few moments checking his hydrophone, before resuming.

"Anyway ... back to the male sperm whale. Another interesting fact for you ladies. A male sperm whale can ejaculate about a gallon of semen!" Billy now winked at the young lady who was still blushing from his earlier comment. "Wow! This makes me feel pretty inadequate," Billy joked.

Me too!

"Oh yeah, here's another one," continued Billy. "I am not so sure regarding sperm whales, but I remember a year or two ago that they had found a southern right whale in possession of two 500-kilo testicles. Yeah, you heard correct ... 500 kilos! Wow guys! Fancy carrying those about?"

Billy was a fun character, but he also knew about the wildlife. He talked about the whales being able to stay underwater for 90 minutes or more, diving down to below 3000 feet, having one of the loudest known clicking sounds in the ocean, and producing vomit (ambergris) that was used in high-end perfumes. This was all most impressive, but it was the wedding tackle that would surely remain in the memory of most people on this excursion.

As we searched for whales, there was also other wildlife to see, including dozens of seals, terns and petrels and also a little blue penguin, which was fabulous to see, even if just for a few moments. The backdrop of the mountains behind Kaikoura was also spectacularly beautiful. And then, the first sighting of a sperm whale was something really special.

Surfacing gradually like a submarine, a large black torpedo eased itself through the water. 40 tonnes-worth of squid-eating monster appeared alongside our boat less than 20 metres away. It was awesome. It snorted loudly a few times as it expelled water through its blowhole. It then appeared to be resting while, presumably, it was allowing its lungs to refill with fresh air. This magnificent beast remained at the surface for only a few minutes, but it was sufficient time for the other boat to speed over towards us to see it. And then, as suddenly as it had appeared, it gave us a wonderful arching flick of its tail, before disappearing towards the deep. This was the only sperm whale sighting we had, but it had been fabulous, and worth every effort and every dollar to come to see it. It was breathtaking, and so close. Perhaps the only disappointment to the ladies on board, was that we never got sight of its genitals!

♦ ♦ ♦

I was dropped off outside the YHA hostel on returning to Christchurch. I walked back to the Ambassador Hotel, stopping for some fried chicken and chips on the way.

When I got back to the hotel, I used the pay-phone to make a brief call back home. I hadn't called for a few weeks, so I thought it was probably a good idea to update my parents that I had now moved on from Australia. I knew that it was highly unlikely that they would ever need to try to contact me, but felt I should update them on where I was. I suspected they would probably only start to worry if they hadn't heard from me for a couple of months. But if I suffered an accident, or was murdered by an axe-wielding maniac ... well, it would probably be helpful for them at least to know which country I was in, and also a bit about where I was intending to go next.

With a 12-hour time difference, I had to call them either at the beginning or at the end of the day. After a lengthy dialling tone and, I imagined, probably a brief argument of "oh, you go ... no I went last time ... no, you get it ... oh, alright I suppose I'll have to go again," I managed to get through to my mum. She was nearly always the one who would answer the phone when it rang, and always complained that my dad never answered it.

There didn't appear to be much news from home. My grandfather had suffered a minor fall in the house a few days ago. He had lived with my parents since just after my gran died. They had called the doctor in to give him a quick check up. Apparently, he was a bit shaken, but otherwise fine, and he was quickly back to savouring his whisky again.

I felt some sympathy for my parents. They had really wanted to travel more now that both Alex and I had left home, and they had saved hard for many years to allow them to do so. But, with my grandfather living with them, they now felt that they couldn't go away for too long. They hadn't wanted for him to try to look after himself, but they weren't keen on leaving him in any sort of care home. I hate the thought of me growing old myself ... but I guess the alternative is worse.

I told my mum briefly about where I had been in the last few weeks: a bit about Sydney, Melbourne, the Great Ocean Road, and the fantastic whale-watching. I had a brief word with dad too. I briefly explained my thoughts on my route around New Zealand, and told him that I would probably call again when I had reached Auckland. I didn't mention anything about meeting Suzi. Much as they would have wanted to know about her, my love life was none of their business.

After coming off the phone, I returned to my room and spent a couple of hours watching highlights of the day's cricket. New Zealand continued their great start to the tournament by comfortably defeating South Africa, while the West Indies thrashed Zimbabwe in the other game. The New Zealand media were starting to become quite enthusiastic about their team's chances. A 3-game winning start to the tournament was putting them in a strong position for a semi-final spot. They were also celebrating the fact that Australia, their greatest rivals, had lost both of their first two games.

Sunday 1 March - Christchurch

After helping myself to coffee and some sausage, bacon and eggs from the hotel's buffet breakfast counter, I sat at a table and looked out of the window watching the steady rain. It wasn't tempting me to go outside. So, I decided to have a leisurely morning and get some of my dirty clothes washed. I was pleased that this hotel catered well for backpackers, and possessed its own laundry room. Having put my washing on, I then went back to bed for a while.

I resurfaced late morning, retrieved my washing, and then set off towards Cathedral Square, which did appear to be the central hub of the city. The rain had stopped, and it was transforming into a reasonably sunny day, although still on the chilly side.

I stopped off at a small supermarket to get myself some provisions for a packed lunch for Monday's trip into the mountains, as my excursion didn't appear to provide for anything. I bought a few basics such as bread, cold meats, tomatoes, chocolate ... not terribly exciting but it would keep me going. For lunch, I stood in Cathedral Square eating a hotdog, as I watched some street performers playing a few jazz numbers. After going back for a second hotdog (I find one is rarely enough), I then strolled alongside the Avon River again, just taking my time in the pleasant surroundings. Fewer people were sunning themselves on the grass today. It had been raining and the grass was damp, but there were still several people punting along the river.

I should take Suzi and Megan punting one day. If Suzi and I are still together when I get back to the UK, that is. It would be wonderful just to float down the River Cam, alongside Grantchester Meadows with a picnic, in the company of these two wonderful girls. Megan could do the punting while Suzi and I cuddle and drink chilled chardonnay ... simply idyllic.

I then thought back to my previous visions of the three of us in a boat. It was a little different. It had been when I was at Kakadu, and I had imagined them in a rowing boat, jumping around in skin-tight black pvc bondage gear, trying to tie me down as though I was a small snapping crocodile. *Yes, I had some weird visions back then ... but really sexy ones.* My visions of us all punting along the Cam were definitely more normal, much more grown up ... but far less 'adult'.

Before going to university in Oxford, I had always expected that I would have done much more punting there. I probably did it only half a dozen times during my three years as an undergraduate. In those wonderful summer afternoons when I wasn't working, I guess I just found too many other distractions, such as tennis, cricket and beer ... as well as the endlessly frustrating pursuit of romance with any of the small pool of available and attractive girls. I had never really got to enjoy the romantic potential of punting. Oxford was a dead loss, and while I had been punting on several occasions during my school years in Cambridge, I had never been punting with a girlfriend. I had been punting with friends that were in a boyfriend-girlfriend situation, but never when it was me with the love interest.

Perhaps I was just not cut out for crushes and dates at an early age. Much of the free time in my pre-teens and early teen years were spent mucking around with friends down by the river, sometimes doing a bit of fishing, sometimes catapulting maggots at passing punters ... yeah, I was that kind of kid ... but they were disturbing our fishing. And then in the years which became ever more testosterone driven, I had discovered the game of snooker before I really discovered girls, and I was spending every free hour down at the snooker club. Perhaps it was now, in my early twenties, when I would finally start to find out what love and romance were really about.

I tried to imagine what Suzi and Megan were up to today. *They were probably still in Adelaide, and having a leisurely brunch somewhere. There was a three-hour time difference. Maybe they'd slept in ... although probably not if they were staying in a hostel dormitory.* It had only been a few days, but I really missed them, both of them ... *but especially Suzi ... I missed her touch, her kiss, her laughter. I missed caressing her hair, holding her tight ... I just missed that warmth that I felt when I was near her.*

♦ ♦ ♦

I returned to my hotel room mid-afternoon, and turned on my TV set, expecting to see some cricket. Today, England were playing Pakistan in Adelaide, and Australia were playing India in Brisbane. As four of the top teams in the world, these matches might start to give some indications as to who would make it to the later stages.

I was surprised, but not disappointed, that instead of cricket being shown, there was coverage of a big boxing match that was taking place in Melbourne. It was Jeff Fenech vs. Azumah Nelson II, a rematch following a controversial draw the previous year. Jeff Fenech was an Aussie hero, and the weight of media opinion had been that Fenech had been robbed of victory in their first fight in Las Vegas. The rematch was on home soil for Fenech who, this time, was the overwhelming favourite, and the afternoon fight was to fit with the USA prime-time TV coverage.

I had first started to like boxing when I was a teenager, and ever since then I had been keen to watch the big fights, especially in the heavier weight divisions. This particular fight was at super-featherweight, but was between two World Champions that were quite familiar to me, especially Azumah Nelson, the Ghanaian, who I had seen flatten one of Britain's best boxers in a title fight a few years earlier.

On this occasion, the 30,000 fans packed into Princes Park stadium in Melbourne were to feel more short-changed by their hero Fenech than they had been for the split decision draw. Despite a reasonably competitive showing from Fenech, the underdog Nelson scored a TKO victory in round eight, leaving Fenech with his first professional loss.

At least the Australian sports fans should have been a bit happier in respect of the cricket. In a slightly rain interrupted game, the match with India went right down to the wire, with Australia winning by a single run. This gave Australia their first win of the tournament following their two opening losses. India, however, now had two losses and a no result, and it looked like they might need to win all their remaining games to make the semi-finals.

England's game was far more rain affected. The rain was highly frustrating if you supported England, but a great relief if you happened to support Pakistan. Pakistan batted first, and made a dreadful mess of things, being bowled out for only 74 after 40 overs, with England's Derek Pringle the pick of the bowlers, taking 3 wickets. It was a terrible score. It was one of the lowest totals in World Cup history. England's reply was steady, and they had reached 24 for the loss of just one wicket when the match had to be abandoned due to the rain. A no-result game was declared, which robbed England of a nailed-on win, and at the same time kept Pakistan's hopes alive in the tournament. Another loss for them might have left them all but out of the competition. Although it wasn't a win for England, only New Zealand had won all of their first three games, and England were in second place in the table. England were a step closer to the semi-finals, and I was perhaps also a step closer to my own reward under 'Megan's rules.'

Monday 2 March – Christchurch to Mount Cook

When I had booked my day's excursion out to see Mount Cook, I had not really paid much attention to the distances involved. From the Mount Cook visitor centre, Christchurch is just over 200 miles away, and approximately 4 hours by road. I was going there and back, so this was going to be a long day out.

I was picked up as expected from the Ambassador Hotel at 8:00am, joining a group of two couples, one German, the other British. The plan was to drive from Christchurch on the main road heading south-west, across the Canterbury Plain, before turning west and passing through settlements such as Geraldine and Fairlie, and then on towards Lake Tekapo and the mountains.

For a couple of hours, we drove across a landscape of fertile green pasture, interspersed by a latticework of arable croplands. It reminded me somewhat of home counties England, only on a much larger scale. New Zealand lamb was a major import to the UK, and I could now understand why. There was just so much grazing land here, and flock after flock after flock of sheep … I couldn't recall what the official ratio of sheep to people was here, but there were just so many of them. As we travelled along, I remembered my conversations with Neil, a Welsh backpacker that I had befriended in Darwin when I first arrived in Australia. He was from a farming family, and loved telling some of the Aussie jokes about New Zealand sheep-shaggers (comparable to the English making fun of the Welsh).

Neil was also the person who had introduced me to Suzi and Megan. Tales of Neil's own shagging exploits were what had embedded those first erotic visions of Megan and Suzi in my mind, and in particular one steamy night he shared with Megan in a hostel in Broome.

As we crossed the Canterbury Plains, for most of the journey I gazed out of the minibus daydreaming as I watched the landscape drift by. Much of my daydreaming naturally involved Suzi and Megan ... thinking about what they were doing, where they were, and longing for us to be reunited.

From time to time, to supplement the sparse commentary from our driver-guide, I dipped into my Lonely Planet to see what it had to say about the small towns and villages we passed through. There wasn't too much in the Lonely Planet either. As we passed through the town of Geraldine, I noticed a mention of a small museum with vintage cars and farm machinery, and also a vineyard which specialised in elderberry and other fruit wines ... perhaps these were not high up my own 'to do' list as a tourist. And then the next small town of Fairlie ... neither the book nor the driver had anything at all to say about it. This really was just a rural backwater.

After the largely unspectacular views of the first couple of hours, from mid-morning onwards, the landscape changed. The snow-capped mountains of the Southern Alps became more visible both above and below a thin layer of puffy white clouds. The scenery improved further when we reached the beautiful blue-green waters of Lake Tekapo. The glacial water of the lake made it unlike any other I had seen before. The light-turquoise colouring of the water actually seemed a lighter shade than the clear blue sky above. Most lakes, seas and rivers that I had seen before were many shades darker than the sky above, but here it seemed almost magical ... or perhaps toxic. Although these glacial melt-waters were probably extremely clean, their appearance seemed unnatural ... like a slick of copper sulphate solution created in a school chemistry lab.

Moving on from Lake Tekapo, we continued on past the southern end of Lake Pukaki, and then to a place with the delightful name of Twizzel. Close to Twizzel there was a hydroelectric power station for us to stop and view ... quite impressive for all the aspiring industrialists out there, but I was far keener just to soak up the beautiful montane habitat. From here, we drove back up to Lake

Pukaki, and then up its shoreline to the northern end, where we continued to drive alongside the Tasman River and up to the main visitor centre for Mount Cook National Park.

From the Tasman River valley there were fantastic views of Mount Cook, and its neighbour Mount Sefton. Their peaks and slopes were blanketed in snow, so majestic on such a clear day. If I had taken this same trip on a cloudy wet day, I would have seen next to nothing, and it would really have been a waste of time and money. Eight hours in a bus when you have little visibility is not my idea of a great day out. But today Mount Cook, visible in all its splendour of 3,765 metres, did indeed look spectacular. Named in English after James Cook (and known to the Maoris as Aorangi, the cloud piercer), Mount Cook is the highest peak in New Zealand, and indeed the highest peak in Australasia. Reportedly it was first climbed on Christmas Day 1894 ... a pretty good morning stroll before the Christmas turkey.

We parked up outside the small visitor centre and were given about an hour and a half to wander around, take some lunch, and generally just do what we felt like. Being part of a group of five, with the others paired up, I was a spare part. The two couples went off by themselves, while our driver-cum-guide disappeared somewhere for his lunch.

I was quite accustomed to feeling like a spare part, as over the last few years, several of my best friends had got themselves paired up, while romance always seemed to pass me by. And now that I had found romance, and was half of a pair, the other half was thousands of miles away. I felt alone and, once more, I longed for Suzi. Couples had more fun ... they laughed together, joked with each other, and shared experiences together. Here I was, surrounded by the majestic snow-capped mountains of the Southern Alps, and I had nobody to share it with. The magic of the moment was just far less magical alone.

After I had seen my fill of the paintings and other visual displays in the visitor centre, had taken a comfort break and consumed a sandwich and some coffee, I walked up the road to a viewpoint by the Hermitage Hotel. According to my Lonely Planet, this was the most famous hotel in the country, on account of its wonderful views. Certainly, if I was wealthy enough to come back and stay here, I could not have complained about such views ... unless of course I had a room on the wrong side of the hotel, or if it had been foggy all the time. On this clear day, the scene across to Mount Cook, Mount Sefton and the surrounding peaks were sublime.

As I ambled around in daydreaming mode, I visualised that Suzi was with me, as I lost myself in late 1970's punk music ...

"... And Suzie is a jewel ..."

Although I didn't remember too many Boomtown Rats hits and was not massively into punk music, their hit 'She's so modern' was one that I used to sing to myself a lot. And now, a certain Suzi had just become my jewel, and just like in the song she had a flashing smile and was clever and considered.

"... Magenta is the best ... she really makes me laugh ..."

After my first recital, I replaced Magenta in the song with Megan in order to make the perfect fit. Well, Megan really did make me laugh; she was more jokey than Suzi and more comfortable as the centre of attention.

I suddenly had visions of Suzi and I about to take our marriage vows beneath a small pagoda on the Hermitage lawn. A string quartet was playing Mendelssohn's Wedding March. Suzi was dressed in a gorgeous creamy-white wedding dress and matching veil, as she walked up the path towards me. Behind her, Mount Cook displayed its snowy white slopes, which mirrored the flow of the wedding dress. *Hmm, this was a really beautiful scene ... but wait, who was this?* I had never met any of Suzi's family, so it was not her father walking her up the aisle. The scene became clearer. It was Megan walking alongside Suzi as her maid of honour, dressed (in the loosest sense of the word) in a figure-hugging black leather leotard, with thigh-length black leather boots. *Yeah, that figures ... I had to go for those sexy thigh-length boots.*

I still couldn't shake such sexy visions of Megan from my mind. They had been with me ever since seeing her in a black swimsuit in Darwin 2 months ago. Almost every day, as I had travelled around Australia, I had seen contrasting visions of Suzi and Megan. And, here it was again ... love vs. lust. When I thought of Suzi, I just wanted to hold her, smell her hair and to cuddle up on a sofa watching a weepy film together. In contrast, when I thought of Megan the vision was of ripping clothes off, and of hot, steamy, energetic sex ... it was 24-carat lust.

If I was having such dreams, did it mean it couldn't be authentic love that I felt for Suzi? Could it really be love if I still had such visions of Megan? Can you hold such fantasies for two people at the same time? ... *Well, you certainly can with lust ... in the past, I had definitely lusted after several people at the same time. But is lust so different from love? Does authentic love for someone actually extinguish all your love and lust for others? Would true love really turn off all such feelings? Or is it that you just learn to control your lust for others? ... Well, if I do want things to work with Suzi, I sure as hell had better start to control these lustful feelings I still have for Megan.*

In the past, I had been much deeper than the crush stage, and perhaps properly fallen in love on at least a couple of occasions. Now, I know there are probably a dozen stages between crush and true love but, quite evidently, I am no expert. Anyway, on those occasions, I really couldn't accurately recall whether I had still continued to think about other girls, or whether I had become totally fixated on the single love interest. I think it was the latter. Who knows? Perhaps it had been the lack of single-minded focus back then which had contributed to me being dumped.

As it was, I sang my way quietly through a couple of other Boomtown Rats hits (Rat Trap, and I Don't Like Mondays), before heading back to our bus for the return journey to Christchurch. On the way back, I decided to jump into the seat alongside our driver-cum-guide, Mark, as this front seat looked a little more comfortable, and there was definitely better visibility of the scenic views.

Mark was born in Auckland, but had lived on South Island for most of his life. He was in his mid-thirties, and luckily for me he was a cricket fan, so we had plenty of conversation. As we drove back, we listened to the cricket coverage on the radio, which today featured Sri Lanka against South Africa. Mark had been surprised and delighted by New Zealand's perfect start to the tournament. He also appeared to be overjoyed, as indeed I was, at the poor start for Australia, although both of us expected that Aussie fortunes were soon to change.

The return journey, of between 3 and 4 hours, retraced much the same route as in the morning. As we were driven through the spectacular mountain scenery, I listened to the dulcet tones of the cricket commentary on the radio. It was a perfectly relaxing way to spend the afternoon; so relaxing in fact, that the other passengers had all slept much of the way back to Christchurch.

We arrived back in the early evening just after the cricket had concluded, with Sri Lanka having managed to win a tight game in the final over. This win lifted Sri Lanka back into contention, but left South Africa at serious risk of elimination. Back in the Ambassador Hotel, I watched a few of the highlights on TV before crashing out.

Tuesday 3 March - Christchurch

It was time to move on. Although I had originally contemplated staying in Christchurch another couple of days so that I could go to see South Africa play West Indies, I felt that I had seen most of what I wanted to around Christchurch, and there was so much more of the country to see. I had also sketched out a timetable to get me up to Auckland, and found that once I started to do that, the days began to get eaten up rather quickly.

After a light breakfast buffet in the hotel, I walked up to the YHA hostel again, where I had found the staff so helpful in previous days. I discussed the next stages of my travel plans with the lady on reception, after which she helped me to make a couple of hostel bookings, and also assisted me with the purchase of a bus ticket. The next day I would go by bus down south to Dunedin, and then the following day on towards the resort of Queenstown. Queenstown was New Zealand's answer to Cairns in Australia. It was an adventure playground which drew tourists in from all over the world to try their hand at bungee-jumping, sky-diving, paragliding, white water rafting, sailing, canoeing and so on.

Mid-morning, I emerged from the hostel with my immediate accommodation and transport needs all sorted. I had no special plans for today, so I decided to meander again around the most picturesque part of the city, alongside the Avon River for the remainder of the morning, before returning to Cathedral Square for the 1:00pm performance by The Wizard.

This time his subject matter was a mixture of the inadequacy of the welfare system for looking after the elderly, followed by a full-frontal assault on the education system. One suspected that if The Wizard had ever decided to run for Prime Minister, he might have stood a reasonable chance. However, perhaps if I was local, and had listened to him every week for a few months, he would probably have become as repetitive and tedious as most normal politicians.

The weather had been a bit mixed since arriving in New Zealand, and today, scattered showers and chilly, damp, overcast conditions persuaded me to spend my afternoon hours back at the hotel writing some postcards while attempting to watch the cricket on TV.

Watching the cricket, however, also proved frustrating, as the game between New Zealand and Zimbabwe from Napier was also affected by the weather. It was a day on which everything appeared a bit downcast. I tried to write some postcards, but the only person

I could really think about was Suzi. I forced myself to write to my parents, and to two of my best mates, Chris and Paul, both of whom had still been seeking employment when I came away in January. I also wrote again to Jackie, my soulmate back in Oxford, whom I had last written to when I was back in Alice Springs.

I recalled quite clearly those few weeks ago in Alice when I had written the last postcard. Back then, I was really missing Jackie; she was the nearest thing I had to any love interest back home. We were close friends, connected on a similar wavelength, but the romantic spark wasn't there. Perhaps we would have been one of those 'backup couples' ... if neither of us were married by the time we were 35 ... that type of thing. But so much had changed in the last six weeks. Just like in Alice, today I was alone with my postcards and my thoughts, but now I could look back on the last month and a half, having experienced five different romantic encounters. And, the last of them, with Suzi, seemed really hopeful to be leading to something longer-term. Today I was not missing Jackie, nor anything else back in Britain. I was not looking back, but looking forward to three weeks' time. The one person on the planet that I wanted to be with was probably somewhere in Western Australia, and I was wishing away the time until we met up again in Auckland.

Despite not feeling especially like writing to anyone, I was glad that I made the effort to do it. It also helped that I was inspired by the whale watching trip. The statistics relating to sperm whale genitalia provided me with ample smut to write about. As I did so, my mind drifted back to one particular lecturer at Oxford, who was renowned for his work on comparative anatomy. He so relished describing animal prowess in human terms. He might describe, for example ... 'if a human male had testicles in proportion to those of a pygmy shrew, he would require a wheelbarrow the size of Peru to carry them' ... that type of thing. Unsurprising perhaps, that this particular lecturer appeared to command a substantial fan base amongst the female PhD students.

As I mused more about whale genitalia, I couldn't help thinking about the promise that lay in wait for me if England progressed to the later stages of the World Cup. The prospect of a sexual MOT with Suzi was an exciting proposition to hold onto, even if those rules or promises were made somewhat in jest. Yes, of course it was sordid ... but exciting all the same.

However, when my mind subconsciously drifted towards such erotic visions, it was not Suzi, but Megan that usually appeared. They were Megan's hands, Megan's lips, and it was Megan's naked body that I saw. Ever since Darwin, it had been Megan who had dominated the lustful sections of my imaginative space, while with Suzi it was the romantic candlelit dinners and walks in the park. *Fuck, what does this mean?*

What it means BJ, is that you want to shag both these girls ... but you had better get your bloody mind straight before Auckland.

In a dreadfully dull rain affected game, New Zealand took their record to 4 straight wins, as they comfortably beat Zimbabwe. Zimbabwe, without any wins, were out of the tournament, while New Zealand were on the verge of a semi-final place. A semi-final for England, and my own reward, also beckoned.

Chapter 3: Chocks away ... Dunedin

Wednesday 4 March - Christchurch to Dunedin

Over the past week, I had spent many hours by myself, alone with my thoughts. Staying at the Ambassador Hotel had been a far less sociable experience than what I had been used to while staying in the backpacker hostels in Australia. As an introvert, I didn't mind this too much, but after several days alone I felt it might be good to have a bit more of a social outlet. Having had a room to myself at the Ambassador, I would be sharing a dorm room in the Dunedin hostel, which would certainly force me again to engage with other travellers. This had its upsides as well as downsides.

I had certainly managed to sleep better in my single room, without any snorers, sleepwalkers, or sleeptalkers to bother me. It had also been great to have been able to slob around, and feel more relaxed while watching TV or listening to my radio, as I didn't have to be concerned about others. I was also more relaxed about the security of the belongings that I left in the room. Although I had not lost anything on my trip so far, I had been aware of a handful of other backpackers reporting theft during my travels in Australia.

After breakfasting, and taking several slices of bread and some cold meats from the buffet for a packed lunch, I checked out of my room and made my way to the bus station to catch my transport for Dunedin. The bus departed just before 8:00am. The journey to

Dunedin was around 225 miles, and we were scheduled to arrive there at around 3:00pm.

Newmans buses seemed to be the New Zealand equivalent to Greyhound in Australia, being the main express bus service connecting all the major population centres. The buses were comfortable, and well equipped with an on-board WC, and good air-con. What they weren't equipped with was the ability to control the weather outside. I had hoped to get some lovely views of the Pacific Ocean along the route, which for about half the journey ran close to the coast. However, for the entire journey, a hazy fog seemed to obscure all but the briefest glimpse of anything interesting.

So, for the majority of the journey, I occupied myself by trying to find something worth listening to on my radio, reading sections of my Lonely Planet guide, and also spent significant periods napping. As I re-read bits of my Lonely Planet to familiarize myself with Dunedin, I did make a note that the two most notable things to see in Dunedin were firstly Cadbury's chocolate factory, and secondly Speight's brewery. This signalled to me a town with well-balanced priorities, but not necessarily a place in which to spend too much time sightseeing.

♦ ♦ ♦

I arrived at the Dunedin YHA hostel at around 3:30pm, to find the chap behind the reception desk with his eyes glued to a small TV screen. It wasn't terribly surprising that he was watching cricket ... the World Cup bug was capturing interest.

Today's match was India against Pakistan, perhaps the fiercest rivalry in cricket. England against Australia would be considered by many to merit that title, but the sheer number of fans on the Indian subcontinent is phenomenal. There are many tens, if not hundreds of millions of people who follow cricket in India and Pakistan, more than the total population of England and Australia combined.

Today's game was in Sydney, and from the look of it, there was quite a packed crowd, and certainly much larger numbers than were in the West Indies vs. Pakistan game I had seen in Melbourne. It was also quite an important game for the World Cup standings. If Pakistan won, it would effectively mean India were out of the tournament.

There was another TV in the hostel common room, and several backpackers were watching. However, as I was travelling on to Queenstown the following day, and only had a few hours in Dunedin, I decided to make the most of the late afternoon by strolling around the town. The earlier dreariness of an overcast and damp day had cleared to reveal some late afternoon sun, but I was not really enthused about the sites of Dunedin. Perhaps my lack of excitement was partly because I was thinking so much about Suzi and Megan, and about what they might be doing in Perth.

As per the Lonely Planet description, Dunedin, with its population of over 100,000, really did have a Scottish feel to it. The town had been founded by Presbyterians in 1848 and was given the same name as the Celtic name for Edinburgh. For a while, from a few years after its foundation, it became the largest settlement on the South Island, as thousands of prospectors had flocked to Otago after the discovery of gold. Nowadays Dunedin was second in size to Christchurch.

As I strolled around, the unmistakable smell of Cadbury's chocolate lingered in the air. Not that I could distinguish Cadbury's chocolate as opposed to Nestlé, Mars or another variety, but the factory was certainly emitting a strong chocolatey flavour that wafted across the city. It was like the smell sensation you get when you first open a jar of powdered drinking chocolate. The initial sensations were of a lovely aroma hitting all the right notes with my nasal receptors and taste buds on my tongue. Then, after a few minutes, it became rather sickly, and I soon appreciated the gusts of wind that blew some fresher air through the streets.

Dunedin was pleasant but unspectacular. The grey stone buildings of the railway station, and parts of Otago University, were quite attractive. However, for me, the most memorable sight of Dunedin was a large amount of rusting ironwork, salvaged from the hulls of old merchant ships, that seemed to have been dumped as scrap metal at the side of the harbour. Such industrial waste rather spoilt an otherwise lovely natural waterfront area.

After a couple of hours wandering about, I found a fish'n'chip shop where I bought my supper, before heading back to the hostel to catch the end of the day's cricket. As I got to the common room, instead of finding the cricket coverage, I caught the middle of a newsflash. There had been a major disaster at a coal mine in Turkey, with significant loss of life, and the Turkish authorities still trying to recover bodies and assess the damage. Wherever in the world you are, you are not immune from feeling shit when you see footage of such human tragedy.

When the TV coverage returned to the cricket, I watched the last few overs, which saw a fairly comfortable victory for India. The result left both India and Pakistan with one win, one draw and two losses, and both teams were on the verge of elimination. The tragic news from Turkey, however, provided a stark reminder. This World Cup wasn't a matter of life or death ... it was only cricket.

Thursday 5 March - Dunedin to Queenstown

It was a dreary morning as I left behind my rather dreary memories of Dunedin. I am sure Dunedin was a more inspiring place than my own perceptions of it ... maybe I will return one day to put the record straight. However, as the bus departed for the 4-hour journey to Queenstown, Dunedin disappeared from my view and from my mind, just like many ordinary and unremarkable Scottish towns had done so in the past. (And indeed, many English and Welsh ones too.)

The trip across to Queenstown was also uninspiring and uneventful. There was a handful of stopping places along the way, including at a small town called Lumsden, where there was an intersection for the buses travelling between Queenstown and Invercargill. We had about twenty minutes to take a comfort break, during which time I wandered over to what might have been the main attraction in Lumsden: a small wishing well called Lumsden Lions Wishing Well. The well itself was pretty unremarkable, just a small granite-sided tube, about 4 feet in diameter, with a tiled roof above it. Mounted above the roof there was a handful of signposts to places that I certainly would not be going by bus today: South Pole 4988 km, New York 15264 km, London 17885 km, Wellington 784 km etc. Distances in kilometres always sounded a lot more than in miles, but either way, Lumsden was rather a long way away from anywhere.

As we drove beyond Lumsden, northwards towards Queenstown, our thus-far unremarkable journey became more interesting as we journeyed up the road sandwiched between Lake Wakitipu and the Remarkables (the mountain range to the south east of the lake). From the end of the lake and all the way up to Queenstown the views were spectacular. The scenery reminded me of the Scottish Highlands, just as it must have done for some of the early settlers, who had named the mountain peaks after the likes of Ben Nevis and Ben More. Others settlers evidently saw things differently ... Sugar Loaf, Tooth Peak, James Peak, Mount Dick and Big Geordie weren't quite the same.

As I looked at these mountains on my map, reading these last three names reminded me of Suzi, and also Megan. Both girls were Geordies, from Newcastle and Gateshead in the north east of England, and Megan had a boyfriend called James. As for Mount Dick ... well, not surprisingly my thoughts turned towards smut, and in particular my memories of Megan offering me a blow-job on the bus from Tennant Creek. *Yeah, BJ, you really shouldn't have turned that down.* I shut my eyes for a few moments and tried to imagine what it would have felt like if Megan had fulfilled her offer. No girl had ever made me such an offer before, so I found it difficult to envisage quite how it would feel to have Megan's lips and tongue playing with my wedding tackle. I could remember the soft touch of Megan's lips when we first kissed ... I remembered the taste and touch of her tongue ... I remembered that amazing electricity between us as we began to explore each other ... I remembered ... that I was now dating Suzi and shouldn't really be thinking about Megan. *Yes, it would be better for me to remember that!*

It had only been a week since I had left the girls in Melbourne, but I was thinking about them every waking hour. The few days I had spent with them were so uplifting ... they had made me feel so alive. This was true for our time in Melbourne after getting together with Suzi, but it was also true before that, when I had first met them in Darwin, and then again at Ayers Rock and in Alice. And now, sitting in the bus, arriving in the outskirts of Queenstown, I was reminded that I was by myself again. A warm feeling in my heart was all that I had to cling to, as well as the hope that I would see them again in Auckland.

♦ ♦ ♦

The afternoon and evening turned out to be far more captivating than most of the bus journey had been. Following a short walk from the bus stop in the centre of town, up along the esplanade by the lakeside, I arrived at the Queenstown Youth Hostel.

As I stepped into reception I was greeted by an enthusiastic middle-aged man behind the desk. He was keeping his eyes on the TV in the common room ... oh yes ... it was cricket again! Yes, today the West Indies team were taking on South Africa in Christchurch, while, more importantly, Australia were playing England in Sydney.

"Hey mate," he said. "Are you a cricket fan?"

"Hello," I responded. "Yes, definitely. How's the game going?"

"It's still early in the match, but I reckon England might win this one. Botham seems to be sticking it up the Aussies again. He's old nowadays, but still pretty awesome. And if you guys win, Australia are as good as out. Come on England!" Sharing a common enemy was often a sound basis on which to make friends.

The hostel manager, whose name was Ian, took my passport details and then directed me towards a dorm room containing six bunks. A couple of the beds were already occupied, and I put my backpack on the lower bunk in the opposite corner of the room. It seemed to me that dormitory etiquette was a bit like the etiquette that men have when they visit public urinals ... every new person that arrives ensures that they take the position furthest from each of the other people. You should never stand immediately next to someone if you can avoid it. When I was younger, I had thought that willy-fright, or the inability to urinate if someone was standing next to you, was an affliction that only I had. However, it seems like it is a rather common condition. Even if you are tanked up on beer, and absolutely bursting to release the pressure on your bladder, the prospect of standing in close proximity to someone else at a urinal can have the same effect as sticking a bung in the end of your urethra. Well, perhaps ... it's not that I have actually tried the latter.

Anyway, after relieving myself of my backpack, and then also relieving myself in the toilets, I returned to the common room to catch up on the cricket.

♦ ♦ ♦

It was around 3:00pm, and the coverage initially focused on the West Indies vs. South Africa game. The South Africans had batted first and had made a respectable score of 200 for 8 from their 50 overs. West Indies struggled with the loss of early wickets in reply.

The game was probably more important to South Africa, as they really needed to win it to remain in the tournament, and their players looked as if they were more up for it.

Someone who definitely was up for it today was Ian Botham, the England allrounder, who took 4 Australian wickets in a professional England bowling performance that had restricted the Australians to a total of 171 all out. This was definitely a gettable target for England. A win would leave England almost guaranteed a semi-final position, and probably also send Australia crashing out of the tournament.

I did consider taking a quick walk into the centre of town to orientate myself and start to plan my next few days, but the cricket at this point took precedence. I instead collected a handful of leaflets from reception and started to ponder over the various activities one could do around Queenstown.

There were a couple of other backpackers in the common room, two Norwegian blokes who looked approximately the same age as me. Neither was particularly chatty, nor interested in cricket. Apart from Ian, the hostel manager, who periodically came in for a closer view of the scorecard, and to enthuse about the Aussies poor showing, I watched the remaining overs of the match largely in my own company. I was a bit surprised there was no other interest. If I had been in a backpacker hostel in Australia, I felt certain there would have been more people watching. But there was one obvious difference here. Staying in a YHA run hostel, there was no alcohol on site, and I had to satisfy my thirst with an ice-cold Coke from a vending machine.

Normally when England have a run chase, particularly against Australia, there are lots of shaky moments, and causes for unnecessary excitement. However, this afternoon, the England batting was solid. With the loss of only 2 wickets, the team led by Graham Gooch, who contributed with a steady 58, knocked off the runs with 10 overs to spare. Barring a miracle set of results from other teams, it now looked as though Australia were all but out of the World Cup. England now had 3 wins and a draw from their 4 games, and really only needed one more scoring result to be through to the semi-finals ... and this looked like a nailed-on certainty as they still had to play minnows Zimbabwe.

After the cricket had finished, which was after 8:00pm New Zealand time, I strolled along the road into the centre of Queenstown, looking for something to eat, and considering whether to go somewhere for a beer.

Just as I had previously read about, Queenstown did appear in its own way to be New Zealand's equivalent to Cairns in Australia. It was a backpacker honeypot. If you were a young adventurer wanting to try your hand at bungee jumping, rafting, sailing, skydiving, or just having a good time with other young people ... this was the place to come. Despite being just a small resort of a few thousand people, its compact centre was packed with places to eat and drink, and premises of tour operators and outdoor activity providers, one of which was the now world famous A J Hackett.

A J Hackett had become something of a celebrity in 1986 when he had bungee jumped from the Eiffel Tower. He had seen the potential for this high-thrill activity to become a money spinner, and was doing his best to grab headlines and profile. In 1988 he set up two different jumping operations in Queenstown, and by the following year thousands of people were flocking in to try it. As I stood outside the A J Hackett shop-front, looking at photos of the bungee jumping, my mind drifted back to Kuranda near Cairns, to my day out with Mike and the three German girls, Kirsten, Vanessa and Brigit. The bungee at Kuranda looked like child's play compared to the ones here ... and, to me, the small bungee at Kuranda had been terrifying.

I followed my nose to the Town Fish Shop on Camp Street, where I purchased some rather delicious fish and chips. Unlike in a traditional British fish'n'chip shop where you might order cod and chips, or perhaps haddock or plaice, here there was no identification of the fish. It was simply fish ... but it was still tasty. I took myself and my supper down to the lake shore and sat on a bench looking out over the lake. For several minutes I watched the TSS Earnshaw steamboat as it chugged across the lake with its complement of evening diners. I would have loved to have taken Suzi on such a steamboat for a romantic evening dinner, watching the setting sun cast its different hues over the Remarkables; it was such a beautiful setting. However, being a single traveller, dinner aboard the TSS Earnshaw today was not such an enticing activity; it would have made me feel more melancholic, and not just because of the extortionate dinner prices.

As I sat there, stuffing chips into my face, I watched a group of youngsters (well, they were about my age anyway) emerge from a bar in quite a rowdy state. Two were wearing light blue England cricket shirts, while a third in the group was wearing the yellow of Australia. The banter was evidently quite friendly, but the two English lads were definitely making the most of the rare occasion when they could say that we had stuffed the Aussies at cricket.

It was certainly a great result for me, as not only had England probably knocked the Aussies out of the tournament, but under Megan's rules there was a more intimate reward in the offing. I knew that I would not hold Suzi to such rules, or pressure her at all if she wanted to take things more slowly. I was also sure that I wouldn't hold back if she wanted to accelerate matters either. Regardless, the thought of a sexual MOT when I arrived in Auckland was definitely keeping my mind occupied a lot. A semi-final looked a certainty now ... which earned me a 'manual service', and there was more to come if England got to the final.

As I looked out across the water, my mind was in another place entirely. I was taken back a few weeks to my time with Elaine on Magnetic Island. I remembered her handywork well; I could almost feel it in my loins just as if it were yesterday. *Wow, Elaine had been such a wonderful girl ... I had been so fortunate to meet her.* In fact, I had been a lucky guy over the last few weeks in Australia, culminating in something with Suzi which really felt special. It was Suzi, not Elaine, that I longed to be with right now.

My mind also drifted yet again to Megan, and her offer of a blow-job in the bus from Tennant Creek. I was still a sexual novice and any opportunities back in the UK had been so few and far between. On the rare occasions when sex had snuck onto the end of the menu, the latex hors d'oeuvres rather blunted any appetite, and left the whole banquet distinctly unsatisfying. I had certainly learnt a bit from my brief encounter with Elaine, and also from Jeannie in the cinema in Brisbane, but there were still so many things to be discovered … one of which was what it felt like to have a hot girl's mouth around my wedding tackle. I had never experienced this, and yet, just a few weeks ago, had come so close (so to speak). But what did it feel like? I had experienced hands down there, Elaine's being the last time. That was still quite fresh in my mind. But how did it feel to have a girl's soft lips and tongue working away down there? What did someone sucking you off actually feel like? And, what if she decided to bite you instead? *Oh fuck! What a thought. But it could happen … you are completely at their mercy.*

I didn't at this point know the famous story from the USA a year later (1993) of Lorena Bobbitt, who, in response to (alleged) beating and rape by her husband John Wayne Bobbitt, had taken a kitchen knife and cut off his penis while he was asleep. I didn't know about this then, but painfully similar visions of bite-induced severing flashed through my mind. Two John Wayne quotes also might have occurred to me at this point:

1) "Life is hard; it's harder if you're stupid." *Is it stupid? It certainly wouldn't be hard if it were severed.*

And

2) "A man's got to do what a man's got to do." *Even if a blow-job might be scary as fuck, I still wanted to experience it.*

With such painful thoughts now countering the more pleasurable visions in my mind, I set off along the lakeside, back towards the hostel.

Chapter 4: Remarkable ... Queenstown

Friday 6 March - Queenstown

Every Friday for the last 8 weeks, as I counted each week that went by, I had woken up and contemplated what I was missing from being back home in the UK. The plain truth was: not a lot. Since leaving Oxford, all my friends had dispersed to different parts of the UK, and some overseas, so I didn't have much contact with them. I had no romantic interest back home, nor any indications that this would change. Although I loved my parents, living back in the family fold even for a short time had been driving me nuts. I hated having to account for my time and activities, and tell them every day when I was expecting to be there for dinner. I wanted to be free, to take each day as it came, and to do what I felt like doing. There is a saying that home is where the heart is, and that may be true, but my heart was lost drifting somewhere in Western Australia, desperately hoping to rediscover itself in Auckland in a couple of weeks' time.

Despite the prohibition of alcohol, this YHA hostel was among the best I had stayed in. Although I was in a 12-berth dorm, which was about half full, the beds were well spaced out and reasonably comfortable. The hostel was clean and well maintained, and best of all, it did put on a splendid buffet breakfast.

A handful of people were in the breakfast area, but were all paired up and not looking out for others to share conversation. So, I took a table by myself and settled down with a mountainous portion of sausages, bacon, hash-browns, mushrooms and scrambled eggs. As I chomped my way through this, I flicked through some of the leaflets that I had picked up from reception. I was only intending to be in Queenstown for a couple of days, and needed to make the most of it.

There were two trips that caught my eye. The first was a high-octane thrill ride by jet-boat along the Shotover River, and the second a rather more tranquil excursion across to Fiordland and Milford Sound. Milford Sound was one of the most highly recommended beauty spots that New Zealand had to offer, and its scene with Mitre Peak adorned millions of postcards and was one of the most photographed places in the country. It seemed if you came to New Zealand as a tourist, you had to buy three postcards: one of bungee jumping, another of sheep, and the third of Mitre Peak.

I cross-checked the leaflets I had picked up with the information in the Lonely Planet. Although I had now changed books from the Aussie guide to the New Zealand guide, I had retained the same bookmark that I had used in Australia. This was the note that Suzi and Megan had written for me in Cairns, saying that they had left town, but hoping we would meet up later. I was so grateful that we had done so.

I sat looking at this note which I must have read a hundred times in the last month, and contemplated just what a massive role luck has to play in our lives. Although I was not currently with Suzi, I was still so overjoyed that we had bumped into each other at the cricket game. Any number of things might have changed that turn of events. Even the slightest change in circumstance can lead to major changes in outcomes. Who knows, perhaps if Suzi had come to the cricket with Megan, maybe Suzi and I would have never got together. Maybe, having had that hot encounter on the bus from Tennant Creek, I would have got together with Megan instead ... who could tell? I also knew that it was far from a certainty that we would get to meet up again in Auckland. I didn't feel that I had experienced the best of luck with relationships over the years, and I was really desperate for that to change ... it was high time that lady luck was on my side.

♦ ♦ ♦

After breakfast, I chatted to Ian at the hostel reception to get his lowdown on the different excursion and activity options around Queenstown. One of the things I had found in Christchurch was that by having YHA membership, you could obtain discounts off some of the backpacker trips. This was also true here. I was pretty sure that I wanted to go to Milford Sound and also to do a bit of jet-boating, so I followed Ian's recommended options, which he also assisted me to book. It was to be the Shotover Jet on Saturday, and then Milford Sound on Sunday. Today I would begin by taking the Skyline Gondola up above Queenstown ... it was a beautiful clear day, and a great chance to see the wonderful panoramas of the lake and surrounding mountains.

Just as I headed out of the hostel, Ian called after me.

"Hey Bruce, before you go ... are you really sure you don't want to try A J Hackett's bungee? I hear it's awesome, and I can get you a discount."

I had chatted with Ian quite a bit by now and had built up quite a rapport while watching the cricket. He and I had laughed about our respective lack of success with the fairer sex, and we had also discovered that we both suffered vertigo. I stuck two fingers up at him as I left the hostel.

As I walked down the road towards the gondola, I decided first to pop into a general store to get some provisions for a picnic lunch. A couple of sausage rolls, some tomatoes and a can of Coke did me just fine. I also picked up the latest version of the International Express newspaper, to catch up on some of the headline news from back home. It didn't look like there was too much of note, but at least now there was some coverage of the Cricket World Cup. Being a week out of date, it only reported on the first week of the tournament, and especially on the contrasting fortunes of England, who had won their first two games, compared to Australia, who had lost theirs. It was the Aussies' poor showing that seemed to be bigger news, as we had all expected them to win the tournament.

The Skyline Gondola was well worth the few dollars ticket price. It was, supposedly, the steepest cable car ride in the Southern Hemisphere, and it took you approximately 450 metres up the hill behind Queenstown to a ridge called Bob's Peak. From here, there were magnificent views over Lake Wakatipu and the Remarkables mountain range, as well as several other peaks such as Walter Peak and Cecil Peak. Around here they seemed to have named a mountain top after any Tom, Dick and Harry ... or at least any Bob, Walter and Cecil. I am sure these were all special people, but I never discovered anything about them.

I was in no rush, and took my time at the top, wandering between different viewpoints to take photos, and then inspecting the over-priced souvenir shop. The over-priced souvenir shop stood connected to an over-priced café-takeaway, and also an over-priced restaurant. Still, for those who have the real estate ... where in the world do they not try to milk the tourists for all they can?

At around 12:30, after having munched my way through my sausage rolls, I caught the gondola for the descent. By this time, there were probably two hundred people spread out across Bob's Peak. It was quite popular, but it felt far from crowded. My ten-minute descent was in a car with a young German couple who, having seen enough of the spectacular views from the top, seemed far keener on gazing intently into each other's eyes ... at least when they weren't snogging the life out of each other. They certainly didn't care that they made me feel uncomfortable, and I am sure they would have preferred it if I had not been there at all, as perhaps they might have just had time for a full-on quickie. The thought that I was preventing them from going further did at least console my evil heart. I also thought of Megan ... in an empty cable car, just the two of us ... would I have accepted her proposal of a blow-job in those circumstances? *Shit! Bad boy. Stop those thoughts ... I am supposed to be thinking only of Suzi these days!*

Why could I not shake such thoughts from my mind? Ever since that bus journey from Tennant Creek, I had cursed myself from turning down Megan's proposal ... I so regretted not finding out how it would have felt. *Fuck! Just the thought of Megan's tongue teasing me down there, and the thought of her having been so horny for me ... it was just such a turn on.* But also, nearly every time I had thought about it, I also considered the alternative prospect of ending up behind bars in a police cell.

♦ ♦ ♦

On reaching the foot of the gondola ride, I strolled a few yards along the road before turning into my second tourist attraction of the day ... the Kiwi House and its associated wildlife garden. As a nature enthusiast, I thought it would be a good idea to see some of the native New Zealand wildlife, even if, as in this case, the animals were captive. It was highly unlikely that I was going to see any kiwis in the wild, as they were both nocturnal and extremely rare.

One thing I hadn't realised before setting foot in this small zoo, was that there was more than one species of kiwi. I guess I hadn't even considered the question before; I had just assumed that the was only one, as every picture I had ever seen of a kiwi had looked pretty much the same. But no, there were four species, or maybe even five. Scientists' current opinion, based on genetics, seemed to propose splitting one of them into two distinctly different species ... if that made any sense.

Kiwis are really quite strange-looking creatures ... as indeed are many other nocturnal creatures. It is possible that they hadn't originally evolved as nocturnal animals when New Zealand was free from mammalian predators ... scientists couldn't tell. But if they hadn't evolved in that way, it was the human introductions of cats, dogs and stoats which would have forced the kiwis to modify their behaviour, or risk becoming extinct.

The adult birds (across the set of kiwi species) range between 25cm and 45cm, and they have some of the smallest eyes compared to their size for any bird ... well, most eyes aren't really that useful in the dark. Kiwis are flightless and they have hair-like feathers which create a shaggy-coat appearance. They lay some of the largest eggs compared to body size of any bird, typically up to 5 times the size of a chicken's egg, and perhaps 25% the weight of the female kiwi ... yes, a pretty hefty egg. Just imagine pushing that out! The human equivalent of the kiwi would be an average human female trying to push a 3-year-old child out of her vagina. While being male, I may find it quite hard to understand what childbirth actually feels like, such thoughts do certainly bring tears to my eyes.

Supposedly male and female kiwis exhibit monogamy and pair up for life. However, I rarely believe such assessments these days, following on from studies of other birds, and in particular some research on dunnocks in the 1980s. It had previously been believed that dunnocks paired together in a devoted and monogamous manner, but studies had shown paired-up individuals discretely going off into the bushes and copulating with whichever other willing partners they could find. So, however your own vision might be of idealism and romance in the animal world, it is full of manipulative behaviour and infidelity, just as it is with human society. Sorry to destroy the clean image; that's just how life works.

Having seen several rather docile kiwis in their nocturnal house, and then a handful of other native birds including a gang of noisy keas (a type of parrot), I headed out of the park. I went for a walk around the main shopping area, and then over to the little peninsula of Queenstown Gardens, which turned out to be a delightful place for an afternoon stroll. I sat down on a bench overlooking the lake, and took out my newspaper to see if there was anything that would capture my attention.

It was a wonderful sunny afternoon, the temperature was somewhere in the mid-twenties Celsius, and perfect for just sitting, relaxing and doing nothing in particular. I skated through the first few pages of the newspaper, which were focussed on Norman Lamont's tax breaking pre-election budget. Preparations were underway for an April 9th election, and currently John Major's Conservative government was trailing in the polls to Neil Kinnocks Labour Party. UK politics all seemed such a long way away. As I turned the pages of the paper, I looked at the flaking skin on the back of my wrists. This was the last remaining sign of some painful sunburn I had picked up back in Townsville.

As I gazed out across the lake, my mind went back to that day when I had climbed up Castle Hill, and watched as the skin on my forearms bubbled under the ferocious sun and 40-degree heat. I could remember thinking about Megan and Suzi that day too. It was the day after my bus journey with them from Alice Springs via Tennant Creek. I could recall as I walked down from the hill, I was singing a song by Midnight Oil, and then Dire Straits ... badly of course.

I had been singing Romeo and Juliet, while imagining romantic encounters in the shadows of the Townsville arcades ...

    5"... Juliet, the dice was loaded from the start ..."

Back in Townsville that day, I had been expecting to meet up with Megan and Suzi in Cairns a few days later, but it never happened. They had left for the Whitsundays just before I arrived. Perhaps the dice had been stacked against me; I mean, why would they be interested in me? Or maybe it was just that the timing was wrong ... *or was it?*

If I had met up with them then, maybe I would not have got together with Suzi at all. Maybe it would have been Megan, or maybe neither of them. How could you predict a different roll of the dice? So, how was my luck going to be when I reach Auckland? I so look forward to seeing them both. I just can't wait to kiss and cuddle Suzi again, to feel the warmth of her body against mine, and to lose myself in her eyes. And I also can't wait to see Megan; she is just so alive, so full of energy.

From feeling fairly buoyant and positive, on my walk back to the hostel my mood turned towards bleaker, more negative thoughts. *Why would Suzi wait for me? What have I got that's in any way special? What if she found somebody else on her travels?* There was a pretty good chance that Suzi and Megan would meet quite a few eligible and interested blokes before I saw them again. As I walked, I sang to myself … it was the Beatles this time and 'You're going to lose that girl', and I was even trying to be Lennon, McCartney and Harrison, singing both lead and backing vocals …

[6]*"… You're gonna lose that girl …*

… (Yes, yes, you're gonna lose that girl) …"

… neither of which, to be honest, was I ever any good at.

Being thousands of miles away was not conducive to trying to keep a romance alive. Suzi was bound to get asked out by some smarmy backpacking bastard before we got to Auckland, and there was absolutely nothing I could do about it. I couldn't call her to tell her how I felt about her. I didn't know where she was, and had no way of communicating with her even if I did.

Why couldn't life be more straightforward?

Already in quite a low mood when I arrived back to the hostel, I had at least expected to be able to watch some cricket highlights. However, I was further disappointed to find that today was a scheduled rest day. Then, to add to my misery, when I got back to my dorm room, I discovered that I had run out of clean underwear. I then had a highly entertaining evening, in and out of the hostel laundry room, waiting my turn, first for a washing machine to become available, and then a tumble drier. Some days life is nothing but a dream!

Bruce Spydar

Saturday 7 March - Queenstown

After another full-on buffet breakfast, I waited at the front of the hostel for my pickup for the Shotover Jet. Three others from the hostel, a British couple and a Dutch girl, all around my age, were also waiting. At just after 09:00am, a bright red minibus pulled up, and we then began the drive up to where we were going to catch the boat. We picked up another couple from a different hostel, and then it was about a fifteen-minute drive, northwards from Queenstown following the Arthurs Point Road, until we crossed over the Shotover River. A little further on, down a side road, we came to the operations centre for the Shotover Jet.

After a five-minute safety briefing, the six of us were supplied with red life jackets, and were led down to the riverside, where a bright red speedboat awaited us. As I walked down to the boat, I remembered my rafting adventure on the Barron River near Cairns just a few weeks earlier, and thought of Mike, Kirsten, Brigit and Vanessa, my companions that day. They were a fun-loving bunch of people, somewhat livelier than the group appeared today. My companions today were not so sociable; the two couples seemed to want to talk amongst themselves, and the Dutch girl appeared reserved and perhaps a bit shy like I was. As we boarded the boat, I did at least find out that her name was Marijke, and I did manage to get a few words out of her during our river trip … but not a lot.

A burly young man, sporting an All Blacks rugby shirt beneath his life jacket, was our boat captain. His shirt matched his physical stature as he by no means would have looked out of place in the front row of an All Blacks scrum. He gave us a few further safety tips, the main one being "strap yourself in and hold on tight."

As soon as he turned his key in the ignition, that advice seemed highly appropriate. The jet engines certainly made a different sound to conventional outboard motors … it was a bit like the difference between a well-tuned Aston Martin and an old VW beetle. The jet engines, which were hidden from view beneath the shell of the boat, were not necessarily louder than conventional ones, but the wooshing sound just oozed power.

After a few seconds of gently easing the boat out to the middle of the river, which initially was perhaps only twenty metres across, our captain suddenly let rip with the thrust, and we could feel the G-force as the boat shot forward. For the next thirty minutes or so, we were speeding up the Shotover River as it wove its way through steep canyons. Our captain interspersed some relaxing periods when we floated slowly through some of the trickiest bits, with high-octane speed thrills that left us pinned to our seats. It was incredible just how manoeuvrable these boats were. It seemed like they accelerated from 0 to 60 mph in about 4 seconds, and then similar levels of deceleration on braking. It was a massive thrill going so fast and so close to the canyon walls. The driver certainly needed a lot of boat-handling skill to do this.

The river also needed to be a guaranteed one-way street, as there was no way that you could avoid things if they suddenly appeared in your path. A few years before, in the earliest days of these jet-boat operations, two such boats had collided on another part of this river. This was before it had occurred to anyone that this type of activity was really quite dangerous. As our captain was telling us this story, it crossed my mind that there might not be too many places in the world where you could actually do this with any degree of safety. One thing that allowed it here was connected to the unusual nature of New Zealand; in that it had evolved in the absence of mammals. In this type of environment in most other parts of the world, you might come along such a river and be lucky or unlucky enough to come across a deer, a bear, or a wild goat in your path. If a sizable mammal collided with a jet boat, it might be catastrophic for all involved. Here, if one could relax just a little, the lack of wild mammals was of some comfort.

The turning point for the boat was at Skippers Bridge, where we had a twenty-minute break before the return journey. During this time, we all climbed up the steep path and steps to the bridge. At the start of the 1990s, Skippers Canyon was probably the most famous spot for bungee jumping in the world. Sure, bungee hadn't been a craze for too long, but here was a place with a bridge about seventy metres high above a narrow picturesque canyon. Below the bridge there was a fast-flowing river, with about half a metre depth of water to cushion the fall if your bungee rope failed. The cushioning effect might be the equivalent to dropping a chicken's egg out of a first-floor window onto some concrete, with just a thin piece of paper to cushion the fall ... i.e. no bloody cushioning at all. If the bungee rope failed, you were on your way to the cemetery.

The setting itself was breathtaking. As I walked out across the bridge, unsurprisingly it was time for a spot of vertigo. My legs turned to jelly, and I felt a little queasy as I looked out in both directions up and down Skippers Canyon.

At the middle of the bridge, which spanned perhaps fifty metres across, there was a small cluster of people gathered around a platform on one side of the bridge. Here they were ... the bravest, craziest thrill-seekers that you could find. I thought back to my erstwhile friend, Mike, doing the bungee jump up at Kuranda near Cairns. That jump was from a crane, and probably wasn't even a quarter as high as this one. The Kuranda bungee also had a deep pool of water below it. *Would Mike have had the balls for trying this one?* I chuckled to myself as I also recalled that when he had jumped, his shorts had been pulled up by the rope, exposing his wedding tackle ... leaving the watching crowds to see for themselves what balls he really did possess.

I couldn't even look down over the sides of the bridge, my legs were shaking so much. How on earth could anyone have the bottle, or indeed the inclination, to jump over the side? From the safety of solid ground at the side of the bridge, I watched for about ten minutes before it was time to return to our boat. In that period, I saw two young men dive from the bridge. It was truly awesome ... I wished that I had the constitution to be able to attempt such things.

But then again, if I did have the bottle, where would it stop? Would I be the type of person who goes through life needing a constant stream of ever more dangerous thrills? That type of life might not be so wonderful, and also might not be a very long one. No, perhaps there are good reasons why some of us get vertigo ... and it also probably keeps our insurance premiums down.

The return journey in the boat was marginally less thrilling, as we were going with the flow of the river, which made controlling the boat at high speed marginally harder. But it was still quite a thrill. Was this something I would do again? Yes definitely ... it was really exhilarating, but having just seen people throwing themselves off Skippers Bridge tied to a bit of string, jet-boating did now seem a little tame. If I did go jet-boating again, however, I might also try to go with a few more lively people.

♦ ♦ ♦

Having returned to Queenstown early in the afternoon, I found a bakery from which I purchased a filled baguette. I then sat on a bench by the waterfront while I contemplated how to spend the rest of the day. There were a couple of cricket matches today, and I hadn't had a beer for a day or two ... a bar seemed to be calling.

Just a block away from the waterfront, I found a family-friendly pub, the Mountaineer, which seemed to fit the bill. It had a large TV screen, the cricket was showing ... and being a pub, naturally it served lots of different varieties of beer. I took a seat at a small table with a good view of the screen, and settled in with a pint of DB Export lager. I took out my Lonely Planet and a few postcards to write, and got myself set up for a relaxing afternoon.

Today's cricket was perhaps not the most exciting of the tournament so far. One game involved India, who still had an outside chance of the semi-finals, vs. Zimbabwe who had absolutely no hope. The other match was Australia, who were all but out, vs.

Sri Lanka who were in much the same state. However, the World Cup was the World Cup, and it only came along once every four years, which meant that I felt some compulsion to watch it whenever I could.

Although the weather in Queenstown was glorious, the same could not be said for Hamilton, a few hundred miles away on North Island. There, the India vs. Zimbabwe game was disrupted with intermittent rain, and so the TV coverage concentrated mostly on the Australia match ... perhaps also because the New Zealand media were hoping for another Aussie defeat to rub salt into their wounds.

As I sat at my table, I suddenly noticed a face that looked familiar. A well-built, blondish chap was standing at the bar. *Where did I know him from?* I couldn't immediately make the connection. I racked my brain, and suddenly found the answer I sought. I stood up and walked over.

"Anders, isn't it?" I asked confidently.

"Hey, how are you doing?" he responded with a friendly handshake.

"Good to see you."

"And you too ... uh ..."

"Bruce," I said, helping him find the answer. We had met each other a few weeks before, in Alice Springs, and had spent a couple of days together on a trip to Kings Canyon and Ayers Rock. Anders was from Stockholm, and after his gap year travels would be returning to start a career as an architect.

Anders joined me for a drink, and we got chatting. Coincidentally, Anders had taken approximately the same route as me around Queensland and New South Wales, but we were just a day or two out of sync. We had stayed at a couple of the same hostels, in Cairns and in Brisbane, and had also stayed at the Carlton hostel in Melbourne. It was great to have someone to talk to again who had some similar experiences to share. We compared notes on Sydney Harbour, the Blue Mountains, Byron Bay, the Great Barrier

Reef, Kuranda Bungee, and we reminisced over our shared experience in the Red Centre.

"Hey Anders, do you remember those two girls I met while climbing Ayers Rock?"

"Yes ... just a little," replied Anders trying to recall. "They were quite hot, weren't they? And with really difficult accents?"

"Yes, those two. Well, I bumped into one of them again at the West Indies vs. Pakistan game in Melbourne ... and now we're sort of dating."

"Ah-ha ... cool! Good for you. Is she here with you?"

"Well, I say we're dating ... that might be overstating it right now. Suzi's still over in Western Australia somewhere ... probably in Perth. We are planning to meet up again in Auckland."

As I was telling Anders about this, I had a warm feeling in my heart. Yes, I was actually dating Suzi. And yes, it really did feel right ... Suzi was my girlfriend now. Well, at least, I hoped that she still was.

♦ ♦ ♦

Time flew by as I sat with Anders, chatting about the places we'd been to and a few of the more notable people that we had met on our travels. One pint followed another, and the cricket matches played on towards their conclusions, while I tried to explain some of the nuances of the game to Anders. He didn't yet fully understand cricket. However, here was one of the few Europeans I had met who was actually interested.

India won their rain interrupted game, setting a great target of 203 for 7 from 32 overs, helped by a fine knock of 81 by Sachin Tendulkar, before rain cut their innings short. The rain had led to a revised target for Zimbabwe from fewer overs, but Zimbabwe fell well short, and slumped to five consecutive losses. This was not unexpected as Zimbabwe were still trying to establish themselves amongst the top cricket nations. India now had two wins and a draw from their five games, and were still clinging on to their hopes.

Over in Adelaide, Sri Lanka set Australia a fairly modest-looking target of 189. It had taken a while but today, Australia had finally showed up for the tournament. They reached 190 for 3 wickets with 6 overs to spare. This salvaged a little pride, but probably wouldn't stop them going out, although a mathematical miracle could still work in their favour.

Sometime just before 9:00pm, Anders and I left the pub and went our separate ways. After five to six hours drinking, chatting and watching cricket, I returned to the hostel to sleep it off.

Sunday 8 March – Milford Sound

I woke up with a sore head, the result of alcohol still swilling around my blood vessels. I was not particularly enthused to have a long day in a minibus ahead of me. I was booked onto a whistle-stop tour of Fiordland, culminating in a boat trip along Milford Sound. It was around 180 miles by road from Queenstown, so 360 in total, and a long, long day on the road.

The minibus picked me up from in front of the hostel at 8:00am sharp, together with a Dutch couple, probably in their mid-thirties, and two German girls who were early twenties like me. Already on board there were two Japanese couples, also probably in their early twenties. I don't know whether it was just me as a singleton, but once again I felt that the world worked in pairs. Once again, I was the spare part … each pair was quite talkative between themselves, but with hardly any communication beyond.

With the effects of alcohol still in my system, I wasn't in a lively mood anyway, so just settled down next to the window and began to watch the world go by. From Queenstown we drove south along the shore of Lake Wakatipu, the reverse of my trip into Queenstown just a couple of days before, and were treated to some more wonderful views across the lake towards Cecil Peak and Bayonet Peak. From Lake Wakatipu we took the road south, and it took just over two hours on the road, across the rolling lowland hills via Mossburn, before reaching the small town of Te Anau, a delightful place, set beside the lake of the same name.

Here we had a 30-minute comfort stop, as well as an opportunity to purchase some food to take with us for a picnic lunch. We were warned that, although we could buy sandwiches and snacks on the Milford Sound boat, everything there was at highly inflated prices. There was a small bakery just across from where our minibus stopped, and it was more than adequate for our lunch needs, which in my case was a pasty and some crisps. I am sure this bakery received a solid regular passing trade from tours such as ours.

In such a short time, I didn't see much of Te Anau, but from what I did see, it seemed like a pleasant little centre, and it was evidently a hub for hikers and trekkers exploring the Fiordland walking trails. It was a quieter and smaller centre than Queenstown, and probably attracted more of the tranquil types, rather than the high-octane thrill seekers that swarmed into Queenstown.

We moved on and headed northwards along the eastern shore of Lake Te Anau, which is the largest body of freshwater on South Island. There were dramatic views across the lake to the Murchison Mountains beyond, with their peaks now obscured by dark gloomy clouds ... reminding us that Fiordland was normally the wettest part of the country. Much of this area is covered with temperate rainforest, with annual rainfall commonly in excess of 6 metres.

We left the lake and turned inland along the Eglinton River valley. The landscape reminded me of the Scottish Cairngorms, but some years later this area would become familiar to millions worldwide as the land of Hobbits and Orcs from the filmsets of Lord of the Rings. It was a beautiful, but relatively barren wilderness.

At around 11:15am, still in the Eglinton Valley, we pulled in at a scheduled stop; a beauty spot known as Mirror Lakes. Here, just a stone's throw from the road, there were some of the best still-water reflections I have ever seen. A small lake, just tens of metres across, provided us with almost perfect reflections of the mountain backdrop. There was hardly any breeze to ripple the water, and the earlier overcast conditions had shifted to leave a few cotton-wool clouds in an otherwise clear sky.

As I moved around to different viewpoints to take some photos, I watched some of the others try to capture reflections of themselves as well as the scenery. I was asked to take a few such pictures by one of the Japanese couples, who told me that they were on their honeymoon. Who could blame them for wanting some great romantic reflection shots? It was a wonderful spot for it, but seeing this couple so much in love made me long to be with different company. I started to think of how different it might have been, were I here with Suzi and Megan. It would have been a wonderful experience to share with them. So, instead of fully savouring the beauty of the reflections from this glass-like surface, I was reflecting on my own glass being half empty rather than half full.

After leaving Mirror Lakes we continued north, passing across a landscape the name of which entertained my dirty sense of humour … Knob's Flat. Open to the imagination, but I am sure this might be the term for at least one type of erectile dysfunction. Now even if the usage of the word 'knob' was, in this case, referring to a rounded hill, I didn't really see how you could have a flat one. It either was a knob, or it wasn't.

That aside, we continued past Knob's Flat, and past Lake Gunn, which presumably fired blanks, and then continued on up to the Hollyford Valley Lookout. From here, there were more scenic views along the Hollyford River, which flowed through a densely forested valley. A little further up the road we stopped again to go for a short walk down to the riverside and once again, the views along the valley were tremendous. Our driver-cum-guide told us to keep our eyes peeled in case we would catch sight of a kea. This was, according to the guidebooks, quite a good area in which to find them.

Kea are intelligent, inquisitive birds, and come armed with an exceptionally strong beak-and-claw combo. This has allowed them to extend beyond their normal foraging behaviour, enabling them to tear through canvas-topped car roofs and break into picnic baskets and cool boxes. Kea were fast getting a reputation as pests at many roadside picnic sites. I rather wanted to witness this for myself, but the nearest I got was a quick glimpse of one as it flew over some nearby trees. Not much, but at least a glimpse.

From this stop, we then set off through the kilometre-long Homer Tunnel, which cut through the mountains by Mount Talbot, and then, on the other side, we continued down the Cleddau Valley and on towards Milford Sound.

◆ ◆ ◆

Shortly before 1:00pm, we boarded a small cruise boat to take us for a 90-minute trip up Milford Sound. Looking straight up the fiord, Mitre Peak was clearly recognisable, despite its summit being partially obscured by low cloud. This was not the picture-perfect postcard scene with clear blue skies and bright sunlight ... this was gloomy, dark and dramatic.

As we set off up the fiord, I found a seat near the front of the boat, and consumed my pasty and crisps. Unlike what I had found at Byron Bay, the bakery had not tried to claim this pasty as Cornish ... a good thing too, as Cornwall was not far off being the furthest point on the planet from here. The lamb-and-veg pasty was tasty nevertheless, and amply satisfied my hunger.

The weather remained overcast and dramatic as we chugged along up the ten or so miles of sheltered water towards the open sea. The scene reminded me of Hardanger Fjord in Norway, which I had been to as a teenager on a summer holiday with my parents. Steep cliffs rose out of the deep water, and several waterfalls poured down sheer rockfaces. Two of particular note were Bowen Falls, a 150-metre fanning-cascade, and Stirling Falls, a similar height single-drop shower.

Having read in the excursion information leaflet that whales, dolphins and penguins could all be seen in the fiords, I kept a keen eye on the water as we travelled out towards the sea. We passed by Seal Rock, which appropriately hosted about fifteen 'sun-bathing' fur seals on the rock's flat surface.

Then just past Dale Point, from which we could gaze out to the open waters of the Tasman Sea, the boat turned for the return journey. No whales, dolphins or penguins this time, but dramatic landscape and waterfalls aplenty … I could hardly complain.

♦ ♦ ♦

Before boarding our minibus for the return to Queenstown, I noticed that our driver was trying to get a signal on the radio. I enquired whether he knew the cricket scores; there were two games today, West Indies vs. New Zealand, and South Africa vs. Pakistan.

"I don't know mate," he responded. "You tell me. It's so bloody difficult to get any radio signal down here."

Despite the well-developed tourism industry, the mountains still provided some major challenges for communication. Without the cricket commentary to occupy my mind on the long drive back to Queenstown, I dozed off intermittently when the scenery was unable to maintain my attention. Despite some areas of the landscape being breathtaking, after a while it loses its novelty, and there is only so much of it you can take in.

I caught up with the cricket again later that evening in the hostel, to discover that New Zealand had beaten the West Indies in a close match in Auckland. New Zealand were out on top of the group with a perfect 5 wins, and had safely qualified for the semi-finals. West Indies were now struggling with a record of 2 wins against 3 losses. In the other match, a rain affected game in Brisbane, South Africa struggled over the line to beat Pakistan. This improved their record to 3 wins against 2 losses, and left Pakistan with only 1 win and a draw from their 5 games. Just like Australia, Pakistan would now need miracles to move on.

I had decided that it was also time for me to move on from Queenstown, and through the hostel reception I booked ahead for my next night's accommodation to be at the YHA hostel at Franz Joseph.

Chapter 5: Glacial ...
Franz Joseph

Monday 9 March - Queenstown to Franz Joseph

After an early buffet breakfast to set me up for the day, I checked out of the Queenstown hostel at around 7:30am, and made my way into the town centre to catch the bus for Franz Joseph. I had decided that I wanted to see one of the two major glaciers on the west coast, either Fox Glacier or Franz Joseph Glacier, but didn't want to spend the time doing both. Ian, at the hostel, had suggested that it would be easier to do Franz Joseph Glacier by myself, as this was just a few miles from the YHA hostel in the small Franz Joseph settlement. For Fox Glacier, you ideally needed your own transport, or else a tour. So, being a backpacker on a tight budget, I naturally opted for the easier, cheaper alternative.

The trip to Franz Joseph was approximately 220 miles and would take over eight hours ... so another long day in a bus. Although not quite on a par with some of the journeys I had taken in Australia, New Zealand was still quite a sizable country, much larger than many people expect.

There were a dozen or so other backpackers also taking the same bus, as well as a couple of rather elderly locals, who I suspected were probably not travelling the full eight hours, as they had no luggage with them. I sat down on a double seat towards the rear of the bus, and settled in for the long day ahead.

We left Queenstown in an easterly direction, and followed the Kawarau River valley for about an hour over to the small town of Cromwell before heading north. On the way, we passed A J Hackett's bungee operation at Kawarau Bridge, which was the more popular of his two bungee centres, being a little more accessible than the one at Skippers Canyon. As we passed by, I felt a bit disappointed in myself for not having the constitution to attempt a bungee jump, but I knew that in the bigger scheme of things bungee jumping was unimportant.

From Cromwell, we headed north for the next hour, beside Lake Dunstan, and along the Clutha Valley up to Wanaka, where we had a short comfort break beside the beautiful Lake Wanaka. The views reminded me of the Argyle region of Scotland, perhaps around Loch Fyne, with its backdrop of windswept moorlands and bleak mountain tops, together with a handful of tiny boats venturing out on the water, perhaps fishing for trout or salmon.

From Wanaka, we then set off up along the shoreline of Lake Hawea, another sizable lake, with another wonderful mountain backdrop. This part of South Island was certainly scenic. From Lake Hawea we continued north beside the Makarora River and up to the pretty cascade of Thunder Creek Falls, where we had another scheduled break and photo opportunity. Here we were now only about 30 miles as the crow flies from where I had been a week ago at Mount Cook.

From Thunder Creek, it was then up to the Haast River, and along Haast Pass to the small town of Haast ... evidently this was Haast country. I consulted my Lonely Planet to discover that these places were named after Julius Haast, an Austrian, who had been exploring these lands in the 1860s. Apart from this bit of self-indulgence, he had also named Franz Joseph, but after the Austrian Emperor ... perhaps Haast Glacier would have been one Haast too far.

The small settlement of Haast is situated where the river meets the sea, and was quite a pleasant stop for another comfort break and the chance for a quick picnic lunch, which I bought from a general store situated close to the bus stop. A short way along the coast road, we stopped again at Knight's Point, where we were allowed off the bus to take photos of the beautiful rocky coastline. I was quite impressed by this type of bus service which acted a bit beyond just getting you from A to B. The stops at Thunder Creek Falls and Knights Point appeared to serve little other purpose than for the photo-shooting travellers, but I guess this probably helped to encourage more tourists to travel this way by bus.

The next point of note was driving through Bruce Bay ... it's always a bit special passing something with your name on it, isn't it? Or perhaps it's only me? At the following stop, we were now at Fox Glacier, and about half the passengers disembarked. As we were parked up, I was gazing at a big signpost pointing towards the glacier, and I drifted towards thinking of Fox's Glacier Mints, a wonderful British travel sweet with a polar bear as its logo. On most of my summer holidays as a small child, my parents had kept a supply of these mints in the car in order to keep me and my brother quiet. I hadn't eaten one of these for several years, but now that I had thought of them, I suddenly had a craving for them.

The last leg of the journey took us up to Franz Joseph, and the bus took us right up to within a stone's throw of the YHA hostel. It was about 4:30pm, and I was glad that I had booked ahead, because there weren't too many other options for accommodation around here. The small settlement looked to me like a rather windswept backwater which only really survived on the back of the glacier-visiting tourists.

♦ ♦ ♦

I checked in at the YHA reception and, after a few questions, I was directed to a four-person dorm room in which there was one other occupant. As I opened the door, I found an attractive slim blonde lady in her mid-twenties lying on one of the lower bunk beds, intently reading a novel. On first impressions, her appearance reminded me a little of a young Agnetha from ABBA ... Mm-hmm, quite a hottie.

"Hi!" I introduced myself. "I'm Bruce, from England."

"Oh, hi!" she responded.

"Have you just arrived today like me?"

"Yeah."

"Are you staying long?"

"No."

"And your name is ...?"

"Brigit ... Now can't you see that I'm reading?"

"Oh. Sorry."

That was the end of our opening conversation. This frosty reception suggested to me that we might not instantly become friends. I set down my backpack next to the opposite bed, and sat on the lower bunk.

So, another Brigit then. Hmm ... this one is somewhat different to the last one. The last Brigit had been friendly and quite engaging, even if she was sometimes abrupt and to the point. Physically, I hadn't found her attractive, despite having let my guard down to fall for her forceful advances in a nightclub in Cairns. This Brigit who, from the flag sewn onto her backpack I guessed to be Norwegian, was physically drop-dead gorgeous. But she appeared ice cold, and with piercing blue eyes to match. Still, today I had not the slightest interest in pursuing anything romantic. *When was the last time I could say the same about a gorgeous girl that came my way?* No, I had no interest today ... no, today I could consider myself attached.

I thought for a moment or two, wondering where Suzi and Megan were now, and trying to figure out how many days I had to wait before I might see them again. Today was the 9th, and we were aiming to be in Auckland around the 21st, give or take a day. It was still nearly 2 weeks to wait. As I glanced across towards Brigit, still reading her book, I imagined that it was Suzi lying there. *Oh, how I wished it was Suzi. How I wished that I could just go over to her, lift up the book, and plant a big kiss on her lips. How I wished I could lie down beside her and hold her tight.*

Just then Brigit looked up.

"Why are you staring at me?"

I snapped out of my daydreaming.

"Oh, sorry, was I? Apologies, I didn't mean to stare. I was just thinking of something … well, somebody actually. I was miles away."

"Well, do you mind looking at something else?"

"Oh … uh … sure … sorry."

Fuck … this girl really is hard work. But I'm sure I wasn't ogling her … or, shit! … perhaps I was? I thought it better to be safe than sorry, so I unpacked my towel and some fresh clothes from my backpack, and left the room to go for a shower.

♦ ♦ ♦

When I returned to the room 20 minutes later, to my relief Brigit wasn't there. I could relax a bit. I sat on the bed and retrieved my Lonely Planet guide, together with a couple of leaflets that I had picked up from reception, which included information about how to get to the glacier. I took out my radio and tried to tune in to see whether I could pick up the cricket coverage. There was a TV in the common room, but it had been switched off and, in any case, at this moment I didn't feel like company … particularly if it was as forbidding as Brigit.

I soon picked up the signal for the coverage, and found that the game between England and Sri Lanka from Ballarat was in its later stages, and appeared to be heading England's way. England had batted first, and had scored a competitive 280 off their 50 overs, with Fairbrother top-scoring on 63. In reply, the Sri Lankans were really struggling as they lost wickets. In the end, they were bowled out for only 174, with Chris Lewis taking 4 wickets and earning honours as man of the match. While Sri Lanka had now lost all but a glimmer of hope of a semi-final slot, England now looked certain to qualify, having achieved 4 wins and a draw from their 5 matches.

Rather inevitably, my mind returned to thoughts of Megan's MOT rules. A manual service was on the menu as my semi-final prize, assuming that Suzi was still game. I hoped that this jokey game Megan had thought of, but which Suzi had agreed to, was not weighing heavily on Suzi's mind. I did hope that she wasn't getting cold feet about me if she felt like she wanted to take things more slowly. I certainly didn't mind taking things slow, I just wanted any intimacy to be special, and not forced in any way. But the prospect of greater intimacy was really exciting, and a semi-final prize would also mean I would give a similar reward to Suzi. The rules were mutual and recently I had learnt one or two extra tricks to try out, from that night in the cinema with Jeannie. I could visualise the expressions on Jeannie's face, and the reactions of her body, as she had guided my fingers to her pleasure zone. *Hmm, I would so love to share such an experience with Suzi.*

As the radio played in the background, I tried to study the information about the walk up to the glacier, while intermittently entertaining further sexual fantasies. One of the leaflets had a pretty large-scale map which showed in detail all the hiking tracks in the area, and was definitely the one to take with me tomorrow. Apart from studying the direct route to the glacier, my eyes were drawn to some other interesting names on the map. In one direction, away from where I wanted to go, was Canavans Knob Track. *Another knob,* I thought, as I remembered Knob's Flat from my excursion to Milford Sound. At least this time I knew that a knob was a type of hill. But my mind wandered. For some reason, seeing the word 'Canavan', my subconscious made a random association with Caernarfon Castle and then, by further association, the Prince of Wales. I now envisioned a long winding path up a hillside that was lined with 6-foot tall cartoon phalluses, each with the head of Prince Charles on the top ... *Blimey what a thought!*

And then returning to the map, further on towards the glacier, there was Lake Wombat Track, which also led to Alex Knob Track. The latter progressed, in my visions, to the removal of Charlie's head, replacing it with that of my brother. As we were growing up, I may have called my brother a dickhead quite frequently, but this was the first time I had actually visualised it. *Gruesome!*

In my daydreaming, my mind also drifted to wombats, which then led me back to thinking of Elaine on Magnetic Island. *Sweet Elaine ...* I wondered what she was doing now. My groin stiffened a little at the thought of her, as in my mind I re-lived the hands-on experience that she had given me that night in Horseshoe Bay. *Hmm, that girl was really something.*

I must have drifted off to sleep shortly after these thoughts, as the next thing I remember was waking up in the dark at around midnight, with Brigit in the other bed fast asleep, and my radio with a flat battery.

Tuesday 10 March - Franz Joseph

I awoke to the rustle of plastic bags, and looked across to see that Brigit was re-packing her backpack. It was around 7:00am.

"Good morning!" I said.

"Uh-huh," Brigit replied.

"I hope I didn't snore too loud," I continued, trying to be friendly.

"No."

"So, not enough to keep you awake then?"

"No."

"Good." I could do one-word answers too. There was an uneasy silence ... and I broke first. "Are you going to the glacier today?"

"Uh-huh." Brigit then shut her backpack, took her towel and washbag, and left the room.

Bloody hell, why is she such hard work? I couldn't understand. I wondered whether it was something particular about me, or if she was like this with everyone. Perhaps her abruptness was because she didn't want to share a room with a male, and in most of the hostels she wouldn't have had to because the dorms were usually segregated by sex. *But, when I arrived, they did ask me whether I minded a mixed dorm ... surely, they would have asked her too?* Perhaps I was overly sensitive to such matters, but I never liked to be the cause of someone else's annoyance ... it always left me feeling uneasy.

As I looked at my alarm clock, I felt it was too early to jump out of bed, especially as I was not planning anything more than a leisurely hike up to the glacier for the day. I found some spare batteries for my radio, and tried to tune in to some international news.

Apart from a reminder of the cricket games for later in the day, the main news was that China had just ratified the Nuclear Non-proliferation Treaty. Great news! So, today the world was now a much safer place ... at least until everyone decided to ignore the treaty, which was bound to happen someday.

Today was 10th March, now two calendar months since I left home. What was I missing? Apart from having my own room that I didn't have to share with some ice-cold unfriendly girl, this morning, for some strange reason, I was thinking about Sunday lunches ... and the traditional English Sunday roast. *Hmm, it would be great to have roast beef and Yorkshire puddings for lunch today,* I mused, in my state of semi-dozing.

As I dozed, I thought back to my days at the hostel in Glebe Village in Sydney. Then it had been pizza that I craved. At that point, I was sharing a room with Heidi, a pleasant, but rather particular young German lady, who complained a lot. However, she did have a pretty good reason. Primarily her grievances were directed towards our other room-mates, Jan and Ingrid, who breached hostel rules by engaging in rampant sex, while both Heidi and I were just trying to get a good night's sleep.

Anyway, it was the pizza craving that I'd had back then. Today it was the Sunday roast. Back in Sydney, I had been hoping to cross paths again with Suzi and Megan. Today, I also held hopes to meet up with them again soon, but I knew it would not be until I reached Auckland. I so ached to see Suzi. I longed to hold her, to chat about meaningless things, and to laugh together at inane jokes that weren't funny. Suzi and Megan were just so easy-going, and so warm and caring, and there was no greater contrast to the ice queen who was my current room-mate.

Brigit returned to the room to hang up her towel and sort out what she was taking with her for the day. Then she was off out with no further words being exchanged. Once she was gone, I slowly got myself out of bed and dressed, and then went along to the hostel breakfast room to see what food was available. Having consumed a large bowl of cereal, I helped myself to some cold meats and some sliced bread, with which I made some sandwiches for my lunch. This all seemed a bit underhand and, at first, I felt a bit guilty, as I had only paid for a buffet breakfast. Then I realised that everyone else was doing exactly the same.

A noticeboard by reception indicated that the weather forecast for the day was 'changeable' ... no more than that. So, I packed my waterproof jacket into my daypack, together with my lunch, camera, Lonely Planet guide and maps, and then I set off for the glacier.

♦ ♦ ♦

It took approximately an hour to walk the 2.5 miles up the valley of the Waiho River, along the Glacier Road to a small car park at the end. On the way, I passed signposts to Lake Wombat Track and to Alex's Knob ... which made me chuckle again as it brought back my cartoon visions from the previous day.

The sky was a little overcast, but there were a few patches of blue, and it looked to be clearing. So, before proceeding further, I decided to take a short detour to see Peter's Pool where, on good days, supposedly you could get wonderful reflections in its clear water. Indeed, this proved to be true. The most beautiful picture could be seen in reflective duplicate; a view all the way down the valley, with the glacier just visible at the end. The scene was tremendous, and I could imagine that with a clear blue sky, this would have made the perfect postcard or calendar photo.

I had only passed a handful of people on my walk along Glacier Road, and it felt wonderful to be a bit out in the wilds by myself. From the end of the road, it was a short walk through a patch of forest to reach the riverbank, at which point I got my first top-to-bottom view of the glacier in all its splendour. From here, the path went along the shingle of the river bed and took me past a pretty fantail waterfall, and then further up to a viewpoint close to the glacier's leading edge.

Along the way there were several marker posts and information boards that charted the retreat of the ice up the valley. Apparently, this glacier was quite a special one, as it was unusual to find a glacier which descended so close to sea level at this latitude. Franz Joseph Glacier starts nearly 8 miles away, over 3000 metres up in the Southern Alps, and then descends to less than 300 metres above sea level. The glacier's ice sheet was generally advancing 30 to 50cm per day, but depending on how fast the leading edge melted, the glacier was either moving forward or retreating back up the valley. In most of the period since 1865, when it had been named after the Austrian Emperor, the Franz Joseph Glacier had been in retreat, and overall had moved nearly a mile back up the valley. During the last year or two it had actually been advancing again, but nobody appeared to understand why. While evidence from other places around the world was starting to indicate global warming, scientists here had not yet managed to see the correlation that they might have expected with the local weather patterns.

A dozen people stood up at the viewing point near the glacier's leading edge, one of whom I recognised.

"Hi Brigit! Pretty fantastic sight, isn't it?"

"Uh-huh," she responded. "We have better ones in Norway."

"Ah-ha."

OK ... I give up. Well, why make the effort when it is clear that someone doesn't like you, and doesn't wish to converse. Thankfully Brigit started on her way back, leaving me to wander around and marvel at the glacier without feeling that I ought to continue to try to chat with her.

The front edge of the glacier, in places, was several metres tall. It was streaked with dirty greyish-brown lines where the ice had lifted up mud and stones from the substrate beneath. There was a fast-flowing stream, perhaps only about eight feet across, gushing out from underneath the ice. Some of the public information signs warned people not to get too close to the ice flow. It was in constant movement, and the cracking and reformation could easily crush you if you were unlucky enough to be standing in the wrong place. They also warned that small changes in melt rate, such as brought on by rain, could cause water levels in some creeks to rise by up to a metre in as little as 15 minutes.

As I stood reading some of these information boards, I realised that all the other visitors had now gone, and were heading back down the valley. As they did so, the residual sounds of voices subsided. I was left standing there, just listening to the sounds of the glacier as it creaked and cracked. If one was to put a 100-metre-high cube of ice into an oversized gin and tonic ... that's what the cracking sound was like, I imagine. Impressively powerful. *I wonder how many normal sized G & T's that would be.*

Standing alongside this majestic ice flow, I suddenly felt quite alone. In the space of a few minutes, the sky, which had been overcast with a few intermittent patches of clear blue, had now become much darker, and a mist was steadily descending from the higher reaches of the glacier. It was suddenly gloomy, and became quite eerie. It was like being out on Dartmoor in the fog, only with the backing track of massive blocks of ice being ripped apart and squeezed back together again.

As is often the case when left alone, I began singing to myself ... it was the words of 'Wonderful life' by Black that had forced their way into my head ...

> [7]"... Look at me standing
> ... Here on my own again ..."

The Franz Joseph Glacier really was an inspiring sight to behold, and a pretty awesome auditory experience too. Perhaps by being alone, I had experienced the eeriness of the place in a way that I could not have done if I had been with others. But I missed not being able to share it. *Well, although I would have enjoyed it more with Suzi, boy am I glad that I am not still trying to converse with Brigit.* I think it was George Washington who said "It is far better to be alone than in bad company."

On my return towards the hostel, I decided not to take the road, but to follow the river bed further along to where there was a light suspension bridge which connected the two walking paths on either side of the river. On my map it suggested that I ought to be able to take one of these paths along the other side of the river, and get back into Franz Joseph village via another route.

As I crossed the river on the small bridge, I was singing again. This time it was Whitesnake, and 'Here I go again'. As I mentioned before, this was not a band that I was ever really into ... but here I went again as, this time, it was another one of their songs which just happened to enter my head ...

> "[8] ... I don't know where I'm going ...
> ... But I sure know where I've been ..."

Today, I really wasn't too sure where I was going, but I did think that I had a rough idea where the path was going to lead. But in life, and in particular my future working life, I really didn't know in which direction I wanted my path to go. I had been keen to pursue some sort of career in ecology or conservation after leaving university, but the opportunities hadn't appeared in the months when I had been looking. There had been a handful of jobs which I had applied for, but I hadn't even got through screening for an interview ... several of them hadn't even bothered to respond. I was not in great demand.

I didn't really want to go back to start a business training in London: firstly, because I was not keen on the hustle and bustle of London, and secondly, because I wasn't really that interested in money and business either. But my circumstances were possibly changing. *Perhaps it would be OK,* I consoled myself. *At least it would be bearable if Suzi was also in London. Well, probably I would actually want to be there if Suzi was too.* The prospect of being a couple, in a proper relationship with Suzi, was really uplifting. But it was also really uncertain. Perhaps it had something to do with the gloomy damp weather, but I started to become pessimistic again. *What if she doesn't meet me in Auckland? What if she has cold feet and never wants to see me again? It wouldn't be the first time something like that had happened.*

I thought back to a girl I was keen on back at secondary school. Dates were so rare for me back then but, I recalled, there was a girl who I was really keen on, and I had just started seeing her before the end of summer term. Then along came the summer holidays, and I had to go to Cornwall with my parents for a couple of weeks. When I returned, her perspective had changed, and I was history. To this day, I had still never really understood why.

While I started to contemplate different scenarios in which I was being dumped by Suzi, I sat on a rock overlooking the Waiho River, and ate the sandwiches which I had made for lunch. I probably only sat there for about ten minutes, but while I did so the cloud had descended so low, it was almost at river level, and it totally obscured my view of the other side. Today, in so many ways, I felt a real lack of clarity in my life.

♦ ♦ ♦

I made it back to the YHA hostel soon after 2:00pm, just as it began to rain. Luckily, I had just made it into reception when the heavens opened and it really started tipping down. With hindsight, it had been a wise decision to venture up to the glacier in the morning. As I went past the hostel reception and through to my dorm room, I was pleased by two more things. Firstly, there was cricket being shown on the TV in the common room, and secondly, I didn't bump into Brigit.

As the weather was so poor, and as there wasn't a lot else to see or do in Franz Joseph besides visiting the glacier, I decided that an afternoon in front of the TV, writing a few postcards, might be a good way of killing a few hours. I would also use the opportunity to get some laundry done.

I grabbed all my dirty clothes, my Lonely Planet and some postcards which I had bought in Queenstown, and then went back past reception to the laundry room. That was where I found Brigit. She was sitting on a plastic chair, immersed in a book, while waiting for her washing to finish.

"Oh. Hi again," I said.

"Hi," said Brigit, briefly looking up from her book.

"Is this machine free?" I asked politely.

"Uh-huh."

I quickly put my clothes into the washer and then tried to persuade a wall-mounted vending machine to release a tablet of washing powder. I tried several times putting the dollar coin in the slot before pulling the release lever, but nothing happened.

Brigit then rose from her chair, walked across, and hit the side of the machine. In doing so, she released the washing powder.

"Oh, thank you. I can never get the hang of these machines."

"You're welcome," she replied, and then returned to her book without another word.

I set the washing machine working and returned to the common room. There were two German backpackers, guys a little older than me, sitting there, intermittently watching the cricket, while chatting with each other about their travel itinerary. I took a seat and settled in to watch.

Today's games were key ones for the tournament. We were now into round six out of eight, and the India vs. West Indies game was critical for both sides, while South Africa also needed victory against Zimbabwe. Zimbabwe were now playing only for national pride.

As I started to write my first postcard, I thought about the next stage of my journey. I didn't want to stay another day in Franz Joseph, but hadn't decided where to stop next. I went to talk with the hostel manager at reception to discuss my options. There weren't too many. I wanted to be in Wellington before Sunday in order to see the England vs. New Zealand cricket match, but I still had a few days in hand. There didn't appear to be much of interest if I stopped in Greymouth or Westport, so I decided I would take the bus all the way up to Nelson in one day. The hostel manager helpfully booked me into the YHA hostel in Nelson, and provided me with a bus timetable, assuring me that I wouldn't need to pre-book the bus. With tomorrow's plans now sorted, I returned to the cricket.

Of the two games, by far the more interesting was India vs. West Indies. Although Zimbabwe pushed South Africa quite close in the other game, South Africa were always in control and came out comfortable winners, thereby keeping their World Cup hopes alive.

India only managed a total of 197, being bowled out just short of their 50 overs. There was then a weather interruption, which took out a few overs, following which West Indies, anchored by a steady 58 from Keith Arthurton, slowly and surely knocked off the total required in 44 overs. West Indies were now on 3 wins 3 losses, and remained in the hunt, while India, with only 2 wins, looked to be going home.

It wasn't the most entertaining of afternoons, but I had written several postcards, organised my next day, and done my washing, so it wasn't entirely wasted. I had a quiet evening. After obtaining a fairly poor version of a lasagne from the hostel kitchens, I retired to my room to read, and listened to the BBC World Service before having an early night. I exchanged a few words with Brigit ... a few words only and, unsurprisingly, nothing of great significance.

Wednesday 11 March - Franz Joseph to Nelson

08:30am. I had checked out of the hostel, and stood at the bus stop awaiting the bus for Nelson. A few yards away stood Brigit, beside her backpack, waiting for the same bus. We had still shared no more than a few words. I kept trying to break the ice, but had barely even chipped away the surface.

Thankfully, there were half a dozen other backpackers also waiting with us, so the uneasy stand-off between us was somewhat dissipated. I still wondered what it was that made her so closed off towards me. Although I knew I didn't have the most magnetic personality, I also didn't believe I was that repulsive.

The bus departed at around 8:45am, and it would be a long journey up to Nelson, where we were scheduled to arrive close to 7:00pm. It wasn't quite equivalent to the mammoth trips of the outback, but long enough. I sat midway to the back of the bus, on the coastal side as we headed northward. I was several rows back from where Brigit sat. It wasn't as if I would have felt any compulsion to chat to her if she was in the next seat, but being further apart definitely made me feel more relaxed. I couldn't think that I had ever come across someone who appeared quite so repelled by me. Well, perhaps that wasn't quite true ... in one or two nightclubs, there had been occasions when I had tried to chat up some girl, and I had been given the look that would have been given to a bit of dog poo that she had just trodden in. But apart from that, and in normal daylight hours, this really was quite unusual.

As we turned onto the main road north out of Franz Joseph, I noticed the name Canavans Knob on a small signpost, which again triggered the cartoon images of the royal phalluses dancing up the road. This was not an image I was likely to forget in a hurry. With hours ahead on the bus, I decided I would play a game of trying to spot more strange signposts ... I wondered whether there might be more knobs to be seen on the journey.

As it turned out, the only further knobs to be seen were in my imagination. The morning's journey was not terribly exciting, and views out of the window were somewhat hampered by persistent drizzle. I dozed off a little while half-listening to the bus radio, which was playing a mixture of music interspersed with local news and sport. When they got talking about the cricket, there was a palpable sense of excitement about New Zealand's brilliant unbeaten start, and there was even talk of them as potential winners. I looked forward to their game against England in a few days' time.

My mind also drifted more than once to Megan's MOT rules. At one stop, the bus had pulled in at a garage to fill up with diesel. I noticed an inauspicious sign on the wall ... 'WOF and Car Servicing While You Wait'. It was at the back of the garage, where they evidently had vehicle repairs and maintenance. WOF stood for Warrant of Fitness testing, the equivalent to MOTs back in the UK, and was to certify vehicle roadworthiness. My mind was in the sewer again as I chuckled to myself, thinking of Megan's rules ... *MOT was Manual, Oral and Total servicing. So, what was WOF? Wank, Oral, Fuck? ... Yeah, that would still work.*

I was also daydreaming about the royal knobs again. I now pictured Suzi and Megan semi-naked, with me at their mercy, having been tied to a bed. This started a little like the visions I had back in Darwin, not long after I had met them. This time, however, I was being prepared for a ceremonial blow-job, as my reward for England reaching the World Cup Final. *Cartoon phalluses were dancing behind the two girls, as Suzi began to unzip my flies. She licked her upper lip, and her eyes betrayed pure lust. She pulled out my manhood, and then teasingly engulfed it in her mouth. As she did so, I closed my eyes momentarily as I felt the caressing movement of her tongue. As I opened my eyes, she lifted her head ... and ... Oh fuck! ... Suddenly I was gazing up at icy-Brigit. Her steely cold eyes were full of loathing, and she was baring her teeth ... gnarling like a hungry wolf. Suddenly she went down for a bite* ... and I was shaken from my dream.

Blimey! I was shocked, and even shaken by what I had just visualised. *That was so not what I wanted to imagine.* Such disturbingly erotic thoughts were going to be hard to shake. For a while, each time that I closed my eyes to get some rest, I was soon awakened after a recurrence of these visions. Perhaps over the last few weeks I had spent far too many long hours alone with my straying thoughts. *I really need to get my head sorted out.*

♦ ♦ ♦

The bus pulled in for short comfort stops in Harihari and Hokitika during an otherwise dull and uneventful morning, and then stopped again for a slightly longer break for lunch and a driver change in Greymouth. Here, several of the people I had travelled with from Franz Joseph left the bus, including Brigit, whom I was now somewhat pleased to see the back of. I also hoped that my warped mind would get rid of her too.

Although populated by only about 12,000 residents, Greymouth was quite a big town by New Zealand standards. It was the largest population on the west coast. Standing alongside the Grey River, it had been an important gold mining centre. In the 30 minutes or so that I had to find some lunch and stretch my legs, I was left rather underwhelmed by the place. There certainly wasn't anything particularly worth writing home about. It is funny how often in life

I have used that phrase, but when you are on the far side of the world, and you do write home, it actually does become more meaningful.

Near Punahaiki, however, an hour or so later, there actually was something much more worthy of writing home about: some extraordinary rock formations called Pancake Rocks. On this part of the rugged rocky coastline, there was a large accumulation of curious horizontally stratified rocks, which took on the appearance of large stacks of pancakes, hence the name. Over millions of years, the limestone cliffs had been moulded into these weird formations. There were also several gorges, caverns and squirting blowholes to be seen. It was a fascinating place, and certainly a welcome break from an otherwise tedious journey.

After Pancake Rocks there were further comfort breaks at the small towns of Westport and Murchison, before we finally arrived in Nelson at just after 7:00pm. By the late afternoon and early evening, the weather had improved and, once in Nelson, there was cloudless blue sky above us.

I walked just over half a mile from the bus stop to the YHA hostel and checked in. A pleasant, clean, friendly hostel; it was a fairly typical YHA-run building. I was allocated to a four-berth dorm, with two other backpackers already in occupation. As there wasn't much daylight left, after quickly enquiring about onward travel to Picton, I then headed back into the town centre to have a quick look around and find something for dinner.

◆ ◆ ◆

Nelson seemed a rather unassuming and tranquil town. For a place that boasted over 45,000 residents, there was hardly anyone to be seen in the town centre. Of course, this was after 8:30 on a

Wednesday evening, and all the shops were shut. There were a few bars and restaurants open, but I settled for a couple of slices of takeaway pizza, and ate them on-the-hoof, as I wanted to take a stroll around the town. Apart from an attractive central park and a cathedral with a distinctive 35 metre free-standing bell tower, I didn't feel that there was too much here to keep me in Nelson for another day. Perhaps I was starting to get travel fatigue after moving on every few days since early January; my enthusiasm for sightseeing seemed to be diminishing. Tomorrow I would try to catch the Picton Ferry across to Wellington, and begin my exploration of North Island.

Heading back towards the hostel, as I passed a bar, I heard 'I want to know what love is', one of my favourite songs by Foreigner, which prompted me to begin my tuneless singing ... and return to thoughts of Suzi ...

[9]*"... I wanna know what love is ...*

... I want you to show me ...."

... And boy did I want to know what love was. Like in the song, I'd felt my share of heartache and pain, and now I'd also travelled to the other side of the world on my journey to find romance ... although there were other reasons for my travel too.

As I sang, I also remembered some of my days at college, most of which had been spent in pursuit of some girl or other, and most often resulting in disappointment. As I walked on away from the bar and up the road, the music grew faint. I then moved on from 'I want to know what love is' to another track from Foreigner's greatest hits, and very much in keeping with the mood ...

[10]*"... I've been waiting for a girl like you ..."*

With Suzi, I was most definitely smitten. I had certainly been waiting for a girl like Suzi to come into my life. I so longed to hold her again, but I also couldn't wait to see Megan; she was so lively, and her joie de vivre and dirty sense of humour were so great for recharging my own batteries.

As I got back to the hostel it was nearly 10:00pm. I clarified with the lady on reception about getting the bus to Picton, and then the ferry crossing, and also enquired about hostels in Wellington. She offered to book me into the YHA hostel, which I guessed might be as good as anywhere.

Apart from the first few days in Christchurch when I had stayed in the Ambassador Hotel, my other accommodation in New Zealand had all been YHA-run hostels. In contrast, in Australia, I hadn't stayed in any YHA hostels, but had used those of the Backpackers Association. I guess each association only recommended their own hostels, but it often seemed easier to take their advice and assistance with bookings. Whether it was the hostel type or the difference between Australia and New Zealand, I didn't know, but the Aussie hostels had certainly seemed a bit livelier. Most of the Aussie hostels had seemed quite vibrant, whereas in New Zealand they were perhaps for the more serious traveller. The cooler weather in New Zealand as well as the absence of alcohol in the YHA hostels might also have had a part to play.

Before returning to my dorm room, I caught sight of the cricket highlights on the common room TV. Today's game from Perth had been played between Australia and Pakistan, teams with between slim and no chance of progressing further. The loser was surely going home, and even the winner would probably not qualify.

For Australia, today looked as though it was the final nail in their coffin. It was their least impressive game of the tournament. Pakistan batted first and put up a competitive score of 220 for 9 from their 50 overs, following which, in their best display of the tournament, they bowled Australia out for just 172. Pakistan still had a glimmer of hope, and that half point that they got from the wash-out match with England might yet prove of importance.

Thursday 12 March - Nelson to Wellington

I caught a bus from Nelson at around 9:30am, intending to arrive in Picton at around noon. This would enable me to take the early afternoon sailing across to Wellington. It wasn't the most direct of bus routes, but some of the scenery overlooking the Marlborough Sounds, and the sight of all the vineyards growing Sauvignon Blanc, were pretty impressive. Ever since I had started getting a taste for wine, Marlborough Sauvignon Blanc had been a favourite … I could either blame or thank my father for this.

Arriving at the Picton ferry terminal just after midday, I had a couple of hours to kill before the ferry departed. After purchasing a ticket, I headed off for a walk around the few shops and along the waterfront. There were a couple of small arcades and a frontage of shops which overlooked the harbour that sheltered more than a hundred small boats. It wasn't spectacular, but everything here appeared to be pretty well maintained; all the buildings and the majority of boats looked freshly painted and well cared for. I bought myself a crab sandwich from a local delicatessen, and then sat on a wall as I watched the inter-island ferry come in.

Picton, and the whole operation around it, reminded me of catching the ferry from Lymington to the Isle of Wight. Nobody here was rushing; all the passengers and vehicles were disembarking, and being replaced by new ones, at a leisurely pace.

I either stood or sat out on the open decks of the ferry for most of the three-hour crossing to Wellington. As we sailed out from Picton, the first stretch was quite scenic, and was littered with small islands before reaching the more open water of the Cook Strait. Once out in the rougher waters, I kept my eyes open in the hope that I might be lucky enough to spot some whales or dolphins, but had to be content with several seabird species, including gulls, petrels, and also a handful of albatrosses.

The weather had changed markedly from one side of the crossing to the other. In Picton it had been warm and sunny, whereas on arrival in Wellington just over three hours later, it was damp and overcast. It is never great arriving in a new city when everything looks grey, and my first impressions of New Zealand's capital were less positive than they might otherwise have been. Beyond a tidy but unremarkable harbour area, the waterfront seemed to be full of non-descript office blocks, and not terribly inspiring.

The ferry docked just to the north of the main waterfront area and city centre. It was conveniently on the right side of the centre for the YHA hostel, which was just a 10-minute walk along one of the main roads. By the time I reached the hostel, at just after 6:00pm, I was thankful that I had booked ahead ... the hostel was nearly full. I was allocated to a 4-berth dorm room, which seemed quite a standard arrangement for the YHA hostels. Such rooms were flexible for use as either family rooms or small dormitories.

As I opened the door to my room, I was pleasantly surprised to find myself greeting Anders again. This was the same chap that I had seen a few days ago in the pub in Queenstown, and that I had climbed Ayers Rock with in mid-January. It was always good to catch up with friendly faces.

"Hey Bruce, good to see you again." We shook hands warmly. "I am just off to the laundry room, but I'll get back to the common room in a minute. The cricket is getting interesting."

"Who is playing today?"

"They are showing New Zealand and India, and it's very close. But England and South Africa are also playing ... I don't know how that one is going."

"Ah-ha ... both are key games."

I dumped my backpack by the free bunk-bed and, after a quick freshen up in the washrooms, made my way to the common room. As I did so, I was diverted by the smell of hot food. The hostel evidently had a small kitchen, and seemed to produce a bit of pub-style food to order. I could smell chips ... it was enticing. I had a quick look at a blackboard which described the rather limited, but welcome, menu options: beefburger and chips, cheeseburger and chips, sausage and chips, egg and chips. *It was no bloody wonder that I could smell chips.*

While I pondered over the food, I walked through to get a view of the TV. The India vs. New Zealand game from Dunedin was in the final few overs, as New Zealand were chasing down India's total of 230. India had to win this game to remain in the tournament and the tension in the team was palpable. New Zealand, with a 5-game winning streak, were already safely qualified, relaxed and enjoying the tournament. I only got to see a handful of overs as New Zealand chipped away at the target, and comfortably reached the total with 3 overs to spare. With a 6 – 0 record, New Zealand had established themselves as potential World Cup Winners, while India, with only 2 wins and a draw from 7 games, were now out.

While the post-match interviews were underway, I ordered a cheeseburger (and chips of course), and then returned to the TV to catch up on the other match. Both England and South Africa were still contenders, with England having already got sufficient points to be safe. South Africa really needed to win.

The match was being played in Melbourne, and had been interrupted by rain. South Africa had set a competitive total of 236 from their 50 overs, but England were chasing down a revised target of 226 from 41 overs. I couldn't understand how such a revised total was set. It seemed absurdly unfair on England that they were losing 9 overs, but only 10 runs were reduced from the target. How could this be? The TV commentators couldn't seem to explain it. I certainly didn't understand, and poor old Anders was left totally bemused.

As England had already qualified for the semi-finals, I wasn't particularly concerned at the result. In any case, it seemed that with that pressure off, the England batting effort was also significantly more relaxed. Just as my cheeseburger eventually arrived, with just one ball of the match left, England reached the 226 target and had won the game. South Africa were now on 4 wins from 7 games, and had to win their final group game against India to go through. England were now 5 ½ out of 6, which was highly satisfying ... as indeed was my cheeseburger.

Part III:
North Island,
New Zealand

Chapter 6: Going barmy ... Wellington

Friday 13 March - Wellington

It was nine full weeks since the Friday on which I set out from Heathrow. Home seemed a long way away, and quite a long time ago now. While I occasionally thought of people or things back home, I was far more focussed on what lay ahead when I got to Auckland. I found it difficult to stop thinking about Suzi, both independently from, and together with, the potential outcomes of England's attempt to win the World Cup. And, ever since last Wednesday, most of my frequent visions of sexcapades under Megan's rules, not only included Suzi and Megan as they had done before, but they also now usually ended up with ice-queen Brigit biting chunks out of my wedding tackle. Today was Friday the 13th ... perhaps it was fitting for me to have such nightmares. *But why Friday the 13th? What was so special about Friday 13th that made people believe it was unlucky? That was one to look up later.*

I was determined to go and watch the New Zealand vs. England game in Wellington on Sunday but, unlike when I was in Melbourne, I was less confident of being able to just turn up on the day to buy a ticket. As far as the tournament was progressing, New Zealand were flying high, as indeed were England. Therefore, it would likely be a popular game and, also being at the weekend, one could expect a higher turnout. So, I decided that my first priority for today was to try to get a ticket.

While there were probably ticket outlets and touts in the city centre, I decided to walk to the Basin Reserve cricket ground, because any tickets purchased there should at least be sold at face value, rather than an extortionately inflated price. Basin Reserve was the other side of the city centre, and about an hour's walk. As I arrived at the ground, I was pleased to see a ticket office cum merchandise store open, and tickets clearly on sale.

After a few minutes queueing behind about five other eager spectators, I purchased a ticket for the match. Also, on impulse, I bought myself a replica England shirt to wear to the game. This time I would be a full part of the 'Barmy Army' of touring England cricket supporters. I don't often impulse buy, and indeed I don't normally buy such sporting uniforms ... but when in Wellington ... I was really starting to catch the World Cup fever.

Not since 1966, before I was born, had England won a world cup in one of our flagship national sports (football, rugby or cricket). The 1966 football triumph was the only one ... although admittedly the Cricket World Cup had only begun in 1975, and the first Rugby World Cup was only in 1987. However, it was the principle! England was a great sporting nation, and winning was a matter of national pride. Despite all the left-wing rhetoric that I had grown up with, encouraging participation rather than success, just taking part was never enough for me ... we had to win.

Pleased and relieved at having safely acquired a ticket, I decided to do the other thing that I knew I wanted to do in this part of town. A short walk along the road from the Basin Reserve was the National Museum. The weather was overcast, and there was light rain forecast, so today was a good day to spend indoors. So, from around 10:30am until around 2:30pm (4 hours was a long time for me in any museum) I wandered around the National Museum and the National Art Gallery which were conveniently both housed in the same place.

In the museum, there were two things of particular note. First, having always been enthusiastic about natural history, I found the displays of indigenous wildlife interesting, and in particular the diorama of extinct moas. Here, they had decided to create a mock-up of what they believed a real one would have looked like. They had used feathers from dead kiwis and emus to try to replicate more than just the skeleton ... it didn't really work too well.

One of the fascinating things, which I hadn't known before, but which I had also not really thought about, was that moas were principally vegetarian. Scientists, on examining their gizzards, had concluded that they were primarily grazers. Moas had filled the types of niches that in other places around the world would be filled by deer, antelopes and llamas. This made sense, as New Zealand's fauna had evolved without mammals ... well, at least until those bloody humans appeared and introduced rats, cats, pigs and goats, which then started destroying everything. However, from what I had seen before, the curators who displayed moa skeletons, and artists who painted their pictures, seemed always to portray moas in a similar way to fearsome carnivorous dinosaurs. For some reason, moas just had to appear aggressive. Perhaps it was to reduce human guilt ... as I'm sure most people feel worse about driving more cuddly creatures to extinction.

There were several species of moa, with the largest of them being up to 12 feet tall, and probably weighing over 200 kilos. All species were thought to have been extinct by the middle of the 15th century, and the conventional scientific view was that it was humans that had driven them to extinction. The Polynesians, who arrived in New Zealand around the 13th century, were known to have hunted them, but the recorded history did appear rather sketchy.

The second part of the museum, in which I also spent a significant amount of time, was the Polynesian cultural section. It was full of impressive wooden carvings, and also displayed models and descriptions of different outrigger-type boats that were typical of those that early settlers must have used to colonise new islands across the Pacific.

Mid-afternoon, when I emerged from the museum, I was quite hungry. On my way back towards the city centre, I took the first opportunity that I saw to rectify matters ... a street vendor, selling hotdogs. If my mother had any idea of the amount of fast food I was consuming, I am sure she would have given me an earful about the benefits of a balanced diet. I wasn't about to tell her, as she was on the other side of the world ... out of sight, and mostly out of mind.

However, this afternoon, as I sat on a convenient wall while I ate my hotdog, I thought about my parents, and in particular I wondered about what they might think of Suzi, were they ever to meet her. I had only rarely introduced my mum and dad to any girlfriend (neither romantic nor platonic) as conversation always became stilted and embarrassing. *They would definitely approve of Suzi ... well, to be honest, they would approve of anyone. They just want me off their hands and married, with a decent 9 to 5 job and 2.4 children.*

The thing is, with Suzi, I could visualize this kind of life too. Only a month or two ago, the thought of settling down like this had appalled me. Today, it really had started to seem quite appealing. *Well, perhaps not the 9 to 5 job ... and the more I think of it ... perhaps not the 2.4 children either ... but settling down with Suzi, definitely.*

I walked at a leisurely pace through an area overflowing with Chinese and other South East Asian restaurants, and then continued along into one of the main shopping and eating areas of Wellington that was lined with the ubiquitous MacDonalds, KFC, Pizza Hut and so on. It was as I was ambling past a KFC that I bumped into Anders again. By chance, he had also spent the morning looking around the National Museum and was now also on his way back towards the hostel. So, after a short chat, we set off together.

However, we didn't progress far before we were drawn into a sports bar that was conveniently located along one of the main routes back towards the YHA hostel. The bar had an open frontage with pavement seating, and extended quite a long way back from the road to a wall displaying an enormous TV screen which, naturally, was showing today's game between West Indies and Sri

Lanka. It was now just after 4:30pm, but lunchtime for the cricket, which was being played at the Berri Oval. No, I had never heard of Berri either, but it turns out to be a small town on the Murray River, situated about 150 miles north east of Adelaide. Berri is in the middle of nowhere ... well almost, it is actually in the middle of 'wine country.' I guess the tournament organisers didn't think that this game was going to be a big box-office draw.

The game in Berri wasn't such a big draw for the boozers in the sports bar either, as most of the pub-goers were on the pavement outside. However, at this stage of the competition, it was now knockout cricket. Both West Indies and Sri Lanka had played six matches, and both needed to win, or they were going home. Having watched the West Indies team in Melbourne (well, watched some of the game, interspersed with attempts to steal kisses from Suzi), I was supporting them.

After lunch, West Indies built a challenging target of 268 from their 50 overs, helped by an outstanding 110 from Phil Simmons. At the gap between innings, Anders and I consulted each other on whether to return to the hostel to watch the Sri Lanka response. The beer talked, so we remained in the pub. In the end, we lost interest and didn't stay to watch the finish. Sri Lanka's batting was dismal ... it was almost as though they weren't even trying to win. Although they batted out their entire 50 overs, they only scored 179, leaving them 91 runs short. Having had their early overs choked of runs by solid West Indian bowling, the Sri Lankans seemed to give up and just be intent on surviving through to the end. This was a poor advert for cricket. Sri Lanka deserved to be out of the tournament, while West Indies hopes remained alive.

For me, several beers later, after returning to the hostel at around 8:00pm, I crashed out on my bed, dead to the world for the rest of the night.

Saturday 14 March - Wellington

I awoke on Saturday morning to the sound of heavy rain against the window. I was not in any great rush to get up. I had to make sure that I was out of the room before 10:00am when the hostel turfed everyone out for cleaning, but I had no reason to get up too early.

Wellington had a reputation as 'the windy city', but so far all I had really seen was a mixture of overcast skies, damp and now wet. My impressions so far probably didn't do the city any justice. In the Lonely Planet guide, the city is described as "hemmed in around its magnificent harbour, the buildings marching picturesquely up the steep hills." Perhaps because I had recently been in Sydney, I had an unfortunate comparison to make with a far more magnificent harbour, and impressions of Sydney had been enhanced with a daily filling of glorious sunshine.

Although Wellington is the capital city with a population of just over 325,000, it is less than half the size of Auckland. As I walked from the hostel towards the downtown area, I wandered past a number of foreign embassies. I stopped to take a look around the outside of the new Parliament building, which was far less impressive than I had expected, and also less impressive than the Old Government Building next door. The new building was known as the Beehive. It was a concrete and glass rotunda, which perhaps resembled a certain type of beehive ... well, perhaps ... if anyone else actually made concrete and glass beehives in that shape.

When I had been in Canberra, I was reasonably impressed by some of the design elements of their newish Parliament, although I had found the clinically-clean modernism more fitting for a conference centre ... which I suppose, when you think about it, is more or less what a parliament building needs to be. Here in Wellington the new parliament was certainly modern, but the styling did remind me more of a 1960's hospital building. *Whatever! ... I am sure the locals love it.*

After seeing the Parliament building, I decided to check out two of the other recommended highlights in my Lonely Planet book. First was Old St Paul's Cathedral, which was a pleasant, if unspectacular, 19th century church; then after 15 minutes walking around inside, I set off to find the Cable Car. The Wellington Cable Car, which was opened in 1902, took passengers up the hillside to a district called Kelburn, where you could get good views over the city and the harbour beyond. Although there was still some rain in the air, it wasn't too windy, so I thought it might be worth the trip. An hour or so later, I was not so sure it had been. It was inexpensive, but the lowish clouds and persistent drizzle had ruined any prospect of good views, and the weather also meant it was not a good day for stopping to admire flowers in the Botanical Gardens on the walk back down.

At midday, rain-drenched and hungry, I sat in the window at MacDonalds with a BigMac, fries and a Coke, gazing out aimlessly at other people getting soaked as they passed by. This was not really a day to do much. *This also wasn't much of a lunch.* After finishing this meal, I was still hungry. I usually find meals at MacDonalds are just not quite filling enough, even when you 'go large'. So, looking out of the window, and not feeling enthusiastic about venturing outside again, I decided on buying myself a second meal; this time a smaller one of just a cheeseburger and coffee.

After finishing my second meal, and without immediate prospect of better weather, I decided to head back to the hostel. I did hope that the weather would be better by tomorrow, otherwise the prospect of much cricket was pretty bleak.

♦ ♦ ♦

Arriving back at the hostel, my clothes were soaked. Instead of trying to dry them, I thought it would be a good time to put them plus my other dirty clothes in for a wash. Unlike when I had last done my washing, in the laundry room at the hostel in Franz Joseph, at least this time I didn't have the prospect of ice-cold Brigit to deal with.

Back in the dorm room, I changed into a different polo shirt and jeans, and then collected my clothes to take to the laundry room. There was a notice on the laundry room door to tell me the coinage that I needed in order to operate the machines. I checked my pockets and thought I had sufficient, so I pushed open the door.

Oh fuck! Déjà vu. Sitting on a plastic chair beside a washer-dryer, quietly waiting for her clothes to be ready, dressed in tight blue jeans and a grey woolly jumper, head down, immersed in a book, with her long blond hair tied back ... there she was.

"Hi Brigit!" I said by way of a friendly greeting.

"Oh, hello," she responded, lifting her head momentarily from the book to acknowledge my existence.

I knew that I should not have expected more. There was no 'how nice to see you again' or 'what a pleasant surprise' ... but there didn't even appear to be a glimmer of recognition that she had ever seen me before.

Wow! ... I really had made a wonderful impression.

I quickly loaded my clothes into a washer-dryer. I then took out a couple of dollars from my pocket to get a powder tablet from the vending machine. "Please behave" I told the machine as I tried to put the first dollar coin into the slot. I didn't have a great record with such machines. I put a second coin into the slot and then pulled the release handle.

Nothing.

"Fuck."

I tried the handle again.

Still nothing.

I tried the handle a third time, and then hit the side of the machine, just as Brigit had done to help me with a similar machine in Franz Joseph. This time it worked.

"Hallelujah!" I said, as I sensed a smirk come across Brigit's face from behind her book.

After a few more moments of uneasy silence while I set the washing machine to run, I then left the laundry room. I didn't feel comfortable remaining there for any longer than I had to.

Wow! ... What is it with Brigit?

With the washing on, I waited in the common room, trying to watch the day's cricket match. Seeing Brigit again had unnerved me, and had left me feeling unable to relax.

The cricket proved to be exceptionally disappointing and of little entertainment value. For a start it featured Australia and Zimbabwe, teams which now had little to play for; then the play was affected by rain delays; and lastly, the cricket itself was so terribly one-sided that Australia didn't even need to break a sweat to win.

This Saturday had been a highly forgettable day in many ways, but not in respect of Brigit, whom I found impossible to remove from my thoughts. I just couldn't understand why she was so frosty towards me ... and it really bugged me.

Sunday 15 March - Wellington

At around 9:00am, I sat in the hostel breakfast room, attired in my England cricket shirt, and eager to go to the match. Thankfully, the weather system had moved through during the night, and there was glorious morning sunshine streaming through the windows.

Sipping my coffee, I was then joined by a couple of lads who were also wearing England shirts.

"Hi! Are you going to the game?" one of them asked.

"Yes ... and you?" I replied.

"Yeah, we certainly are ... it should be good. I am Steve, and this is Neil," said Steve who bore a passing resemblance to a young Mel Gibson. His friend, Neil, looked a little similar to me; about the same build, with blond hair like mine ... only he was better looking, and his hair wasn't receding.

"Why don't you come with us?" said Neil.

"Yeah, sure," I responded. They seemed like friendly chaps.

We got talking over breakfast, and it turned out that they had been in New Zealand for about a month, and were heading over to Melbourne after this game, with the hope of seeing England in the World Cup Final ... a hope that was steadily turning into a reasonable expectation.

We walked across town to the Basin Reserve cricket ground, stopping at a small supermarket on the way, to pick up a supply of beer and some snacks for lunch. As we got nearer to the ground, progressively more and more cricket supporters appeared. This was different from how it had been in Melbourne when I had seen West Indies and Pakistan. Here in Wellington, this was a home game, and the home team was flying high having just won six games on the spin. There were New Zealand replica shirts everywhere. There was also quite a contingent of England fans, perhaps several hundred if not into the thousands. This was a pretty good turnout for the 'Barmy Army,' and I was pleased to be among them.

When we got into the ground and took up seats near the back of the main stand, it didn't feel like there were so many England supporters after all. The three of us were surrounded by Kiwis. There wasn't another England shirt for fifty yards. However, unlike this type of situation in some football games, being surrounded by 'the enemy' was not at all intimidating. People were just here to enjoy it; cricket was a friendly game, and attracted a friendly crowd. The people immediately around us were even hospitable enough to share some of their more than plentiful supply of beer.

Although this was a World Cup game, the match didn't seem to have much of an edge to it. Both teams had already qualified for the semi-finals, and it was just a case of who was going to finish top of the group and perhaps have an easier route to the final. There wouldn't be much in it, but the result probably meant a little more to New Zealand because, if they finished top of the group, they could expect a home semi-final in Auckland, which would be preferable to playing in Sydney. However, it did seem that both sides lacked much sparkle and were saving themselves a little for the games to come.

The game itself was certainly no classic. England batted first and struggled to set a competitive total in their 50 overs, finishing on 200 for 8, with Graeme Hick the only batsmen to make 50. It wasn't a great total, but it was good to see that Hick had at last found a bit of form for England. He was not long established in the England side, despite an outstanding county record which, in 1988, had included a record-setting 405, playing for Worcestershire against Somerset. If only he could replicate that sort of form for England, there were real reasons for optimism that we could actually win the World Cup. Today, however, the total of 200 didn't really look enough.

Indeed, it wasn't. New Zealand's batsmen set about the run chase in a highly professional and controlled manner. Steered by a contribution of 78 from Andrew Jones, they reached England's total for the loss of only 3 wickets after just 41 overs. It was a comfortable win for New Zealand, which left them top of the group on 7 straight wins, while England were clear in second place with a 5-1-1 record.

It was an enjoyable match, even if the cricket itself had not been gripping. It had been a memorable day out, but the day's excitement in the cricket had been elsewhere, with the other teams fighting to remain in contention. On returning that evening to the hostel, I caught up with the highlights of the other matches. South Africa had a must-win game against India, who were now only playing for pride. And Pakistan were also playing for survival against Sri Lanka, who, again, had no more than pride to play for.

Both these games were close nervy affairs, and each match went down to the last over, to be decided in favour of South Africa and Pakistan respectively. South Africa were now safely in the semi-finals, and Pakistan were still clinging on, but only just. They now had to defeat New Zealand in their last game, and rely on other results to go their way.

Monday 16 March - Wellington

While Sunday had proved to be lucky for the weather if not for an England win, Monday was damp, gloomy and a little windy. I decided that I didn't wish to spend too much longer here, especially if the weather remained poor, so with the help of the hostel manager, I booked a bed in the YHA hostel in Rotorua for the Tuesday night.

I also checked on bus timings, and was shocked to find just how little I had studied about the shape of New Zealand. By now, I had a reasonable grasp of South Island; it was long and thin, and of course I had just spent a couple of weeks travelling around it. But North Island? I had in my mind that it was a squarish blob of land, with Wellington at the bottom, Rotorua in the middle and Auckland at the top, and had thought that this blob was about half the size of South Island. I hadn't really noticed that Wellington was stuck on a long thin bit at the bottom, and that there was also another long narrow strip above Auckland. Nor had I noticed that Rotorua was not situated in the middle of the squarish bit ... no, actually, Rotorua was around 300 miles away from Wellington, rather than the 100 or so that I had thought. It was over 6 hours by direct bus, and I was a little disappointed to discover that I had to travel more than double the journey I had envisaged.

Nevertheless, I wanted to start heading north towards Auckland to ensure I made it there in advance of the semi-final on Saturday. Although it looked certain now that the England match would be in Sydney, I still wanted to go to the semi-final if possible. Of course, even more than the cricket, I was longing to meet up again with Suzi and Megan, who I hoped would also be arriving in Auckland at the weekend.

Ever since that Sunday four weeks ago at the cricket in Melbourne, when sparks of romance had truly been ignited with Suzi, my mind had struggled to come to terms with it. I wanted to be in a relationship so badly ... perhaps too badly. I felt so insecure; it felt that whatever Suzi and I had captured could disappear at any moment. Perhaps it had already disappeared. I had insecurities about my character; why would someone as bright, intelligent, witty and great looking as Suzi be interested in me? In respect of both looks and personality, I was trying to punch well above my weight, and sooner or later, surely, I would be found wanting.

With such gloomy thoughts in my head, matching the gloomy overcast weather, I spent much of the middle part of the day wandering around Wellington's downtown shopping area. Aside from purchasing the latest copy of the International Mail newspaper and one or two more postcards, I wasn't really shopping for anything specific; I was just passing the hours by browsing in the clothes shops, and in a few of the music stores and book shops.

As I emerged from one of the book shops, a sizable one called Unity Books, I wasn't paying enough attention to where I was going, and stumbled into two familiar faces. England cricketers Graeme Hick and Derek Pringle were out and about on their day off, just wandering round the streets of the capital. These guys didn't know me, although both had actually met me before, and one of them on several occasions.

"Oh ... sorry!" I said, as I just avoided bumping into Pringle.

"No problem," came the reply, as they walked away ...

A moment or two later, once my thoughts had caught up with the picture in front of me, I added ...

"Oh ... and good luck in the semi-final."

"Thanks," acknowledged Pringle, peering back at me over his John Lennon style spectacles.

It had been a few years since I used to watch Pringle playing at Fenners, the University of Cambridge cricket ground. In those days I was a regular visitor there from April through June, when the University hosted county teams and the occasional international touring side. I used to go there after school, and I occasionally got the chance to bowl at Pringle and other University players as they practised in the nets. More recently I had seen Hick playing there for Worcestershire, and indeed Pringle for Essex, when the county sides had played against the University. Both these players probably had more than their fair share of expectation heaped upon their shoulders for this tournament. For Hick, the expectation came due to his phenomenal record in the county game, while eyes were focused on Pringle because English fans were desperate to find an allrounder who could succeed the legend that was Ian Botham.

Although neither Hick nor Pringle really acknowledged my existence, I was lifted a little out of my earlier gloomy mood as I began to think about the World Cup again. Despite their fairly poor showing against New Zealand, England still appeared to have a pretty good shot at winning the tournament, as there weren't really any outstanding teams in the competition. Australia, the pre-tournament favourites, were all but out, and even if they miraculously scraped through to the semi-finals by virtue of run-rate mathematics, England had already beaten them, so they were certainly not a side to be feared. And New Zealand, despite having won all their matches and having just beaten England, did not look overly impressive either ... it was more that their opponents had largely failed to deliver.

For the first time, I was imagining the World Cup Final ... *It was New Zealand against England at the Melbourne Cricket Ground. I was watching it on a big screen in a sports bar in Auckland, together with Suzi and Megan. New Zealand had won the toss and put England into bat, but unlike the match I'd seen in Wellington, England's openers Gooch and Botham were in tremendous form and smashed the New Zealand bowlers around the park. Gooch, the captain, scored a century and England batted through to a total near 300. In response, the New Zealand openers went cheaply, but were then rescued by their captain, Martin Crowe, who also scored a century as he kept New Zealand in the game.*

It all went down to the final over ... New Zealand required ten to win, but only had one wicket left. I was nervous ... standing up, eyes glued to the screen, a beer in one hand with the other holding Suzi tightly around the waist. I couldn't look but I had to watch.

Pringle is bowling the final over. The first ball is a dot ball ... that's good. The second ball ... oh, no ... bad delivery ... Crowe square cuts for 4. Now only 6 more runs are needed from 4 balls. Then the third ball ... another dot ball ... now 6 from 3. The fourth ball of the over goes just outside the off-stump ... Crowe slices the ball down towards Lewis at third man. Oh no! ... Lewis fumbles it. Crowe returns for a second run ... Oh, it's going to be close. Lewis throws the ball straight into Stewart's gloves above the stumps, and Stewart whips the bails off.

Was Crowe out? ... It's a tight one.

Everyone looks across towards the square-leg umpire. His finger goes up, signalling that Crowe has been run out.

Yesssss! ... It's all over ... England have won. England have bloody won! I leap for joy.

I hug and kiss both Suzi and Megan.

I can barely believe it ... England have just won the World Cup. They've done it. This was a dream. England have bloody won it!

I hold Suzi tight, and then kiss her firmly on the lips. Seconds later, Megan then suddenly passes Suzi a door key ...

"Here you are babe ... Room 64, at the Hilton up the road. I got you two lovebirds a little pressie ... Now just go and fuck each other stupid!"

I snapped out of my daydreaming, as I almost bumped into an elderly couple crossing the pavement in front of me.

Who knows? Perhaps it could actually happen for me this time, I thought. But BJ ... just don't get your hopes up.

This scenario was still not a high probability, for either aspect. With England, although they were in with a shout, one always felt they would somehow manage to grasp defeat from the jaws of victory. And with Suzi, she most probably would have got cold feet about me by now. It was true that she liked me three weeks ago, but three weeks was longer than any of my previous relationships had lasted.

Chapter 7: Steamy ... Rotorua

Tuesday 17 March - Wellington to Rotorua

There was a lot of time to kill on the journey today. I caught the direct bus for Rotorua from near Wellington train station at just before 8:00am. It was scheduled to arrive in Rotorua at around 3:30pm. There was a handful of short comfort break stops along the way, most notably at Taupo, the small town at the north end of Lake Taupo. Apart from some wonderful views of this large expanse of water, the rest of the journey was quite uneventful and uninteresting. In fact, I spent much of the journey with my eyes closed and dozing, and sometimes dreaming up various different endings to the daydream that I'd had yesterday.

In the first ending, after England's World Cup win ... *Suzi and I had gone from the bar up the road to the Hilton and had taken the lift up to the sixth floor, where we arrived at room 64, and turned the key. The door opened to reveal a moonlit room, with curtains open and a view across the lights of Auckland below. In front of us lay a huge king-size bed ... pristine white sheets ironed to perfection ... heart-shaped velvet cushions lay against the pillows on either side of the bed. Suzi and I turned to look at each other, then shut the door behind us. Hand in hand, we walked across past the bed to the window. Bathed in the moonlight, our lips met in a firm embrace, followed moments later by our tongues. I untucked her white blouse from her cut-off jeans, as she tugged at my sky-blue polo shirt. We struggled to pull each other's tops over our heads, still trying not to part our mouths from each other. We kicked off our trainers and then with our tops thrown to the floor, Suzi steadied herself against a large oak dressing table.*

I unclipped Suzi's black satin bra, allowing her sumptuous breasts to be released before my eyes. My lips then began to work on gently kissing her nipples, before I then took to one knee, while continuing to kiss and caress her breasts. My fingers moved to stroke Suzi's tummy, and then down to unbutton her cut-off jeans, which fell to the carpet to reveal her black satin knickers. A few caresses over the satin, and then the knickers were also released to the floor. There Suzi stood, gloriously naked but for her white half-socks.

My head moved down as I kissed her belly button, and then further down to her tightly-trimmed pubic hair. Suzi leaned back against the dressing table, as my fingers caressed up and down her inner thighs, and eventually met up with my mouth, as fingers, lips and tongue converged on her pussy ... oh, it was so wet and inviting. Suzi gripped my head with her hands, as her head tossed back with pleasure while my tongue began to work inside.

After a few minutes I could feel the muscles of her bum clench and release as she felt waves of pleasure run through her body. Then Suzi struggled to push me off and onto the bed, where she pulled off my jeans and removed my boxers. "Now it's my turn," she said as she knelt at the end of the bed, as she began teasing my stiffy between her fingers. As our eyes met, she licked her lips and slowly eased herself down to lick the tip, before rolling her tongue underneath the head and then engulfing it fully. She clasped the base in one hand, and then lifted her head up for air, before ... SUDDENLY I was being stared at by ice-queen Brigit, with her fangs sharpened for a killing bite ... I woke up, startled.

♦ ♦ ♦

A second time, an hour or so later as I was dozing off, the dream began again ... *Suzi and I had gone from the bar up the road to the Hilton and, having taken the lift up to the sixth floor, we had arrived at room 64 and turned the key. The door opened to reveal a moonlit room, with curtains open and a view across the lights of Auckland below. In front of us lay a huge king-size bed ... pristine white sheets ironed to perfection ... heart-shaped velvet cushions lay against the pillows on either side of the bed. Suzi and I turned to look at each other, then shut the door behind us. Hand in hand, we walked across past the bed to the window. Bathed in the moonlight, our lips met in a firm embrace, followed moments later by our tongues. I untucked her white blouse from her cut-off jeans, as she tugged at my sky-blue polo shirt. We struggled to pull each other's tops over our heads, still trying not to part our mouths from each other. We kicked off our trainers and then with our tops thrown to the floor, Suzi steadied herself against a large oak dressing table.*

I unclipped Suzi's black satin bra, allowing her sumptuous breasts to be released before my eyes. My lips then began to work on gently kissing her nipples, before I then took to one knee, while continuing to kiss and caress her breasts. My fingers moved to stroke Suzi's tummy, and then down to unbutton her cut-off jeans, which fell to the carpet to reveal her black satin knickers. A few caresses over the satin, and then the knickers were also released to the floor. There Suzi stood, gloriously naked but for her white half-socks.

My head moved down as I kissed her belly button, and then further down to her tightly-trimmed pubic hair. Suzi leaned back against the dressing table, as my fingers caressed up and down her inner thighs, and eventually met up with my mouth, as fingers, lips and tongue converged on her pussy ... oh, it was so wet and inviting. Suzi gripped my head with her hands, as her head tossed back with pleasure as my tongue began to work inside.

After several minutes, I looked up ... her back was arching as she was approaching climax. As I resumed my oral work, I glanced at the dressing table mirror behind her. Her long blonde hair rolled down her back. Wait ... blonde hair! Somewhat startled, I looked up ... to see Brigit's face snarling back, her hand clasping a knife that she was about to plunge into my back ... I woke with a start.

Fuck – I must have been watching Basic Instinct too many times. Ice-queen Brigit did perhaps bare a passing resemblance to Sharon Stone … with her clothes on. *Oh, please come back, Agnetha?*

♦ ♦ ♦

A little later on, I was dozing off yet again, and the dream began again in the same way … *Suzi and I had gone from the bar up the road to the Hilton and, having taken the lift up to the sixth floor, we had arrived at room 64, and turned the key. The door opened to reveal a moonlit room, with curtains open and a view across the lights of Auckland below. In front of us lay a huge king-size bed … pristine white sheets ironed to perfection … heart-shaped velvet cushions lay against the pillows on either side of the bed. Suzi and I turned to look at each other, then shut the door behind us. Hand in hand, we walked across past the bed to the window. Bathed in the moonlight, our lips met in a firm embrace, followed moments later by our tongues. I untucked her white blouse from her cut-off jeans, as she tugged at my sky-blue polo shirt. We struggled to pull each other's tops over our heads, still trying not to part our mouths from each other.*

As I finally released her blouse over her head … aarrgghh! It was Brigit staring back at me. "What the fuck do you think you're doing?" she said in her Norwegian accent. "Rape! Rape!" she shouted' … at which point I woke up startled again.

Why had Brigit got into my head like this? Yes, she was the most incredible mix of fantastic looks and monstrous obnoxiousness that I had ever come across … but why did she have to keep invading my mind?

♦ ♦ ♦

I arrived in Rotorua shortly after 3:30pm, and stepped out from the bus. Instantly, the reason that Rotorua was famous hit me. It was unavoidable; the air was saturated with sulphur ... rotten eggs, and then some. I could taste the pungent air on my tongue; it was overpowering, even burning my nostrils ... it was inescapable. My initial thoughts were that I should get straight back on the bus. How could I remain here if I could hardly breathe?

After a few minutes, however, my body and mind had acclimatised a little. Although the sulphur was still noticeable and unpleasant, it did become somewhat more tolerable.

I was one of eight people who got off the bus here, and I was the last to retrieve my backpack from under the bus. As the others departed, I took out my Lonely Planet to consult the map and see in which direction I needed to go for the YHA hostel.

Luckily the hostel was only a block or two away, and straightforward to find. I was assigned to a 6-berth dorm, and went there to dump my backpack. I only intended to stay in Rotorua a short time, so needed quickly to arrange a trip to see the main tourist sights. Just as with previous YHA hostels, this proved uncomplicated to do. The hostel manager was extremely helpful, and in no time I was all booked up for a 'see the sulphur sights' excursion the next morning.

Feeling quite satisfied that I had booked on a great day trip that should take in the best of the hot springs, geysers and also some Maori culture, I set out from the hostel to look around the town of Rotorua in the few remaining daylight hours.

♦ ♦ ♦

The small town of Rotorua was something of a tourist hotspot. Thousands flocked in from all around the world to see the thermal activity of the area. The town itself had a population of just over 50,000, and it looked as though most of the adult population probably worked in something connected to tourism. The compact centre was contained in a 500-metre by 500-metre square just north of the railway station. It was full of small hostels, hotels, eateries, tour operators and shops.

As I walked along the main road north from the hostel, there was a curious phenomenon which I had never encountered before. Steam was rising up through the ground all over the place, sometimes through cracks in the road or pavement, and in other places through drainage vents. Everywhere I looked there was steam ... and foul-smelling steam at that. Despite having become somewhat accustomed to the sulphur, it was still really unpleasant. This was most definitely not a place where I would want to live. In fact, since I had left the UK, I hadn't really found anywhere that really grabbed me as somewhere I would want to stop and settle down. Well, perhaps Sydney. For a big city, Sydney was really a pretty awesome place, as long as you spent most of your time around the harbour. Having said that, I had much fonder memories of Melbourne ... but, admittedly, that was primarily down to Suzi. Places were nothing without people; it is the people that make somewhere good or bad, and people more than places that determine how happy you feel. Perhaps I could feel happy even if I lived in Rotorua and had to wear a gas mask every day ... as long as I was sharing the experience with Suzi.

I walked along Tutenekai Street, one of the main north-south roads through the town, which took me to the side of Lake Rotorua. The lake, which was approximately 6 miles across, thankfully provided a light breeze with fresher air that gave some respite from the sulphur.

A few yards along the lake shore I came to Ohinemutu, a small Maori village site which contained a church and traditional meeting house. The meeting house was highly decorated with reddish stained wooden panelling, intricately carved with a variety of different shapes, figures, and monsters. It was certainly interesting, but I wasn't terribly convinced about how old and traditional it really was. It appeared in such great condition; it was almost as though it had only just been finished.

Along back into town, I walked over to see the other main building noted in the Lonely Planet; the Tudor Towers building, otherwise known as the Bath House. This was a fabulous mock-Tudor style building, set back behind the beautifully manicured bowling greens and croquet lawns of the Government Gardens. Around the turn of the century the building had been used as a bath house, but more recently it had been converted into a museum and art gallery. It was said to contain some interesting Maori artefacts but, as it was after 7:30pm, it was shut, so I would have to see it on another day.

From Tudor Towers, I took a short detour to see where the thermal pools were. This was one of the main attractions of the town. For a few dollars you could take a dip in the sulphurous hot spring water, which was meant to work miracles for your skin and bones. I noted that there was no indication of the sulphur being a magical cure for male pattern baldness ... so, *maybe not tonight ... perhaps another time.* The only thing for tonight was to get some food inside me, and also to buy something for a packed lunch tomorrow.

Along one of the main streets I managed to find a small supermarket that was still open, so I headed inside. As I walked in through the door, to my surprise, a familiar face stood paying for some groceries at the cash-till. *Oh, not her again,* I thought, instantly recognising Brigit, as I snuck in behind her and disappeared to the far end of the shop. *Bugger! ... I cannot get her out of my mind, and now she seems to be following me around New Zealand.* I didn't bother to say hello this time. What would have been the point?

I picked up a couple of Cokes, a pack of sausage rolls, some cherry tomatoes and a pack of two scotch eggs. Perhaps, considering the sickly smell of rotten eggs in the air, scotch eggs might appear a strange choice. However, despite the sulphur-saturated air, scotch eggs were exactly what I felt like eating. (So, there's a marketing tip for the supermarkets back home. If you want to sell more eggs, just fill the store with pungent rotten egg smells! No? Probably a bad idea.)

Having paid at the counter, I exited the shop and walked a few yards along the street to where there were some wooden benches. I sat there for a while, sipping my Coke and munching my way through the scotch eggs, which were actually rather tasty. At least I thought so, despite the fact that my taste buds seemed also to be rather saturated with sulphur. Sulphur and Coke, sulphur and scotch egg ... a weird combination. I kept looking around to see whether I would see Brigit again, but there were to be no more sightings for me today. Well, at least not in the flesh ... my dreams during the night were another matter.

Wednesday 18 March - Rotorua

I got up at around 7:00am, took a shower and breakfasted to be ready for an 8:30 pick up for the excursion. The tour that I had booked, which they called the 'Waimangu Round Trip', was one specifically recommended in the Lonely Planet as a great way of seeing some of the best sites with thermal activity.

As I waited at the hostel reception, I was joined by a German chap, perhaps three or four years older than me, who introduced himself as Carsten. He was booked on the same trip. And then a few minutes later, a couple of Dutch girls (Annika and Helen), also in their early twenties, joined us to wait. Shortly, our transport arrived. It was a fifteen-seater minibus, complete with driver, guide, and three passengers already picked up from another hostel. As I stepped into the bus, my heart skipped a beat again.

"Oh! Hi Brigit!" *It just had to be her again.*

"Oh ... hello," she replied.

"Ah-ha, do you two know each other?" asked Carsten, rather highlighting the obvious.

As I squeezed into the bus, the other passengers made space enough to ensure that I sat close to Brigit. I guess they assumed that we must be old friends.

Awkward was an appropriate word to describe it.

"So, which hostel are you staying at?" I asked, trying once more to break the ice.

"Oh ... uh ... I'm at the YWCA, just up the road," Brigit replied. *Well, I suppose it was harder to completely blank me with others here.*

"Is the accommodation there OK?"

"Yes, it's fine." Still a minimal response.

"How does it compare to a YHA hostel?" I prodded further ... *without being able to escape, she would have to talk.* "How is it compared to the hostels in Wellington or Franz Joseph?" *Third sentence in ... we might even start a conversation.*

"Well, I have my own room. So, thankfully, I don't have to put up with any snorers."

Clearly mindful that the others were listening in, I smiled ... "But Brigit, I thought you said that I didn't snore?"

At last she cracked, as a smile appeared on her normally stern face.

"Bruce, you snored like a fucking elephant!" she replied, finally laughing. Giggles spread around the minibus. *Perhaps she's finally softened ... but shouldn't the phrase be 'snores like a rhino' rather than an elephant? ... I'll let it pass.*

"But Brigit, why didn't you tell me, or hit me ... or something? ... Oh, sorry guys," I explained to the others. "For your benefit, Brigit and I were put in the same dorm room back in Franz Joseph."

"I am so sorry Brigit," I continued, "I guess it's no wonder you looked annoyed with me."

"No, I am sorry," Brigit responded. "It wasn't just that. I am sorry, I just didn't want to talk ... it wasn't only you." I looked at her quizzically. Suddenly, the face that I had seen as ice-cold and emotionless, now showed genuine signs of warmth. "A couple of days before arriving in Franz Joseph, my boyfriend dumped me.

We'd travelled together from Norway; we'd gone around Australia together. Then we get to Queenstown, he goes bungee-jumping, and then he goes off and screws around with some local girl. So now I'm travelling alone."

"I am so sorry," I said, sympathetically.

"Yeah, so I am still fucking pissed with him ... and now ... well, I've got a few more days out here before flying home. I have been in a terrible mood since Queenstown, and I am right off men. I probably snapped a bit when you first arrived because I didn't like the way you were staring at me."

"I am sorry Brigit; I didn't think that I was."

"Well, you were. You said your mind was elsewhere, but it looked to me like you were staring, so I found you a bit creepy. Sorry!"

"I really don't know what to say." *Was I really creepy?* "Well, Brigit, I am still sorry if I snored like an elephant."

The whole bus laughed, as did Brigit. A weight had been lifted from my shoulders; at least I now understood more about why she had been blanking me. *But was I creepy? Why would she think that? Maybe I had talked during my sleep ... I can't deny that I do have some dirty dreams. Or perhaps she had sensed the content of some of my daydreams ... but what if other people could do that too? Fuck ... perhaps I do need to clean up my mind. But creepy? Really? Even if I was someone who thought about sex rather too much, it was good sex ... I mean consensual and enjoyable, and I visualise mostly giving a girl pleasure. (Not Brigit ... but generally). Surely that's far less creepy and depraved than the millions of people who enjoy watching violent films, psychological thrillers and murder mysteries. My mind is oriented towards providing pleasure, not pain or death. There ... I've said my piece.*

♦ ♦ ♦

We had a couple of guides on this trip: one was a tall and lively bespectacled lady called Jill, who was primarily the guide; and the other was a shorter, rotund man called Graham, who was mainly the driver. The trip required two of them, as we were going to leave the minibus to walk and travel by boat, and afterwards get picked up again from different places.

We were heading for two different thermal areas which were both relatively close to Rotorua. One was Whakarewarewa, which most people call Whaka, as it is not the easiest word to get your tongue around. The other, and our first stop, was the Waimangu thermal area.

The Waimangu Valley and hydrothermal system lies about 10 miles south of Rotorua. In geological terms it is a baby, having been created by the eruption of Mount Tarawera as recently as 10 June 1886 ... yes, it even has a specific birthday. Every year, the Waimangu area attracts thousands of visitors from around the world to see its wonderful and strange natural creations.

The first part of the trip was itself a great creation; our tour began with a 10:00am Devonshire cream tea at the Waimangu Tearooms, while we listened to an introductory talk about the area. From here, we then wandered down the valley, passing a range of different thermal sights.

First there was Echo Crater, containing a steaming greyish-blue pool called Frying Pan Lake ... *Such a frying pan would cater for some whopping sausages ... perhaps a hundred feet long. That'd make a rather impressive hotdog.*

Next were the Cathedral Rocks, which were a bit like a set of large termite mounds, pressed together with jets of steam escaping from every possible crack in the rock. And just along from this, there were streams of clear water which flowed over bright white silica sheets and emerald green algal blankets. This was followed by the duck-egg blue Inferno Crater Lake, which was steaming like a massive bucket of liquid nitrogen ... and then after that, a spectacular terrace of green and dirty-brown algae.

Such sights were breathtaking. However, taking deep breaths was not really advisable with such toxic sulphurous air all around. Brigit and the two Dutch girls, and indeed Jill, all wrapped head scarves around their faces to try to filter some of the air. I couldn't help feeling that this probably had little effect.

We did get some welcome fresher air for twenty minutes or so as we took a boat across Lake Rotamahana, towards the Maori village of Te Wairoa. While Lake Rotomahana was created by the 1886 eruption, the village of Te Wairoa had been destroyed by it. Lava, ash and mud had buried the settlement, and more than 150 people were known to have lost their lives. Te Wairoa had become known as the Buried Village (and also as the Maori Pompeii). There were still excavations going on, but a range of different artefacts was on display. Thankfully, these were mostly stone ovens, metallic jewellery, tools and cooking pots, rather than the more gruesome ossified bones and skeletons of those who had perished.

After a comfort break, we sat in a picnic area to eat our packed lunches. I was glad I had kept the sausage rolls for today, rather than the scotch eggs ... I had really had enough of sulphurous eggy smells by now! I took the chance to sit with Brigit. I was still curious about why she said that she found me creepy. After a bit of light discussion about some of the sights we had just seen, I approached the subject.

"You know earlier this morning you said you thought I was creepy ... well, that's been bothering me. Is it something in particular that made you think that? I would really like to know."

"Oh, I am sorry ... I guess it's mainly my insecurities. So, if it helps, I actually don't think you are so creepy now."

"Well, yeah, I guess that helps a little," I responded.

"But back then in Franz Joseph, you were actually staring ... it seemed like you were mentally undressing me."

"Oh God ... sorry. I can assure you that I wasn't." (No, really, I wasn't.) "If it came across that way, I do apologize. I do daydream a lot, and I was probably thinking about my girlfriend at the time."

"Look Bruce, think nothing of it. I get that with so many guys, so don't worry about it. I even quite like it sometimes. But after my boyfriend dumped me, I have really been in a foul mood."

"Really. Do you get stared at a lot?"

"All the time ... and I know it's not such a bad thing. I mean, I also often look at handsome guys and imagine them naked ... why not?" Brigit smiled.

"You do?"

"Yeah, sure. It's natural isn't it?"

"Well, I guess it is. I admit I certainly do it sometimes when I see someone I fancy, but I wasn't with you. Shit! ... I mean, it's not that I don't find you attractive ... but ... oh shit, I am digging a hole for myself again." *Such eloquence BJ.*

"Hey, no worries Bruce!" Brigit smiled.

"Did you pick that phrase up in Australia? No worries?"

"Oh yes ... I love it. It's a great phrase isn't it?"

It certainly is.

Having had this brief chat with Brigit, I did feel it had been great to clear the air (not from the sulphur, obviously), and I did feel a little better about myself. I wasn't really creepy ... or perhaps I was, but, if so, at least I was the same as most other guys. At least it wasn't only me.

♦ ♦ ♦

After lunch we headed off by road to Whakarewarewa. At the Whaka thermal area, we were treated to some spectacular displays by two related geysers: Pohutu (or "big splash" in Maori), which ejected water and steam 20 to 30 metres into the air, and the slightly smaller Prince of Wales Feathers geyser. The latter always seemed to act as a trigger for setting off the bigger one. I had never previously seen geysers, and I was pretty impressed. Such ejaculations, and indeed the Prince of Wales name, did also act as a trigger for me to see those cartoon phallus visions again, which I had first imagined in Franz Joseph. *But no, I am not weird ... Brigit said so ... or ... at least, not creepy.*

After the geysers, we were entertained by a display of some traditional Maori dancing and music, in the form of a show that was set up for tourists in a traditional style meeting house. I was not so impressed by this. Perhaps I am always a bit sceptical of the authenticity of 'indigenous culture for tourists'... especially when they then try to sell you hundreds of their 'traditional music CDs' and 'traditional' wood carvings.

All in all, the excursion had been a great day out, and indeed it was also great to have buried my insecurities about Brigit. I never felt that I could have been that awful. And now that she had appeared warmer and more human, hopefully she would not turn up again in my nightmares.

◆ ◆ ◆

When we got back to Rotorua, Brigit was dropped off at the YWCA, and minutes later, Carsten, the two Dutch girls and I were set down in front of the YHA hostel. I walked through to the common room to check on the cricket (no surprise there), while Carsten stopped at reception to ask about a message he was expecting. A few minutes later, Carsten reappeared.

"Hey Bruce, do you want a lift up to Auckland tomorrow?" He waved a note in his hand. "I've now got a hire car that I need to drive there."

This sounded like an interesting prospect. I had been planning to remain in Rotorua for another day, perhaps to visit the thermal baths and the museum, but the offer of free transport to get to Auckland a day earlier sounded great.

Carsten explained a bit more. He had been travelling around New Zealand this way, by arranging to drive hire cars for the likes of Avis and Hertz. They frequently needed their cars to be moved from one depot to another. In this case Avis wanted one relocated from the small airport near Rotorua to Auckland's international airport, while Carsten also currently had a vehicle which he needed to return to the Avis Rotorua depot.

With this now established as a plan, Carsten and I both organised booking ourselves into the main YHA hostel in downtown Auckland for the following evening. There wasn't too much I would be missing out on by leaving Rotorua earlier than planned. Perhaps I might have enjoyed the thermal baths, but my skin and bones were still young enough, and I didn't feel that I needed the miracles of sulphur to delay the onset of rheumatism quite yet.

I had also had sufficient sulphur-saturated air for one day, so I decided to spend the remainder of the evening in the aircon-ventilated common room watching the end of the cricket, while munching my way through several packets of crisps. I didn't feel like venturing onto the streets for anything more substantial, and certainly wanted a rest from my lungs being filled with the smell of rotten eggs.

It was the last day of group games in the cricket, and two of the three games still held substantial interest. New Zealand, England and South Africa had all already qualified for the semi-finals, but the last place was still up for grabs between West Indies, Pakistan and Australia.

The calculations were complicated. West Indies, with 4 wins, just needed to avoid a disastrous defeat by Australia to secure a semi-final spot. A win or draw would see them through, and even a narrow defeat could see them through if Pakistan failed to win. Australia (on 3 wins) needed to thrash West Indies, but then could only go through with a Pakistan defeat. Pakistan needed Australia to win, and they also needed to defeat the unbeaten New Zealand. The other game between England and Zimbabwe was inconsequential.

Anyway, not to go into much detail ... Australia did thrash West Indies, Pakistan were victorious over New Zealand, and England put up a really dreadful performance, and were beaten by Zimbabwe. So, not all turned out quite as expected.

What this all meant was that Pakistan had qualified for the semi-finals and would now have a repeat match with New Zealand in Auckland (the one I would try to see), while England would face South Africa in Sydney. Although England had beaten South Africa in the group game, their dismal showing against Zimbabwe did nothing to inspire any confidence in them now going on to lift the trophy. However, what all today's matches had done was to level off the odds for all the remaining teams with the bookmakers. The World Cup was now a toss-up ... or in my case a toss-off, under Megan's rules.

Chapter 8: Garden of Eden ... Auckland

Thursday 19 March - Rotorua to Auckland

I met Carsten in the hostel breakfast room at around 8:00am, ready for the journey ahead. I was now really looking forward to arriving in Auckland; it meant that it should only be a couple more days before I could hold Suzi in my arms again. Today I definitely had a spring in my step.

We both checked out of the hostel and I waited with our backpacks, while Carsten went to fetch his car which was parked a couple of blocks away. For the last week or so, Carsten had been driving a white Toyota Corolla which he had brought up from Christchurch. It was now due at the Avis depot at Rotorua airport, where he would exchange it for another car to take us up to Auckland.

When we arrived at the Avis depot there was quite a bit of paperwork for Carsten to sort out. The Avis staff also took a copy of my own driving licence, as it allowed us the option of me driving, should Carsten need a rest. Having done all that, we were then taken out to the car yard by an Avis rep, and directed to a small blue Holden Barina hatchback. After a few words of explanation, Carsten was handed the keys, and we put our baggage in the back. We were free to go.

"OK Bruce, you can drive," said Carsten immediately.

"What? Don't you want to drive first?" I asked, somewhat surprised.

"Nah, I could really do with a break from it. It's over 200 k's and more than three hours' drive ... I'll take over when we get nearer to Auckland. There will probably be more traffic later on. It's simple driving around here ... there are so few cars on the road."

"OK, fine," I agreed, although still a little apprehensive. I was far from an experienced driver, and had only driven overseas once before, although that had been in a rather more chaotic environment, in Venezuela. Here in New Zealand, just like in the UK, people drove on the left-hand side, and here they also obeyed road signs and traffic lights. It wasn't like that in Venezuela, where drivers seemed to treat both stop signs and red lights as 'for information only'.

As we set off, I was actually quite enjoying driving again. The Holden was a nice little car with plenty of zip, and the roads were well surfaced, and empty. We quickly made headway, and before long, Carsten had turned the radio on, and we were listening to familiar music ... Elton John, Madonna, Eurythmics, INXS ... plenty of stuff I would frequently listen to back home. Luckily Carsten and I had reasonably similar music tastes. We were also equally out of tune as we sang along with many of the wrong lyrics.

Somewhere just to the north of Hamilton, we pulled into a service station to refuel, take a comfort break, and swap over driving. After this, it was only an hour or so along the motorway up to Auckland airport to drop the car off. I noticed another 'WOF and Vehicle Servicing' sign at the rear of the garage, which again made me chuckle as I thought of Megan and her MOTs.

We reached the Avis drop off point at around 1:00pm, following which Carsten decided that he would pay for a taxi into the centre of Auckland. Although, like me, Carsten was mostly staying in the YHA hostels, he didn't seem to be too tight with his money. However, to be fair, he was saving a lot on his transport.

♦ ♦ ♦

We arrived at the YHA hostel near the Queen's Street/City Road junction at around 2:00pm. This left plenty of time in the rest of the day to explore, which was useful, as I still needed to try to get a ticket for Saturday's cricket semi-final. So, after dumping my backpack on a bed in a triple room, which I would initially be sharing with Carsten, I decided to get back outside and take a half-hour walk up to Eden Park, the cricket ground.

As I walked back through the hostel reception, I spotted a message board. I checked it quickly just in case ... but I didn't expect that Suzi and Megan would be in Auckland until Saturday or Sunday. There was no note for me.

I remembered well when I had found their note in Cairns, and how crushed I had felt that they had left without me seeing them. Back in Cairns, it had been Megan that I was more hopeful about getting to know better, following on from our snog on the bus from Tennant Creek. This time it was Suzi that I couldn't wait to see.

As I passed through the lobby and stepped out on the street, I looked up to see the high-rise tower of the Sheraton Hotel. *Ah, so it was a Sheraton, not a Hilton,* I chuckled to myself. I recalled vividly what I had dreamt about in Wellington, relating to events following an England World Cup victory. Gazing up at the tinted glass of the hotel tower, I mused ... *Perhaps it could be in the Sheraton ... and it could still be room 64.*

As I took out a large map of Auckland which I had picked up at reception on checking in, I oriented myself, and set off in the direction of Eden Park. As I walked, I began daydreaming about Suzi and Megan again. *They should be arriving anytime now from Perth.*

Having been listening to Eurythmics tracks amongst others on the car ride to Auckland, I was now in a Eurythmics mood, and began singing to myself as I walked.

[11]*" ... And you know that I'm gonna be the one ...*

It was the song 'When tomorrow comes' and my anticipation for the next few days was building. I was so itching to see Suzi. Perhaps, with any luck, it might be as early as tomorrow ... more likely Saturday or Sunday, but it shouldn't be long now ... I was now in a pretty buoyant mood.

" ... *Wait until tomorrow comes ...* "

... Buoyant mood yes ... tuneful, perhaps not.

It turned out to be a 45-minute walk to the Eden Park stadium, and thankfully when I arrived, I found a ticket office open. I was pleasantly surprised that there were still hundreds of tickets unsold, but, with New Zealand playing in a home semi-final, I thought that would definitely change before Saturday.

After purchasing a ticket for the game, I decided to head over a few blocks to the east, to climb up Mount Eden. Although hardly a mountain at just under 200 metres high, Mount Eden was an extinct volcanic cone and, according to my Lonely Planet book, it was one of the best places to go for views over Auckland and beyond.

As I walked along the road which took me up to the top of the hill, I was reminded of a similar walk I had done up to the top of Castle Hill in Townsville two months ago. Today I was thinking about the same two girls as I was back then, and I had even started to sing [12] 'So far away', the same Dire Straits song as I had been singing that day.

Back in Townsville I had been looking forward to catching up with Megan and Suzi again in Cairns, but it didn't turn out that way. Here in Auckland, two months on, and again I was excited about seeing them ... only a hundred times more so. But where were they now? I cursed myself for not having written down their flight details but, from memory, I thought that they were scheduled to be flying in from Perth this weekend, arriving in Auckland on Saturday evening. *Oh, please let it go according to plan.*

Once I had climbed up to the top of Mount Eden, I was able to walk around the rim of the extinct volcanic crater. Over centuries, grass had grown over everything, and it was only really the crater shape itself that was suggestive of any previous volcanic activity. The panoramic view from the top was tremendous, a full 360-degrees ... out across downtown and the harbour to the north, and over to One Tree Hill and the suburbs to the south. From the vantage point of the hilltop, Auckland also looked quite green for a big city. Unlike most of the large cities I had visited, here the views in all directions appeared full of parks, gardens and trees. The city was still just under one million people, about a third the size of Sydney or Melbourne and, as yet, it didn't have quite the size of commercial centre that I had expected. The downtown area certainly had plenty of high-rises, but away from that central downtown zone, most buildings in the suburbs were only one- or two-storey.

After spending about half an hour up the hill familiarising myself a little with the layout of the city, and taking a few photos, I made my way back down Mount Eden and headed back towards the hostel. In the evening, I became familiar with another hostel laundry room, where once again I demonstrated my incompetence with powder dispensing machines. I also spent an hour or so in the common room, mostly watching international news, the main focus of which were recent voting reforms in South Africa that would officially end apartheid. The South African cricket team, who would play England in Sunday's semi-final in Sydney, were having to field more media questions about the political changes happening back home than about their own impressive return to international cricket. *Hopefully it would prove to be a big distraction for them.*

Friday 20 March - Auckland

Another Friday morning, after another not so great night's sleep. This time it had been Carsten's snoring that had kept me awake for much of the night. Perhaps this time, having been told a couple of days ago about my ability to snore like an elephant, I was not so quick to get frustrated by it. Snoring was a common affliction. *I am still sure that the phrase should be 'snores like a rhino.' Do elephants snore? I suppose they do.*

It was now 10 weeks since I had left home. I had seen a lot in that time, and had met some wonderful people, although, to be fair, most of those had been in Australia rather than New Zealand. Carsten had been quite good company the last couple of days, and then there was Anders whom I had bumped into a couple of times, but most of the time I had been pretty much on my own.

The YHA hostels in New Zealand had not seemed as conducive to making new friends as the Backpacker Association hostels had been in Australia. Perhaps it was partly the colder weather further south, and maybe also the more outdoor-oriented lifestyle in Australia, with several hostels having swimming pools and barbecues. However, the biggest contributory friendliness-factor was probably that the Backpackers Association hostels frequently had bars. Sitting at a hostel bar with a beer on a warm evening in Australia had been a good way of meeting new people. The YHA hostels in New Zealand had been much like the YHA hostels in Britain, with no alcohol allowed on the premises. I guess this made them more family-oriented, which was fine, and they were still full of backpackers mostly my age, just not so engaging. However, as I was not normally the most sociable of people, I probably had no right to complain.

As I lay awake pondering over whether to get up and take a shower, I contemplated my journey ahead. My scheduled flight was due to leave Auckland on Thursday evening, which was just under a week away. If Suzi and Megan did arrive over the weekend, it wouldn't leave us many days to spend together.

We hadn't really talked around what their plans might be when they arrived. I didn't think they were planning on staying in New Zealand too long, but I couldn't remember whether they had mentioned it. Suzi and I had certainly talked about being in Auckland around the days of the World Cup semi-final and final, but little besides that. Perhaps we were too preoccupied with ensuring that we aimed for the same YHA hostel, and that we wrote down each other's home phone numbers in case we lost each other again.

Bruce Spydar

We didn't really think about what we might do together in Auckland, nor perhaps afterwards.

Should I delay my flight? I am not in such a great rush to get over to Canada, and I certainly want to spend as much time with Suzi as possible. If only I knew what their plans were. With this uncertainty in mind, I decided to leave it until after the weekend before I tried to re-confirm my onward flight.

♦ ♦ ♦

Before setting out from the hostel, I decided to leave a note for Suzi on the message board. Unlike in Cairns, at least this time I knew Suzi's surname.

> To Suzi Wheeler
>
> Dear Suzi,
>
> Just gone out for the day. Expect to be back by 5 – 6pm. I am in room 23. Please leave a message if I'm not here. Can't wait to see you. Love BJ. XXX

What's this? I am now writing kisses at the end of the note, and I had done it automatically. I can't remember having ever done that before, but this time I just did it, and somehow it felt right. And 3 kisses felt the right number too. Do blokes do this sort of thing? Perhaps I am turning into a girl. Why am I so bloody ignorant about these things? The language to be used in such notes had been a mystery to me when I received Suzi's note back in Cairns, and although Kirsten, Vanessa and Brigit had tried to enlighten me a little, I was definitely still a novice.

I pinned my note up to the message board, and then set out from the hostel. Once again as I stepped out of the front door, I glanced along the street towards the Sheraton, and was quickly sucked back into a daydream. I looked up towards one of the corner rooms on around the 6th or 7th floors. *That would be the room,* I thought, as my mind became lost. This time I was envisaging the scene, not from my own perspective, but as how it might appear if I had been a window cleaner looking in on it. *There we were, right in front of the window ... Suzi, looking so pure and beautiful, leaning back against a chair in front of the dressing table. I was on my knees in front of her, and my face was hidden from view, between her thighs. Suzi's head was tilted back and her eyes were shut as she bathed in the moment. Her naked body was a perfect vision of womanhood ...*

"Hey Bruce!" A voice disturbed me from behind. "You left this on your bed." It was Carsten, who had just come rushing out of the lobby, carrying my camera. "You probably don't want to leave this lying about."

"Oh ... thanks Carsten," I responded. "I am not thinking so clearly today."

"Suzi on your mind, is she?" asked Carsten. I must have bored him rather a lot in the past couple of days with my story.

"Was it that obvious?"

"Well, just take care," he continued. "You are no good to her if you walk under a bus before she gets here."

"Yeah, I know. Thanks mate," I said, as Carsten handed me my camera and then strolled off down the road.

I was heading the opposite way, off towards a big park called Auckland Domain, where I thought I would spend the morning visiting the War Memorial Museum. Both the park and the museum were recommended in my Lonely Planet guide, with the park being rather politely described as 'lovely', and the museum being described as a 'if-you-are-only-going-to-do-one-thing, go there' type of attraction. I discovered that both of these descriptions were rather pushing it. The park was large, with open expanses of grass and lots of trees, but it was hardly overflowing with ornamental fountains or flower beds or anything that would add some colour. It was pleasant more than lovely.

The museum did look quite impressive; it was the type of neo-classical style which could have passed as a museum or government building in most European capitals. Inside there were interesting displays of Maori cultural artefacts, and some fine displays of New Zealand's natural history, including re-creations of moas, as well as some rather moth-eaten displays of stuffed kiwis and keas. Perhaps it was because my mind was drifting elsewhere that I wasn't really taking in most of the information. This was clearly a day when I wasn't in a museum mood. At least the entrance was free.

♦ ♦ ♦

After emerging from the museum at around 12:30, I headed out to the east of the Domain, and into the Parnell Village district. Now this was definitely my kind of place. It was a semi-pedestrianised zone, full of boutiques, arts and crafts shops, and open-air street cafes. On a pleasantly warm Friday lunchtime, it was an excellent place to stop at a street-side café for a bit of lunch, a beer or two, and just watch people milling around. So, for a couple of hours, that is precisely what I did. I stumbled across a quasi-Italian restaurant, and enjoyed a tasty seafood linguine, washed down with a couple of bottles of Steinlager.

Parnell Village was a lovely, relaxing place. Although the restaurants along the street-side appeared to be quite busy, nobody seemed to be in a rush. As I sat, I took out my Lonely Planet and contemplated what to do in the afternoon. I also started to think about what places might be good to visit with Suzi and Megan, if and when they arrived. *I could certainly come back to have another meal here,* I thought, as I looked over to another table where a couple were sharing a delicious-looking and mountainous seafood platter of crayfish, mussels and prawns.

After leaving the restaurant, I browsed a little around some market stalls, where I picked up a couple of cheap polo shirts. I then headed north along through Parnell and continued on up to the harbourside. I walked past a bit of the commercial port area, before arriving at a rather pleasant marina in which several high-spec millionaires' yachts and cruisers were moored alongside the more average boats. There was certainly quite a bit of money in Auckland, and people here definitely loved their sailing.

In view of the attractiveness of this particular part of the harbourfront, I was a little surprised not to find more in the way of harbourside bars and restaurants, especially considering what I had just experienced in Parnell Village. The harbourfront had one or two hotels and the odd shopping arcade, but it seemed like they hadn't yet developed this area into a leisure attraction. There were a few ferry boats signposted to various places around the harbour, but there wasn't the same hustle and bustle as in Sydney ... not by a long way.

After meandering around the harbourside for an hour or so, I walked along Queen Street back towards the hostel. I arrived just after 5:00pm, and immediately checked the message board. My message was untouched. I took out a pen from my daypack, and amended the note, crossing out the first sentence which said I was out for the day, but leaving the rest. I hadn't really expected Suzi and Megan to have arrived yet, but from tomorrow it really could be anytime.

Saturday 21 March - Auckland

I woke up around 5:00am, and couldn't get back to sleep. Today was a big day. It was the World Cup semi-final but, more important than that, the day when I hoped to be re-united with Suzi after the last month thinking about her almost non-stop. After these last few weeks, I now realised that having such feelings for someone could really be exhausting. An aching heart and twitchy groin are such a difficult combination.

I don't think I had ever experienced such a mix of emotions. There was most definitely a significant lust-overlay, thanks mostly to Megan and her MOT rules ... but when I imagined sex with Suzi, it was slow, sensual, warm and gentle. My feelings for Suzi were so much deeper: the way my heart skipped a beat when she smiled at me; the warmth I had felt when she had been so caring about my asthma attack at the zoo; the way that she had eaten her pizza in such an orderly and precise manner. It was all the detail, and it built together into a vivid picture where I could imagine a future life together. Was this true love? Well, if not, it was the closest I had ever been to it.

There was no point in getting up so early, so I found my radio and tried to pick up the BBC World Service while using some rather tinny-sounding earphones. I couldn't find much of interest, but I eventually tuned in to Voice of America, which must have done the trick, as I woke up again around 8:00am.

I showered, then had some coffee and muffins in the breakfast area. It seemed that muffins were the main breakfast currency for hostels both in Australia and New Zealand. They were easy for the hostels to provide, and probably at a reasonable mark up for them.

I thought for a few moments about wearing my blue England shirt, but decided against it, realising that this would be a little stupid in a New Zealand vs. Pakistan game. Instead I put on the maroon polo shirt which I had picked up in Parnell Village.

At about 9:30, having left another message for Suzi on the board, I set out for Eden Park. A semi-final of the Cricket World Cup ... this was the biggest sporting event I had ever been to. I was excited. So, OK, it wasn't the England semi-final, but in some ways that was better ... less downside if we lost. And, after their performance against Zimbabwe, I was so unimpressed that I wasn't sure I even wanted to watch the game against South Africa. *I am sure I will do ... even if it might be painful.*

Anyway, I was not in Sydney to see England, and today was the day when all of New Zealand were willing their team to make it to their first World Cup Final. A few days ago, they had played an inspired Pakistan team, and were fairly comfortably defeated. But that match hadn't mattered to New Zealand, while it was everything to Pakistan. Now, New Zealand also had everything to play for, but had all the additional pressure and expectancy of playing at home.

Today it was the light grey shirts of New Zealand against the lime green of Pakistan ... perhaps not one for the fashionistas. As I arrived at the gates of Eden Park there were hundreds, maybe even thousands of grey shirts, and only a handful of light green ones. Inside the ground, I found my allotted seat in an open-air section, opposite the main covered stand, with a great view of the pitch and scoreboard. As long as it didn't rain, or didn't suddenly become fifteen degrees warmer with blazing sun, this was the perfect spot for a summer day.

Just like in Wellington, I sat in a New Zealand section of the 40,000 strong crowd ... although to be fair, everywhere today was a New Zealand section of the crowd. Looking around the ground, I could only spot a couple of small areas where there were any more than a handful of Pakistan supporters.

The excitement was building and, at about 10:30, team captains Martin Crowe and Imran Khan walked out to the middle with one of the umpires for the coin toss. Crowe called correctly, and decided that his team would bat first. A cheer went up around the ground, but only with hindsight would we see whether this was a good call.

For those who do not follow cricket, of whom there are many (well many millions), the decision on whether to bat or bowl first is not always an easy one. There are different opinions as to whether it is advantageous to bat first or second. If you bat second, you know what your target is, but you also may feel the pressure of the total. You then have additional parameters of the pitch, the weather and atmospheric conditions to take into account ... considerations for how much the ball might swing or spin. Some players also have superstitions, or claim that divine inspiration influences their choices. Anyway, whatever factors are taken into account for such decisions, you only know whether they are good ones with hindsight … which, naturally, the captain never has.

♦ ♦ ♦

As they took to the field for the start of the game, this looked like a different Pakistan team from the one I had seen in Melbourne, and from the one that I had seen on the TV a few times earlier in the tournament. The players were the same but, having won their last three matches, they had a swagger about them … their confidence was high. A few days before, it had been New Zealand, coming off a seven-game unbeaten run, that had looked the more relaxed and confident of the two sides when they played each other in Christchurch. Today looked distinctly different.

The New Zealand openers, Greatbatch and Wright, slowly settled in and survived the first few overs. There was a palpable sense of relief from most of the crowd, who didn't want to see early wickets go down. It was into the 10th over, with the score on 35, that Greatbatch was bowled by Aaqib Javed. This loss was followed almost immediately by a second, as Wright was caught by the keeper off Mushtaq. There was a growing concern for the home nation.

The crowd were now calling for a captain's innings from Martin Crowe, and that's precisely what he delivered. First with Jones, and later with Rutherford, Harris and Smith, Crowe anchored the New Zealand innings with a knock of 91, that steered New Zealand up towards a competitive total of 262. This was one of the highest totals in the tournament, and would set Pakistan a tough target. The home crowd were in a buoyant mood; their team were performing well, and everyone was enjoying the spectacle, looking forward confidently towards the final.

When Aamer Sohail and Ramiz Raja came out to open the batting for Pakistan, it was crucial for them to settle. Sohail fell with the total on 30, but then Imran provided a solid backbone to the Pakistan innings as the score steadily accumulated. Pakistan lost Ramiz with the score on 84, but then Javed joined Imran, and together they took the total on to 134, before Imran was caught out. They were now 3 wickets down, with half the total still needed, and with 17 overs remaining. The game still looked quite evenly poised. However, when Pakistan lost the wicket of Salim Malik just moments later, the game looked to be turning in favour of New Zealand. Enter Inzamam-ul-Haq.

Inzamam was young, relatively new to the Pakistan side, and not yet a name that was familiar on the international stage. The next hour changed all that. After taking an over or two to settle, Inzamam hit a rapid-fire 60, from only 37 balls faced, and accelerated Pakistan's total to 227 by the time his wicket fell. His performance appeared to have broken the morale of the New Zealand team, and the home crowd had fallen into a depressed silence. The match was slipping away, and New Zealand needed a miracle.

No such miracle came, and Pakistan knocked off the required runs with an over to spare. It had been a fantastic game, and had been settled by the individual brilliance of Inzamam shining through at the critical moment. Pakistan were now through to their first World Cup Final, while New Zealand had to lick their wounds and wait four more years for another shot.

♦ ♦ ♦

There was a sombre mood as I left Eden Park, and the air of disappointment was tangible in the streets as I walked back to the hostel. In contrast, my own mood was fairly upbeat. I hadn't really cared too much about whether it was New Zealand or Pakistan who won; the semi-final that really mattered was tomorrow. I had a spring in my step because by now there was a real possibility that Suzi and Megan had arrived in Auckland.

It was around 7:00pm that I arrived back at the hostel, and found that my message was exactly where I had left it. Just like yesterday, I took a pen and crossed out the part saying I had gone out, and returned the message to the board. I was certainly a little disappointed, but I knew that it was most probable I wouldn't see the girls before tomorrow, even though it was possible they could arrive at any time.

After freshening up a little, I walked back out and along Queen Street, and found a Subway fast food outlet, where I got something to eat before swiftly returning to the hostel. I sat out on the hostel roof terrace chatting with Carsten for a while, and then watched some of the cricket highlights in the common room. It was quite fun to try to find myself in the crowd, as well as watching the highlights on the TV. It really did emphasize just what a fantastic innings Inzamam had played, and Martin Crowe too, although his was now of little importance.

I headed to bed with my mind on Suzi. *Perhaps by tomorrow night I would be able to hold her in my arms again.* I longed to see her smile, to hear her voice and listen to her laugh. I fell asleep dreaming of holding her tight, snuggling up, and feeling the warmth of her body against mine. There were no sexy dreams nor thoughts of the Hilton or Sheraton tonight. ... *Well, if you believe that, you'll believe anything!* There were, however, none that I remembered.

Sunday 22 March - Auckland

I woke up early again, finding it difficult to sleep with Carsten's persistent snoring: *perhaps more like a warthog than a rhino or elephant*, but sufficient to be highly irritating. My mind was also preoccupied and excited about seeing Suzi again. *But what if they didn't come? What if Suzi didn't feel the same way about me as I felt about her? Or what if there had been an accident, or something else bad had happened?*

Some days I can just sense that something isn't going to turn out as planned, and when I have had that feeling in the past, I have often been right. Today, however, was not such a day. Everything seemed fine … in fact I felt unusually optimistic. Today, England had a great chance in the semi-finals against South Africa, and Suzi and Megan were going to arrive in Auckland. By the end of the day, I would be back together with Suzi, and England would be in the World Cup Final. I was sure of it.

Due to the semi-final being in Sydney, in Auckland time, this meant it didn't start until around lunchtime. I didn't want just to hang around the hostel so, after taking a shower and putting another message up on the board, I set out along Queen Street in the direction of the harbour.

Naturally, as I left the hostel, I glanced up at the Sheraton tower again, and chuckled to myself … but this time I avoided getting further absorbed into my erotic dreams. I had looked in my Lonely Planet guide, and discovered that most of the main airlines had offices on or near to Queen Street, and I had also noticed an STA travel office just off the main strip. I would need to sort out re-confirming my onward flight within the next couple of days so, in the absence of anything better to do, I decided to try to find STA on my way down to the harbour.

I passed by a Canadian Airlines office that was closed for the day (it was Sunday). *This might be useful …* my flight from Auckland via Hawaii to Vancouver was with them. Then a couple of blocks further on, I found the STA office. If I wanted to change my schedule, it would be better to go there, as it was through STA that I had made my original booking from Cambridge, and not all my scheduled flights were with the same airline. At this stage I didn't know whether I would want to change, but if Suzi and Megan turned up, I would dearly love to spend more time with them ... *Perhaps we could go up to the Bay of Islands together ... that'd be great.*

At the harbour end of Queen Street, I also noticed the central post office. *Maybe it was time to send some more photos back home.* I was trying to keep prints and negatives separate so that if I lost one part, I didn't lose everything. I had last posted my prints back home from Christchurch, and since then I had used three more films which were yet to be processed.

I wasn't particularly hungry, but at around 11:00am I decided to pop in to a Dunkin Donuts outlet to get a coffee and donut ... just as well, as they didn't serve much else. I don't think that this American chain had yet made it across to the UK ... at least I hadn't seen one yet. But I had heard of it, so I thought I'd give it a try. I ordered a large coffee and a couple of tasty-looking, but excessively sugary donuts. I soon realised that Dunkin Donuts might not be quite right for reserved British tastes. *Bloody hell, this coffee is sweet,* I thought to myself on taking my first taste. *And I did say no sugar. Do Americans really drink their coffee so sweet and sickly? Perhaps they do.* And perhaps they could actually taste the coffee in their coffee when drinking it alongside the even sweeter, even more sickly pink-iced donuts ... I certainly couldn't.

Well, if I had needed a sugar-high to build me up for the England vs. South Africa game, I now had one. I wandered back to the hostel, checked and amended my note again, and then installed myself in a comfy chair in front of the TV, which I switched on ready for the match. I could see the hostel reception from my selected chair, so I could also keep an eye open for the girls arriving.

There was nobody else in the common room getting ready to watch the start of the game. After being there for about ten minutes, skipping through the channels and wondering what was going on, the hostel manager walked through.

"Didn't you know? The semi-final is a day-night game; it won't be starting for another four hours."

"Ah … fuck, that would explain it," I replied. "Thanks mate! I'm such an idiot." *Yep that's me.*

This meant that I had a few more hours to wait for the start. I didn't really feel like doing much, so I returned to the room I was sharing with Carsten. He was out.

I lay on my bed and switched on my radio, and … at around 5:45pm I woke up again.

Shit … idiot … I have probably missed the start.

♦ ♦ ♦

This time, as I arrived back in the common room, the TV was on, and the game was underway. There was a handful of other people watching the game, including a couple of other English lads wearing light blue England shirts. Nobody was particularly talkative. Seeing that the best viewing chairs had already been taken, I slipped through to reception to check the message board. No change … my note for Suzi was still there.

Apart from the later start as a day-night game, the match had also been further delayed due to light rain in Sydney. There was some discussion going on about whether there would be any reduction in overs, but it didn't appear to be clear to anyone.

Anyway, I had missed the start of the game, but joined the action with both of the England opening batsmen, Gooch and Botham, already out. South Africa had won the toss and had elected to field, which looked to have been a wise choice as the initial damp conditions were well suited to bowling first. However, despite the early wickets, Stewart and Hick were settling down and steadily constructing a score.

It was not until the total had moved on to 110 that England's third wicket fell as Stewart, on 33, edged a ball to the keeper off MacMillan. This brought Fairbrother out to join Hick. As he walked out to the middle, I suddenly looked around towards reception, thinking that I had just heard Megan's voice. I must have been imagining it; there was nobody there.

For about the next hour, Hick and Fairbrother steadily built up the England total, and just as they both looked comfortable, South Africa got rid of the two of them in quick succession. England were 187 for 5, and instead of having the foundation for an acceleration of runs, it now meant two new batsmen, Lamb and Lewis, having to reset and begin again.

Near the end of the innings there seemed to be some confusion over the number of overs to be played. Due to the initial delays, and perhaps a slightly slow over rate, the England innings finished after 45 overs, having made a total of 252 for 6. This appeared to be quite a competitive score, but it was a shame to lose the 5 overs, as Lewis and Reeve were scoring quite freely at the end. However, 252 looked a pretty decent target.

At the change of innings, about 8:30pm local time, I walked round past the reception to use a toilet. As I re-emerged, I suddenly heard a voice I recognised.

"Megan," I called out, spotting her at reception talking to the hostel manager.

"BJ ... oh it's so good to see you."

♦ ♦ ♦

As I walked forward to greet Megan, I became concerned.

"Hi, it's so great to see you. Is Suzi with you?" I gave her a massive hug before she could answer.

"Oh BJ ... I am so sorry, Suzi's not here. It's a long story. Can we go and sit down?"

"What? What's happened? Did you fall out? Is she sick?"

"Hey ... just calm down BJ, and let me tell you."

We moved out of the reception and walked through to sit down in a quiet spot on the roof terrace.

"Oh babe ... I am so sorry, Suzi had to go back home. Her dad suffered a heart attack."

"Shit! When did that happen? Is he OK?"

"It was only a few days ago, just before we were going to reconfirm our flights out from Perth. So, Suzi re-arranged her flight to go home. I wanted to go with her ... I probably should have done, but she didn't want me to. Suzi wanted me to come to Auckland, to find you. Oh, I really hope she is OK ... perhaps I should have gone with her."

At this point, Megan became a little tearful. I reached forward, and grabbed her hand to comfort her, before repositioning myself next to her to allow me to give her a hug.

"And Suzi's dad? Do we know whether he is OK?"

"No, Suzi wasn't sure. It was only when she phoned home to tell her parents that we were coming here that she found out. She spoke to her mum. It appears that the heart attack was just a couple of days earlier. When they spoke, her dad was alive, but still in hospital. Her mum told her to stay out here ... but would you have done so if it was your mum or dad? No, Suzi had to go, and I guess she'll probably be arriving home about now. I will try to phone her tomorrow evening to see how things are."

"Oh boy! Poor old Suzi."

"Yeah. So, babe, I am afraid it's just you and me." I hugged her tight, still digesting the news.

"Well, if I couldn't see Suzi tonight, you are a bloody good substitute."

"Thanks babe, and I am so relieved that I found you here. I didn't really want to come over to Auckland by myself, and I thought I might have missed you ... though Suzi said you would be here until after the cricket final. She didn't want me to go back with her because she thought if neither of us turned up, we might never see you again."

"Wow! Well, I am so glad you did ... and you are probably right. If you hadn't turned up, I wouldn't have known why, and I guess I would have assumed that Suzi didn't like me anymore."

"Well BJ, you don't have to worry about that ... she more than just likes you. And, you know, I am pretty fond of you too."

I started to overflow with emotion, and could sense tears welling up in my eyes.

"Did you get a room here?"

"I did pop in briefly over an hour ago just to enquire, as the shuttle bus dropped me outside. But then I decided to check out a hotel just up the road to get my own room rather than sharing in a dorm here. I feel like I now just need to chill out and sleep."

"I don't blame you ... which hotel?"

"Park Towers, just across Queen Street. It's not too expensive, and anyway ... as Suzi and I aren't now going to Thailand, I will only spend a few days here before going home."

"Oh. Are you going straight back from Auckland?"

"Uh-huh ... yes. I didn't really fancy travelling much further by myself, so I thought I'd just have a few days here hoping to find you, before heading home. I have rearranged my flight to go home on Friday evening."

Suddenly I heard a loud cheer come from the common room.

"Oh BJ, don't let me stop you from watching the cricket. I know that it's England's game."

"Hey Megan, don't worry about that; I am just so relieved to see you."

"Yeah, babe, I know ... but I am not Suzi, am I? I know you must be gutted. Suzi was certainly missing you a lot ... oh my gosh BJ, she just couldn't stop talking about you. You really don't know how much I have had to put up with over the last month." Megan chuckled. "Yeah, but then Suzi got the news; she was devastated."

"Well, I really can't thank you enough for coming to find me ... I know you didn't have to. I really don't know what to say ... you're an angel."

Megan laughed.

"An angel? ... Me? ... Babe, you and I both know that ain't true, don't we? But, me coming here ... well, Suzi is my best mate; I'd do almost anything for her. And, I also rather like you too ... in case you didn't know. I couldn't have you disappearing off, thinking that we didn't want to see you again. I know you already kinda got that impression before, when we left Cairns."

"That's true," I responded.

"Oh, and I am so sorry for that too," Megan continued. It wasn't that we didn't want to see you, it's just that ... well, things were complicated. But, anyway, who knows what might have been different if we hadn't gone off to the Whitsundays?"

"Who knows indeed?" I shrugged.

Megan turned from beside me to look into my eyes. "You know BJ ... perhaps I really missed my chance back then. Suzi has caught herself a wonderful bloke with you. I really mean that." As Megan said this, she smiled and tweaked me on the nose with her index finger.

"I know you do Megan, and you know ..."

"No BJ, don't say any more ... you are together with Suzi now, and I am really happy for both of you ... although, with you two being on opposite sides of the world, missing each other like fuck, and with her dad sick, and ... well ... you know what I mean."

"Come here you," I said, and hugged Megan again, refusing to let her go. We held each other in silence for a few minutes before we were interrupted.

"Hey Bruce! Are you not watching the cricket? ... Oh, sorry, was I interrupting?" It was Carsten.

"Oh ... Hi Carsten!"

"Ah-ha, so is this Suzi then? I've heard so much about you," continued Carsten.

Before I could correct him, Megan intervened.

"Oh really? ... Hello. And what precisely has Bruce been telling you?"

"Well, he has been missing you for sure. He has been counting down the days, talking about you in his sleep, daydreaming ... all sorts."

"OK, okaaayyy," I said. "Sorry ... Carsten, this is Megan ... Megan this is Carsten. Megan is Suzi's best friend. Suzi had to return home because her father had a heart attack."

"Oh no ... I am so sorry. And I am sorry that I interrupted; you must have a lot to catch up on. I must leave you to it."

Carsten then disappeared off back to the common room.

"He's my room-mate right now. I travelled up from Rotorua with him; he's quite a laugh, but he also snores."

"Is Rotorua that smelly volcanic place?" asked Megan. "Sorry, I haven't done much homework about New Zealand ... and I guess I won't get to see too much of it now."

I nodded. "You say that you've got until Friday. Well, I fly out Thursday night ... so at least we can have a few days hanging out. Well, that is, if you'd like to."

"Oh, I would love that BJ ... I really would. We don't need to do much, but it'd be good just to hang out and talk."

"Well, I would love that too ... and I really am so glad that you are here. I know I am disappointed at not seeing Suzi ... but ..."

"Yeah I know."

♦ ♦ ♦

Another cheer could be heard from the common room.

"Look BJ, are you sure you don't want to watch the cricket?"

"No worries, I am OK," I replied, although to be honest, I was curious as to what was happening.

"Are you really sure? Well, look babe, it's getting quite late, and I am tired." Megan looked at her wristwatch and realised she hadn't adjusted for local time. "What is it, around 9:30? Look, why don't I go back to my hotel, and leave you to watch the cricket? We can meet up again tomorrow morning."

"Well OK, if that's what you want. Look, how far is your hotel? Park Towers did you say? Why don't I walk back over there with you? It's dark, and I don't know how safe these streets are at night."

"Well, OK then ... if you don't mind."

I quickly nipped back to my room to grab a jacket, and then returned to Megan. We walked out onto the street.

"So, you are not at the Sheraton then?" I asked Megan, glancing up and smiling to myself.

"No BJ, the Park Towers. You don't think I've got that kind of money, do you?"

"No, of course not," I said, chuckling.

"So why did you ask then?"

"Oh ... I ... uh, well, I'll tell you later."

"Park Towers is just over there," said Megan pointing in the other direction.

We walked slowly up the road, and stood in the hotel entrance.

"So, what time would you like me to come over tomorrow? Which room are you in?"

"Um ... room 64."

"No kidding! Really?" I said in amusement.

"Why? What's up? Tell me BJ?"

I glanced through the lobby, and could see a TV showing the cricket in the hotel bar.

"Look BJ ... tell me. Please? OK, come for a drink in the bar ... and then you can tell me. Please BJ?"

"Well, if you put it like that ... I could murder a beer."

Megan collected her key from reception and then we walked through to the bar.

"What beer is good here?" asked Megan.

"Steinlager is OK, and they seem to have that on tap."

Megan ordered a couple of Steinlagers, charging them to her room, and then we went to sit at a table in front of the TV screen. There was nobody else in the bar.

I noticed that South Africa had just lost their fourth wicket, and were now at 140 for 4, with Rhodes and Cronje at the wicket. The match looked like it was evenly balanced.

"How's it going BJ? And, please tell me in terms that I can understand?"

"It is ... poised. That might be the best word for it."

Megan lifted her glass.

"Well BJ ... cheers!"

We clinked glasses, and sipped the beer.

"Yes indeed ... cheers Megan! And, once again, thanks so much for coming to find me. I really don't know what I would have thought, or what I would have done if you hadn't turned up."

Megan removed her jacket and put her room key down next to the beer on the table.

"So, tell me BJ, what was this about the room number? And the Sheraton?"

I removed my jacket, and hung it over the back of my chair.

"It's a bit of an embarrassing story ... well, no ... it's more than a bit embarrassing. Are you sure that you want to know?"

Megan laughed. "Naturally babe, the more embarrassing the better. But you and I share everything, right?"

"Well OK then. But I am not so sure what you will think ... well, no ... actually I can guess exactly what you'll think ... but anyway, don't say that I didn't warn you."

I took a deep breath, and another sip of Steinlager, and began. "You see Megan, it was a dream I had. I don't know if you remember back in Melbourne that you suggested some additional 'rules' relating to the cricket?"

"Remind me BJ. ... Oh, yes, now I remember. What was it, the MOT rules? ... (she whispered) ... Manual for the semi-final, oral for the final and a total service for the win. Yes, I do recall now." Megan giggled. "Suzi was really irritated with me, wasn't she?"

"Well, perhaps," I continued. "Oh, and before going further, the MOT equivalent in New Zealand is 'warrant of fitness', or WOF, which also still works ... wank, oral and fuck ... I just thought you'd like to know."

"That's cool." Megan smiled.

"Anyway, back to the dream. So, several days ago, I dreamt that England had just won the final. We were all watching it together in a bar somewhere. And as I was jumping up and down in celebration, you passed Suzi a room key. It was room 64 ... at the Hilton rather than the Sheraton ... and you then said ... (I hesitated ... *Should I really tell her this? ... Oh, what the hell?*) ... you said, "I got you two lovebirds a little pressie ... Now just go and fuck each other stupid!""

At this point, Megan nearly choked on her drink.

"Well, my dear BJ ... you do have some imagination ... and a very, very dirty mind."

"Well, I am not the only one," I said smiling at Megan. "Weren't the MOT rules your thinking? ... That's how I remember it."

"Mm-hmm ... that's true ... and actually, I can't deny that 'go and fuck each other stupid' is probably something that I would say. OK, so what happened next?"

"Blimey, you want me to continue? No, Megan ... it really is so sordid."

"Come on babe, you know me ... the dirtier the better. You can't just stop the story before the juicy bits. Come on, please? I'll even tell you a naughty dream of mine in return."

"Well, OK. So, we get to room 64 and open the door ... it's a moonlit night, and the light is streaming in as the curtains are open. There's a massive bed to our right, but we continue towards the window. At this point we are kissing ... and we just can't get enough of each other. We start undressing each other ... our tops first, and then Suzi's bra, and then ... are you really sure you want to hear it?"

"Yes. Go on."

"Well, then I get down on one knee," ... (at this point I am really visualising it in my head, closing my eyes as I am re-telling the dream) ... "and next I remove her cut-off shorts ... and then it's Suzi's knickers ... before ... oh yes ... mm-hmm ... before I taste between her legs ... and ..."

"Oh my God BJ, stop it! ... You are beginning to make me horny now too. No, actually don't stop, I really want to hear it ... please continue?"

I opened my eyes upon this interruption. "No ... but just then ... from between her legs, I then look up ... and I see the snarling face of a scary girl that I met in Franz Joseph. And I mean really scary."

"Wow, BJ! I guess you were hoping all this was going to happen with Suzi for real this week? Wow!"

"Well ... yes ... uh no ... uh maybe ... well yes perhaps. Well, you know ... you caught me at that fucking condom machine. Oh Megan, I don't know. I wouldn't have pressured Suzi into doing anything that she didn't want to ... I hope you know that. But ... oh fuck ... that dream ... and ... my God, I so did not want to see that really scary girl, and ... well ... maybe I shouldn't have told you."

"Hey BJ, why not? We're friends, right? And remember, I told you what I did with Neil back in Broome, didn't I? And that one was for real, not just in my dreams."

"Well, I suppose so," I conceded.

"Come on BJ, loosen up! You know you can always talk dirty to me." We both laughed.

"Yeah ... and maybe that's part of the problem."

"What do you mean by that, BJ?"

"Oh ... nothing really ..."

"BJ?"

"Wait. Wait a minute ... it's another wicket."

I looked up at the TV screen. Rhodes had just gone, with South Africa now on 206 for 6, and Richardson was coming out to join MacMillan.

"What's happening?" asked Megan.

"Well, it's still tight, but maybe, just maybe, England are starting to get on top."

Well I hope they are.

"OK. So, what did you mean just then?"

"Sorry, what?" I had lost my thread. "What was I saying?"

"You said I was part of the problem. What did you mean?"

"Sorry, did I?"

"Yes ... after I said you can always talk dirty to me, your exact words were ... "Yeah, and maybe that's part of the problem." So, what did you mean?"

Fuck ... get yourself out of this one BJ.

"Ah-ha ... I said that, did I?" I was trying to backtrack.

"Yes, you did, so ... what ... did ... you ... mean?"

"Well, I suppose ..."

"Suppose nothing, BJ ... you must have meant something ... so what was it?"

My God, she's not going to let up. Well, here goes.

"Well, alright Megan ... but please don't take this the wrong way. Look, Suzi was not the only person I had in my dreams. You know, before we met up again in Melbourne, it was you rather than Suzi that I couldn't stop thinking about. You know ... after that bus journey from Tennant Creek."

"Mm-hmm ..."

"Well ... you remember?"

"Yes BJ, of course I remember ..."

"Well, after that ... you know, when I got to Cairns, I would have done anything to re-light that fire. And I kept having these naughty visions of you ... after what you told me about you and Neil, and ..."

"Maybe I get the picture now ... and perhaps you had better stop before you say something you'll regret."

"I think that's better," I agreed.

"Look, now that you are together with Suzi ... you are off limits. No ifs, no buts ... and whatever I may have felt for you before, I have to put that behind me."

I nodded.

"So, Megan, changing the subject ... have you made a decision about James yet? ... Or shouldn't I ask?"

"Yeah, that's OK, I suppose." Megan clearly didn't want to think about her boyfriend back home in Newcastle. "I think it's over between us ... it's time that James and I moved on. It may be painful, but I need to start afresh in London ... and I just can't see it working for us."

"I don't know whether to say I am sorry, or good for you ... but I know it might be painful."

"No worries, BJ, I'll get over it ... I'm a strong girl. But I know it's the right thing to do. You know, Neil, and then you, both made me realise that my life with James was not all it should have been. And although you are off limits now, you did at least help me to realise I should move on."

"Oh, what's happening?" I asked, rhetorically, looking at the screen. The teams were coming off the field; it was now raining in Sydney. The match was close to a finish; it had reached the 43rd over, and South Africa required another 22 runs to win with just 13 balls remaining. It could still go either way, but England were now marginal favourites to win.

The teams were not off the pitch for long, as the shower passed quickly, and the commentators were speculating on what the situation might be when they resumed. *Would they need to recalculate the target again, based on reduced overs? And if so, what would that mean?* I remembered back to the strange run calculations that had been made when these two teams had played in the group stages. What would they do here?

After what seemed like half an hour, but was probably nearer fifteen minutes, the teams took to the field again. The officials had decided that the game needed to be shortened by two overs due to this rain disruption, and had adjusted the target accordingly.

Surely not!

Before the revised target was announced, the two team captains, and several other players surrounded the umpires and were gesticulating. There was to be further controversy.

The revised target was then shown on the big screen. It was unbelievable ... *surely a joke.* South Africa's new target was calculated so that, instead of requiring 22 more runs off 13 balls, they now required 22 more runs off just one ball.

How could that be?

22 runs from one ball was not only impossible to achieve, but it was also unfathomable that there could be 12 balls lost without any reduction in the number of runs required.

There was much more gesticulation from the South African players and coaching staff, but after several more minutes, and after some kind of appeal being lodged, the final ball was bowled. South Africa had lost the game by 20 runs.

Absolutely crazy.

England were through to the World Cup Final, but the game had ended in farce.

"Well Megan, I have seen it all today. I thought I understood cricket, but I have absolutely no idea how it ended in the way it did."

"But England are in the final, aren't they?" asked Megan.

"Mm-hmm ... yes."

"So, aren't you happy?"

"Well, I have had better days," I said. "This was certainly not how I imagined today was going to turn out."

"I guess not, BJ. OK, look, it's getting late. What time shall we meet tomorrow morning?"

We agreed that I would drop by at around 10:00am. Then we hugged each other, Megan got into the lift, and I returned to the hostel down the road.

Monday 23 March - Auckland

I had hardly slept during the night; there were so many thoughts spinning around inside my head. I was so gutted that Suzi hadn't come, but I also felt really gutted for her, and hoped that her father would be OK. *Perhaps I would get the chance to talk to her tonight or tomorrow*, I thought, although I had no idea whether she would really want to talk with me. It was definitely a good sign that she had wanted Megan to come to find me in Auckland. That meant that Suzi still cared ... or at least Megan did, and it was so wonderful to see her again. I could have been despondent with Suzi not turning up, but Megan had given me a real boost ... she was such fun to be with.

But is it more than just fun with Megan? I could feel that I was still drawn towards her. *It cannot be more than just fun; I can't allow it to be. I really want things to work out with Suzi as, with her, it could be the real deal ... real love. And, anyway, I am off limits to Megan ... and why am I even asking myself this?*

No, I knew that Megan was off limits, but she was great company, and really relaxing to be with. She was lively, and sometimes a bit exhausting, but we just seemed to click in a best-friends type of way ... well, best friends who had previously been snogging passionately on the bus from Tennant Creek.

I thought again about the cricket; it had been such a bizarre ending to the match. *How on earth could South Africa have needed 22 runs off just one ball, after previously needing 22 from 13? It just didn't make any sense.* (And, it wasn't just me ... it didn't make sense to anyone, and following on from this World Cup, the run-rate scoring methods were reviewed and changed).

And connected to the cricket, my visions of Suzi in the Hilton or Sheraton, rewarding me under Megan's MOT rules, were now miles away from any reality ... something like 11,500 miles away. While I had never really expected that the MOT would happen, it had been an exciting prospect to think about. I did so want to become more intimate with Suzi, and indeed really wanted to sleep with her when we both felt that the time was right. It certainly wasn't going to be anytime soon; I wasn't going to see Suzi for 3 months ... maybe a bit less if I cut the time I had planned to spend in Canada. This was a frustratingly long time to wait, for both of us. *Suzi would probably have forgotten about me by then. I know I won't forget her, and I know I can wait if she can. But will she?* This reminded me, *perhaps today I should get my films developed, then at least I would have some photos of her.*

♦ ♦ ♦

After a shower, and breakfasting as usual with coffee and muffins, I set off for the short walk over to the Park Towers Hotel. Arriving bang on 10:00am, I found Megan waiting in the hotel lobby, studying a map of the city.

"Greetings!" I said as I walked in.

"Oh ... Hi BJ!" We gave each other a quick kiss-cum-hug.

"Did you sleep well," I asked.

"Like a log. It was so wonderful to have a large comfy bed and a room to myself. How about you?"

"Certainly not like a log ... although, why do logs sleep? I wonder where that expression comes from. Anyway, no, not so great ... Carsten really snores. And, to be honest, I was thinking about Suzi for much of the night. I really hope she's OK ... and her dad too."

"I am sure that they will be. Perhaps we can try to call her together this evening ... she'll certainly be keen to speak to you."

"Do you think so?"

"Are you kidding, babe? You are all that she has been talking about since Melbourne. Of course, she'll want to talk."

"Well, that's good to hear."

"Have you thought about what you want to do this morning?"

"Yes," I said, "if it's OK with you, I thought it would be useful for me to try to reconfirm my flight for Thursday night, and also go to get some films developed. I saw that there was a 3-hour processing place along Queen Street. We could then go down towards the harbour, and perhaps go for lunch around that area ... but is there anything that you would like to see or do?"

"Well, nothing in particular. I feel like just hanging out and relaxing for a few days ... but the photos bit is a good idea. Wait here a moment, while I just go and get a couple of my films from the room."

I waited for a few minutes in the lobby, perusing some tourist leaflets, while Megan returned to her room.

"OK ... lets go," she said, emerging again from the lift.

We set off north along Queen Street for a few blocks until we came to Victoria Street, and then took a right and a few yards further on we came to STA travel. At the same time as reconfirming my flight from Auckland to Honolulu, I also wanted to do the onward bit from Honolulu to Vancouver for a couple of days later. I did consider whether to spend more than just two nights in Honolulu, but I decided to go with my original plan. This was just a quick stop-over and, as I wasn't on my honeymoon, it wasn't somewhere that I wanted to spend too much time. It might have been so different had Suzi been with me; I could imagine the sunsets and romantic walks along the beach ... but not by myself.

Megan and I were invited to sit at a desk with one of the STA staff, a lady in her mid-thirties, smartly dressed in a light blue blouse with navy skirt. She had dark, shoulder length hair, a knock-out smile, and angular reading glasses perched on the end of her nose. I handed over my paperwork and asked to confirm my flights.

"Are you leaving the girl behind?" the woman asked me, clearly thinking that Megan and I were a couple.

"No, he's abandoning me here," replied Megan, trying to look serious. "He's a 'love-em-and-leave-em' kind of guy."

The STA lady looked up at me quizzically.

"She's kidding," I said. "We aren't a couple ... just friends."

"Shame," said the STA lady. "You look good together."

"I know," said Megan, smiling. "He stole my heart ... but what can I do?"

Megan stuck her tongue out at me, as the lady entered my details into her computer terminal.

"OK ... now then ... hmm ... right ... that's it. You are all set," confirmed the STA lady. "Your flights are all confirmed through to Vancouver, and no changes to the flight schedules."

"Thank you," I said. Megan and I stood up to leave.

"You are most welcome." The STA lady smiled. "But you should re-consider whether you really want to leave this girl behind. Now, you two ... have a nice day."

"Thank you, we will." I replied.

◆ ◆ ◆

Another block further down Queen Street we came to the place I had remembered with the film processing: it was a sort of large pharmacy-cum-health store. Between us, Megan and I had 5 films to process, so we handed them over for the 3-hour processing service. As we stood at the counter, Megan noticed that we were standing beside a display of condoms and lubricants.

"How come I always catch you by the condoms BJ?" asked Megan, just sufficiently loud to be sure that the sales assistant could hear.

I could feel a blush coming on.

"Hey, do you remember when I caught you by that condom machine in Tennant Creek?" Megan was visibly relishing my embarrassment.

"Uh-huh ..." I replied rather wearily.

"You never did tell me who you had in mind."

I was saved by the bell.

"Here you are," the man at the counter said. "Here's the chit with your order number. You can collect your photos any time after 2:00pm."

"Great … thank you," I said. "OK Megan, let's go."

We left the shop and returned to Queen Street, and continued north towards the harbourside.

A few yards along from the pharmacy, Megan tugged my arm, forcing me to stop.

"BJ, you still haven't answered my question. Who were you thinking of back then at Tennant Creek?"

"Well, who do you think it was? Isn't it obvious? You and I started snogging not too long afterwards, didn't we? Or do you not remember?"

"Yeah, yeah, yeah … I know that, but you still haven't really answered. I know it had to be either Suzi or me, and I know that it was also me who jumped you … but that doesn't actually tell me which one of us you had your eye on first."

"Oh fuck, do you really want me to answer that? Why do you need to know? Whatever I say will be wrong, won't it?"

"No. No, honestly BJ, it doesn't matter to me what the answer is … I'm just interested, I really want to know."

"Well, I suppose it doesn't change anything now, but back at Tennant Creek … well, to be honest, I was attracted to both of you. I was a bit scared of you, and based on what Neil had told me, I guessed that perhaps Suzi might be more into me …"

"You were scared of me?"

"Well, maybe scared isn't quite the right word. But, I'm a shy guy … and … uh … well, you aren't exactly the reserved type."

We continued walking.

"But you did fancy me too then?"

"Come on Megan … did you not feel it when we kissed? But … look, you blew me out in Cairns, and it was Suzi who came to find me at the MCG, and … well … I think I really love her now … I so wish she was here."

"Yeah, I know BJ … instead of me."

"Well, yeah … but no … uh … oh, you know what I mean."

Megan gave me a hug. "Yeah, I know babe … and I really do hope that things work out for you both."

"Yeah … so do I, but I now won't get to see her for maybe three months. That's a long time … do you think she'll wait?"

"Hey BJ, don't you worry. I think you and Suzi really have something, and I am quite sure that she'll still feel the same way in a few weeks' time."

"Oh, I do hope so Megan … love doesn't come my way too often. Well, I guess you already know all about my non-existent love life after that bus journey."

Megan laughed. "OK, less of that negativity please. Right, which way do we go?"

We had now reached the harbour, and it was about 11:30am. We decided to walk slowly around the marina area, discussing the merits of different expensive-looking yachts and cruisers, imagining where we would travel to if we were millionaires.

As we ambled round, Megan began humming to herself.

"What song is that?" I asked.

"Oh … I am trying to remember … your words just then put this tune in my head … *Love don't come easy … da-da-da da-da-da-da…*"

"Ah … yes," I said. Then, trying to sound like Phil Collins, I began to sing …

"*[13] … You can't hurry love …*"

I know that the Supremes sang this more than a decade before Phil Collins, but they were a bit before my generation.

Megan then joined in

"*… No, you'll just have to wait …*"

… She was rather more tuneful than me … but who was judging?

"So, do you like Phil Collins then?" I asked.

"Yeah, he's OK … quite sexy. I have a thing for baldies."

219

I laughed. "No, I mean his music."

"Yeah, it's OK. I used to listen to him quite a bit at Uni."

"Yeah ... me too. Perhaps it wasn't the coolest music to be into, but not surprisingly, I was never that cool. I liked it."

We talked a bit more about our tastes in music, and discovered that we weren't so far apart. Most of what we liked was quite mainstream ... Queen, U2, Madonna, INXS, Pretenders, Blondie; other people would probably find us quite boring.

"Sharing a house with Suzi was great. We never used to fight over music ... which is quite important when you both play it quite loud. We've calmed down a bit now ... well, probably."

"And how about cooking? That's another area for arguments, isn't it?"

"Yeah, that was pretty good too. Luckily both of us will eat almost anything. One of the other girls in our house was vegan, which sometimes caused us a few frictions."

"Uh-huh?"

"Oh sure ... and not just with the food. She lived a very green, ethical lifestyle; no meat, fish, eggs ... nor leather or fur, and she wasn't too keen on them in the house either. While I have nothing against this, it can be hard when others try to impose it on you."

"Uh-huh ... I know the sort. Oh sorry, that's so fucking stereotypical and bigoted, isn't it? Well, you know what I mean?"

"Yeah, and if it's not that, its religion," continued Megan. "Oh fuck, sorry BJ ... you didn't tell me ... are you religious?"

"I guess that you aren't then? Hey ... well, that's good; there are still lots of things we don't know about each other. You may know the name of the first girl that I kissed, and indeed how it tasted, but you don't know whether I am a Buddhist or a devil-worshipper. I am not, by the way; I'm probably as atheistic as they come, but I do have respect for what others believe."

"Sarah ... and alcoholic ... wasn't it?"

"What? ... Sorry?"

"The girl was Sarah, and your first kiss tasted alcoholic. Am I right?"

"Blimey Megan, you have a good memory."

"Well BJ, back then on the bus, I was kind of into you. Not any more, of course; not now that you are spoken for ... everything you say now will go in one ear and out the other."

We laughed.

♦ ♦ ♦

As we both liked Italian food, when we spotted an attractive-looking trattoria a block away from the harbourfront, we decided we would try that for lunch.

We were shown to a table, and handed a couple of menus from an Italian-looking (and sounding) waiter.

"Very dishy," whispered Megan, as Giovanni disappeared out of earshot. A few minutes later he reappeared.

"Is the lady ready to order yet?"

"I like that," said Megan. "I like being called a lady."

"A rarity is it?" I laughed.

"Hey BJ ... you just behave. Yes, the lady is now ready, and would like to start with some bruschetta ... followed by pizza al funghi."

"Ah yes," said Giovanni, scribbling the order in his notepad. "And for you sir?"

"Hmm ... I will start with the ravioli. And then ... (Suddenly my mind switched to one of my favourite TV comedies, The Fall and Rise of Reginald Perrin. Putting on Reggie's voice, I continued) ... And for my main course, I'll have the ravioli ... and then for dessert ... hmm ... yes ... more ravioli. I ... like ... ravioli."

"Sorry sir?" Giovanni looked momentarily bemused.

"No, I am sorry, I must apologise. I was just thinking of an old comedy programme I used to love."

Megan giggled. "Reggie Perrin ... I used to love that too."

"Anyway," I continued. "I will have the ravioli as a starter, but then a four seasons pizza. And perhaps we'll have a carafe of house red. Is that OK Megan?"

"Fine by me. I don't normally drink at lunchtimes, but yeah."

"OK then ... a carafe of wine, and a jug of water too."

"Thank you, sir." Giovanni took the menus and disappeared.

"Oh, I love that ravioli scene," Megan continued. "I haven't thought of Reggie Perrin in years."

"Yeah, it was brilliant, wasn't it?"

"Oh, yeah, and I remember those farting chairs, and the "I didn't get where I am today without knowing a good farting chair when I see one.""

"Yeah ... good old CJ. I did sometimes wonder whether mum started calling me BJ after seeing Reggie Perrin, but it might also have been the BJ character from MASH ... did I already tell you?"

"Well, I do remember that you didn't think it was connected to blow-jobs."

"Yeah, I mean, can you imagine your parents doing it? ... Yuck!"

"Hmm, well ... not really; my mum and dad divorced when I was quite young, not too long after my baby sis Beth was born."

"Oh ... sorry, you never told me."

"I know ... there's a lot we don't know about each other. And I am sure there's a lot you don't know yet about Suzi ... although I think she's a bit less fucked up than me."

"Why do you say that? You don't appear the slightest bit fucked up to me."

"Well, Suzi didn't ask to give you a blow-job on the bus, did she?"

Megan started to giggle, which also set me off.

"No Megan ... I suppose you are correct."

I know I am about to regret asking, but ...

"Please forgive me for asking Megan, but did you really mean it back then? Would you have really given me a BJ?"

"Yeah, probably ... I was feeling pretty damned horny on that journey."

"Fuck, really?" *Wow! I really did miss out.* Just the thought of it sent a tingle to my groin.

"But anyhow, as I was trying to say before," Megan continued, "compared to Suzi ... well, she appears to know what she wants in life. She has some direction, she's consistent ... and she now has you. Whereas, I ...? Well, there's James for a start. And then, there's law school ... which I suppose will be a good thing, but I am really not that sure. Oh BJ, I really don't know what I want in life at the moment."

Giovanni returned with our starters.

"Thank you," I said, on seeing my ravioli placed in front of me.

As Giovanni returned towards the kitchen, Megan's eyes followed.

"Oh, now wait BJ ... that really is something I wouldn't mind a piece of."

"Sorry?"

"Oh, I'm sorry babe. Great bum though, don't you think?"

"I wouldn't really know ... he does nothing for me."

"Oh BJ, why is my mind always in the sewer?"

"My God, we really do have so much in common. Now, how's your bruschetta?"

♦ ♦ ♦

Lunch was great ... both the food, and the company. Spending time with Megan was such a joy. She was one of those rare people you find in life who, while being poles apart on many things, you just seem to click with, and are never lost for things to talk about. You can be in the middle of one topic of conversation, then you throw away some random comment, and it just opens up whole new dimensions for discussion.

We conversed about a wide range of subject matter over lunch, from the merits of Italian vs. French waiters and waitresses; to the beauty of the Scottish Highlands; to what was the likely result of the upcoming British general election. At just after 2:30pm, we left the restaurant with our stomachs well satisfied, and in very good cheer … the second carafe of wine I ordered may have helped in this regard.

"I guess we can pick up the photos now," I suggested.

"Yes, but can we go into this shopping mall first? I feel like doing a little birthday shopping."

"Oh, sure … yeah, of course … whose birthday?"

"Mine," replied Megan with a smile. "Tomorrow."

"Hey great! Happy Bir … uh … no … no, I can tell you tomorrow, can't I?"

"Mm-hmm. But while we are on the subject, you should make a note that Suzi's birthday is on April 9th… in case she hasn't told you. And knowing her, she probably won't have done, because she never likes to make a big deal of it."

"Thanks, and no … she hasn't told me."

We walked through the mall, and after browsing in a couple of shoe shops, we found ourselves in a large department store, walking around a lingerie section. Megan knew that I was someone who embarrasses easily, and I am sure she was determined to exploit it.

"How do you think I would look in this, BJ?" Megan turned to face me, clutching a lacy crimson bra and matching panties. They were skimpy and hot, and not the type of thing I should probably be commenting on.

"Yeah, great," I said. "Well, fucking hot actually, if you really want to know." I could feel my face getting warmer, as I started to blush. My skin was turning to match the colour of the underwear.

"And how about these black ones?" she asked, as she held them up to her body, waiting for me to express an opinion.

"I shouldn't be saying anything, considering I am dating your best friend. But yeah … well … you know … you'd look fantastic in anything."

"Even in my birthday suit?" Megan teased, winking at me, and sensing my unease with the current conversation.

She picked up a shopping basket, and then placed both the crimson and black sets of underwear into it, before continuing. "Have you done much lingerie shopping before, BJ?"

"Uh, no, not really. I was forced to go with my mum sometimes as a kid, but I do really try to avoid it."

"I can tell that it embarrasses you … but it shouldn't. And you also shouldn't be embarrassed about looking at a sexy girl. I think most girls actually enjoy it when a guy looks at us, particularly if the guy is a hottie. But don't tell Suzi I told you this … and certainly don't let her catch you doing it."

Megan laughed.

"I'll try." *However hard that might be.*

Megan had now stopped in front of a range of figure-hugging leather hot-pants, skirts and tops.

"Hey babe, how do you think I'd look in black leather?" Megan picked up a top to check in the mirror.

Fuck, please try to control your thoughts BJ.

Too late. My mind exploded with visions that I had seen so many times in my dreams, ever since I had first met Megan in Darwin. From the time when Neil had told me his story of Megan tying him to a bed in a hostel in Broome, my mind had been possessed by sexy visions of Megan in skin-tight black leather.

"Hey BJ! So, tell me … what do you think?"

I was gazing in her direction, but my mind was miles away.

"Hey BJ, snap out of it! So, babe … how do I look?"

As I regained reality, Megan pulled the top across her front, once again waiting for a response.

"What can I say, Megan? It's the stuff of dreams." I smiled.

"So, shall I try it on?"

"Well, if you want to, but please don't ask me to look. I have no doubt that you'd look awesome, but you really shouldn't be trying to turn me on."

"Hey, I'm sorry BJ," she said, returning the sexy top to its peg. Megan slowly moved away to browse amongst some slightly more sober tops. "Sorry babe, I didn't think that you still looked at me in that way."

"Oh, come on. You know it's hard for me not to. I know that I am dating Suzi, but it doesn't mean that my dick's cut off when I see other girls … and you already know that I think you're pretty damned hot."

"OK, sorry. I will try not to misbehave."

We moved around a few other sections of the store, and then Megan found a couple of summer blouses that she wanted to try on.

"How about these ones? Not too slutty, but … yeah, I like them."

We then walked over to some changing rooms, and I stood outside with the basket, while Megan tried the tops on. She then emerged a few minutes later, placing both items in the basket.

"Well, please let me buy you those for your birthday," I said. "It wouldn't look right for me to buy you sexy underwear, but perhaps this would be acceptable."

Megan laughed.

"Really BJ, please don't feel you need to get me anything. But, thank you, that would be lovely."

After paying for the clothes, we left the shop. After briefly visiting a handful of other stores, we walked back up Queen Street to collect our photos. After a quick check that they looked like our pictures, we headed back up towards the Park Towers Hotel.

It was just before 5:00pm when we arrived back. We briefly stopped in the lobby.

"Look babe, it's still maybe three hours until we should try calling Suzi; we don't want to wake her up too early. I feel like crashing out for a while now … how about you?"

"Yeah, I could probably do with a rest too."

"Well, why don't you come up to my room? We can look at the photos together ... and I promise that I'll behave." Megan seemed to sense a bit of reluctance on my part to follow her up to her room. She sensed correctly. I couldn't help but find Megan magnetically alluring, but we both had to behave ourselves. If either of us made a move, it could stuff any chance I had of a relationship with Suzi, but it could also destroy Megan's friendship.

◆ ◆ ◆

We can behave. I'll go up ... what harm could there be in it?
"Well OK. I would love to see your photos from Adelaide and Western Australia."

We both got in the lift, and waited quietly while it rose up to the sixth floor.

I wonder if she is thinking what I am.

I was trying to stop my mind thinking of anything, but it drifted towards sexy thoughts of what Megan and I might get up to if we were stuck in the lift. We smiled at each other, keeping our thoughts to ourselves. It seemed to take an eternity before the lift doors finally opened.

As I followed Megan to the door, I watched as she turned the key.
"Mm-hmm ... yes ... room 64."
"Oh yes ... your naughty dream?"
Megan opened the door and walked through.
"Mm-hmm." I followed into the room. "Oh my God!"
"What is it babe?"
"Wait a minute. The large airy room, the tinted windows, the view over the rooftops, the king-size bed, the dressing table against the wall on the left ... it's ..."
"Exactly like your perverted dream," said Megan, finishing my sentence.
"Uh-huh."

"Oh, come on BJ ... most hotel rooms look much like this." She smiled, and looked me in the eye, sensing the cogs that were turning in my mind. "And don't you go getting any dirty ideas ... I am not Suzi!"

"Yeah Megan, I know." I tried to snap out of my thoughts.

"Do you feel like a coffee?" asked Megan, thankfully changing the subject.

I sat down in a brown leather tub chair beside the bed, while Megan put the kettle on, and looked to see what coffees and teas were in the bowl of freebies.

"May I use your bathroom, Megan?" I asked politely.

"Yes of course you can. There's no need to ask."

"Well, I don't like to assume."

"Don't like to assume what? Of course, BJ ... just go to the bathroom. Don't worry, I haven't left my bullet out on the side."

"Sorry, what?" I looked quizzically as I stood up from the chair.

"Oh, my dear sweet BJ. My bullet? My silver bullet ... you know, my vibrator."

Instantly, I blushed. My God this girl had her way of switching my emotions on and off in a flash. And, whether it was deliberate or not, Megan realised it.

"Hah-hah," I said, making my way to the bathroom, nodding my head at her joke.

"No, the bullet is not out on the side ... but if you want to take a look, you'll find it in my washbag."

I said nothing, and closed the bathroom door behind me. I could sense that Megan was smiling wickedly on the other side of the door; I didn't know whether she was just playing games with me. I really wanted the two of us to become great friends, but there was always a sexual tension. Well, I certainly felt it ... perhaps it wasn't the same for her.

I saw her washbag next to the washbasin, slightly open, and tempting me to peek. I didn't. I walked straight over to the toilet, and stood for a pee. After flushing, and carefully putting the toilet seat back down (as I knew leaving the seat up was a no-no!), I washed my hands. I then used the remaining noise of the flush to hide the sound of me taking a quick look in Megan's washbag ... I just couldn't resist it. Only a sneak-peek, but enough to spot a smoothly polished silver baton, about 4 inches in length. There were also several packets of pills which I didn't recognise, some paracetamol, some lip balm and a couple of packets of condoms. They were almost definitely the same condoms which she had taken from that machine I half-destroyed in Melbourne. On the other side of the washbasin, there was her toothpaste, toothbrush, and a multitude of small bottles and sachets of shampoos, creams, and gels.

I emerged from the bathroom just as the kettle had boiled.

"Hey babe, did you take a peek?" Megan asked, with a knowing smile.

"Oh Megan ... why do you play with me so? Yes, OK then, I did just have a quick look."

"I'm sorry BJ, I don't really mean to. Think nothing of it; it's just the way I am."

"Apology accepted."

"So, what did you think? If you ever need a present for Suzi ... well, I can tell you ... that bullet is extremely pleasurable. Oh yeah! It just takes a triple-A battery and ... oh my God! It's like ... the ... best ... thing ... ever! You would not believe how it makes me feel ... Ooohh baby!"

"Wow! That good, huh?" I had enjoyed how much pleasure Megan seemed to feel only by telling me.

"Yes, really. It ... is ... awesome. I picked that little one up in Melbourne on the day that Suzi came to see you at the cricket. I needed a bit of cheering up."

Megan looked up at me, holding out some coffee sachets, before noticing the intrigued expression on my face. "Well babe, everyone masturbates, don't they?"

"Did I just hear that right? Is this what your girl-to-girl type conversations with Suzi sound like?"

"Uh-huh ... yeah ... sometimes."

"You know, I am now just so glad I wasn't shopping with you when you chose your bullet. Lingerie is bad enough, although, having said that ... despite your love for embarrassing me, I did quite enjoy it."

"I know you did BJ." Megan smirked, while arranging a couple of mugs on the dressing table. "Here. Would you prefer coffee or tea?"

"A black coffee would be fine, thanks."

Megan emptied a sachet of instant coffee into a mug, and poured the water.

"Here you are." Megan passed me the coffee. "So, babe, who's first? Do you want to show me yours, or shall I show you mine?"

I looked quizzical.

"The photos BJ? Oh my dear BJ, no ... I don't always have such thoughts on my mind."

We both laughed.

"OK then," I said. "Shall we do me first? The top ones seem to be mine."

Megan put her own coffee down on the side table next to the bed, following which she kicked off her shoes and lay down next to me. I sat down again in the tub chair.

"Before we start Megan, can I ask you something a bit personal? I am curious about your view on something, but please don't take it the wrong way."

I had to deal with this.

"Uh-huh ... yeah, of course. Sure babe, what's wrong?"

"Well, nothing's wrong Megan. Not really ... it's just ..."

"What? What is it babe?"

Here goes.

"Well, do you think that guys and girls can ever really be just good friends? It's kind of been worrying me. It's easy for me to be best mates with several guys, because hormones don't complicate things. But with girls it's different, it's like ... well ... you know ... like with us. Because ... well ... you know that I still think you are hot ... and we did have that bus journey, and those feelings don't magically disappear. But now ... well, I really think that I have fallen in love with Suzi and ... oh hell ... I just don't want to fuck things up with either of you."

Megan seemed a little taken aback, but after a moment, she leaned forward and grabbed my hand.

"Oh babe ... look ..."

I looked into her eyes, as she smiled back.

"That is such a sweet thing to say, and I am sure that if Suzi were here now, she would think the same. Look ... to be honest, you may actually be feeling quite similar to how I do. If Suzi weren't my best friend, then I'd probably be trying to tear all your clothes off right now. I think you know that I fancy you too ... but nothing further can happen between us. We have to make it work as friends, and I really do want that, because I really enjoy spending time with you. But just because I have to be restrained, it doesn't mean that I don't have feelings too."

"Oh ... wow!" I wasn't really expecting this.

"We just have to control ourselves," she continued. "If Suzi dumped you, or indeed if Suzi dumped me as a friend, then things might be different ... but ..."

"Yeah ... I know. God, how I wish Suzi was here now ... it's not that I don't enjoy being with you, I really do, but ..."

"Yeah, you probably just want to have sex ... I know, but just shut up now BJ, or you'll have me going. Come on, let's just look at some photos."

I quickly checked the films and separated the three that I could see were mine.

"OK, so mine seem to start in Sydney; I sent the previous ones back home already. I thought it was a good idea not to carry prints and negatives around together so that if I lost some, I might still have the photos in some form. I figured that my photos would be the most valuable thing from my travels."

"You're a real brainbox, BJ ... I never thought of doing that."

"Hey look ... there's Her Maj," I said, showing Megan a photo of The Queen speaking outside Sydney Town Hall. "That was the day before coming on via Canberra to Melbourne."

"I remember you saying you'd seen her. I never have. She has been up to Newcastle a few times, but never when I've been around. I would quite like to see her one day; I actually quite like the royals."

"Yeah, I do too ... some of them anyway. You know, I actually felt quite proud to be British when I was standing there taking this photo."

"Ah-ha ... Canberra Parliament," said Megan, as I handed her a couple more photos. "What did you think of it?"

"OK, I suppose ... but a bit too ..."

"Hygienic?" suggested Megan, finishing my sentence.

"Yes ... a good word for it."

We continued browsing through the photos, and soon came to Melbourne.

"Ah, yes, the cricket ground, and the start of the World Cup ... West Indies vs. Pakistan."

"But no pictures of Suzi?"

"Oh ... no ... you seem to be right. I suppose we just had other things on our mind, and it looks like I didn't take any more pictures that day."

"You were just bowled over with love." Megan giggled.

"Ah-ha ... now here's one ... and here's both of you at the zoo. Ah yes ... and here with the koalas."

♦ ♦ ♦

For the next hour or two we enjoyed seeing pictures and reminiscing over a few of the memories we had shared from Melbourne. We then told each other about our separate adventures over the last few weeks, with me in New Zealand, and Megan and Suzi in Adelaide and then over in Western Australia.

The time flew past as we re-lived our memories, and I carefully studied every single picture that had Suzi in it. We chatted and laughed, and after our third refill of coffee, we realised it was nearly 8:00pm.

"Are you hungry," I asked. "Do you want any supper?"

"No, I don't think so. How about you?"

"No, I'm good." I was still quite full from lunch.

"Oh shit, is that the time? I ought to try to phone Suzi ... she should be up by now. It is 12 hours difference, isn't it?"

"Yes, it should be around 8:00am. What day is it today?"

"Monday? ... Yeah, Monday. Well, let me try to call her. I asked down at reception earlier; they said the room phone doesn't cost any more than the payphone in the lobby ... so here goes."

Megan extracted a small notebook from her purse, found the number, and then began to dial. "I can never remember the number. Outside of term time, we didn't really call each other much."

After a slight time-lag, there was a dial tone at the other end.

"I so hope that her dad is OK," I remarked.

"Yeah, me too."

The phone rang again and again. There was no answer. After about the tenth ring, Megan hung up. "Let's try again in a few minutes. It's possible that she's out already. Her mum might have gone to work, or they might have gone to the hospital. Or maybe she's taking a shower ... well, who knows ... let's try again in a few minutes."

Megan tried three more times to get through, and at about 9:00pm tried a final time. Each time there was no reply. We were both deflated and disappointed.

"OK, let's try again in the morning," suggested Megan.

"Fine. Look, it's getting quite late now. Well, I know it's only 9 o'clock ... but maybe we should call it a day. What would you like to do tomorrow?"

"Oh, nothing special ... why don't you surprise me BJ? How about you come over around 9:00am, and then we can try calling her again. Just come up to the room when you get here."

"OK. That sounds good." I stood up to leave, picked up my photos and put them in my daypack. I then gave Megan a big hug. "I really enjoyed today. Thanks."

"Me too, BJ ... it's really been fun. See you in the morning."

"Sweet dreams," I said as I opened the door. "Oh, that reminds me ... yesterday you said you also had some weird dreams ... well, perhaps you can tell me about those tomorrow."

"Perhaps BJ. Goodnight."

I made my way along the corridor to the lift, and descended to the lobby. *What could I think of to surprise her with tomorrow?* As I stepped out into the lobby, I had an idea. I walked over to the receptionist.

"Uh, excuse me. I don't know whether you could tell me if the lady in room 64 orders breakfast? It's her birthday tomorrow, and I wondered whether you could send something special up to her room ... I'll pay for it."

"OK sir, let's see what we can do."

I left the lobby quite pleased with my idea ... I had ordered her breakfast for 07:30am. I had gambled that she might not be an early riser, and that she wouldn't go down to the breakfast room before then, and perhaps wouldn't have any breakfast at all ... she hadn't done so today. Anyway, I had ordered a mini champagne breakfast, with smoked salmon, scrambled eggs and toast, together with orange juice and a quarter-bottle of champagne. It would accompany a note which said: "To my Super-Sub ... Happy Birthday."

I then walked back to the hostel with a spring in my step, and tried to think of what we could do tomorrow. Despite not being with

Suzi, spending time with Megan had really boosted my mood, and her assurances on how Suzi felt about me meant the world. I hoped that I would hear her voice in the morning.

Tuesday 24 March - Auckland

I arrived in the lobby of the Park Towers just before 9:00am. I was excited to see whether Megan had enjoyed her champagne breakfast, and even more excited to speak with Suzi. I checked at the reception desk to confirm whether the breakfast had been delivered. They assured me that it had, and waved me through to the lifts.

I paused outside the door for a moment, just chuckling to myself again at the visions that were triggered by room 64. Then I knocked three times.

"Push the door BJ! It's open!"

Megan sat on the end of the bed sipping orange juice, with a breakfast tray beside her. Her ear was listening to the phone.

"Come on in BJ ... it's Suzi. Come on over ... I won't try it on loudspeaker; I don't want to press the wrong button and lose her. Here babe, you talk to Suzi for a moment while I tidy these things up."

I took the phone from Megan, and as I did so, I received a kiss on my cheek, and a big hug as she whispered "thank you so much."

"Hi Suzi. Hey, it's so good to hear you; how's your dad?"

"Hi BJ, it's so good to hear you too. I'm so glad that Megan found you again. Megan just told me about the breakfast; that's so sweet of you ... I hope you'll treat me like that when you get back."

"You'd better believe it, Suzi ... I miss you so much. So, how are you? ... And how's your dad?"

"Things aren't so good ... well, I wouldn't be back here otherwise, right? But all things considered, at least he seems to be recovering. It was a heart attack, about a week ago now. He's still in hospital, but he is slowly getting stronger again. Fingers crossed ... he might be out again in a few days' time."

"I am so glad to hear that he's improving. So, how are you bearing up? And your mum?"

"A bit exhausted by it all. Both of us are. But we're OK. At least me being here means that I can give them a bit of support."

"I know they will both appreciate it."

"Yes, I guess. It's just such a shame though ... I was so looking forward to seeing you again, and now who knows when we will next see each other?"

"Yeah, Melbourne seems like a long time ago, doesn't it? But I promise I haven't forgotten you ... not in the slightest."

"Well, don't you go forgetting me, you hear? And don't go treating Megan too much like a queen neither ... she could easily get used to it."

"I so wish you were here. But it is wonderful to hear your voice again. I will try to call you as much as I can once I get to Canada. Listen, I don't want to add to Megan's phone bill too much. Do you want another word with her?"

"OK. Look BJ, you take care of yourself, and I will speak to you soon. Take care, BJ ... I love you."

"Yes ... you too ..." *Hang on, what did Suzi just say?* "Hey, hold on ... what did you just say, Suzi?"

"I said that I love you BJ ... you dummy."

"Oh Suzi, you do? That makes me so happy ... because, you know, I think I have fallen in love with you too. Wow!" I looked up at Megan, who was now pretending to vomit.

"I so wish I was out there with you, but we'll have lots of time together when you are back. Look, you put Megan back on ... and call me again when you can. I know it may be difficult."

"I will. Are there particular times that work best for you? Early morning or late evening?"

"Probably evenings, but just call me when you can."

"You bet I will. OK, I'm putting Megan back on. Love you."

"Love you too BJ. Take care."

I passed the phone back to Megan.

I then stepped over to the window, and just stood gazing out across the rooftops of Auckland. I became glassy-eyed ... in a daze. *Wow! ... Suzi says that she loves me ... Wow!*

After a few more words, Megan hung up the phone.

"There, you see, BJ? Didn't I tell you that Suzi was still mad about you?"

"Yeah, you did ... Wow!"

"Oh, and BJ, thanks so much for the breakfast. It was such a wonderful thought ... and, there was also a rather dishy young man who brought it to my door." Megan smiled. "You know, I think you and Suzi have got something really special; I am so happy for you. You are both such wonderful caring people ... it brings tears to my eyes."

"Hey! Come on. Dry your eyes ... and let's go out and celebrate your birthday. Oh, Happy Birthday, by the way."

"Oh, hang on BJ. Just before we go ... what did you mean by the note?"

"Sorry?" I looked back quizzically.

"I want to know what you mean by 'Super-Sub'? ... Sure, I may be a bit slutty, but even I am not that kinky."

"Sorry?" I was still bemused.

"Super-Sub. I am not really into dominants and submissives ... you know, bondage and that kind of kinky stuff."

"Oh my God! Sorry ... I actually meant substitute ... you know, instead of Suzi being here. Oh, bloody hell! Did you think I meant 'sub' in that context?"

Megan started giggling.

"Yes."

"Well, I really did mean substitute," (and I had done), "but now that you mention it ... what was it that you ended up doing with Neil? No bondage, you say?"

"Oh, BJ ... low blow ... very funny." Megan stuck her tongue out at me. "Anyway, regardless ... breakfast was a wonderful thought. Thank you so much."

"You are most welcome."

"OK. So, what do you think?" Megan spun herself around showing me one of the tops that I had bought for her yesterday. It was a smart-casual white cotton blouse that would match with almost anything.

"Yeah ... it really suits you."

"I am also wearing the crimson undies ... but I won't show you."

"Perhaps you'd better not," I agreed, "... as I now appear to be spoken for."

"Oh BJ, Suzi is such a lucky girl. But I guess I am too, because it means I have just found myself another bestie. Oh, and, who knows? Maybe one day I'll get to be a matron of honour. Oh, shall we go shopping for a hat?"

"Perhaps it's a tad early to be thinking of that."

"No, but it's exciting ... two of my favourite people in the world."

"OK. No hats, but let's head on out into Auckland, shall we? Are you ready?"

"Yes, nearly; I just need to brush my teeth. I think there's a tiny bit of champagne left if you want it, and thanks again babe ... it was really wonderful."

◆ ◆ ◆

We set out from the hotel, and began to walk along Queen Street. It looked like it would be a fine day; the sky was blue and the temperature warm enough for shorts and T-shirts.

"Have you got a jacket in your bag, just in case?" I asked.

"Yes ... but in case of what?"

"I thought we might try to take one of the little ferry boats out across the harbour. Do you like that idea?"

"Yeah, sounds great."

"I thought we could do that this morning while the weather looks fine. We should get some good views of the harbour ... we might even see some seals or porpoises, and there is a small hill that we can climb on the other side. Maybe we can get some lunch over there, or, if not, we could head over to Parnell Village where there are a few great-looking restaurants, market stalls and boutiques. I was there a couple of days ago."

"Yeah ... all good for me. I am in your hands, BJ ... just show this girl a good time."

"I'll try."

We walked along Queen Street to the harbour, and within ten minutes or so we had boarded one of the frequent small ferries which ran across to Devonport on the north side of the harbour. The boat ride took no more than fifteen minutes, before we were back on land again.

There wasn't much of interest immediately around the boat jetty: just one or two small shops and a café. So, we continued on our way to climbing up Mount Victoria. This was an extinct volcanic cone, just like Mount Eden which I had climbed a few days ago. It was only a couple of hundred metres high, but again came with a splendid 360-degree panoramic view from the summit.

Although smaller than Sydney, Auckland and its harbour area were similar in the way that the suburbs seemed to stretch out for miles in every direction, and occupy every bit of land possible to build upon.

"What a fantastic view," said Megan, looking back across to the downtown area from which we had come.

"Isn't it just," I agreed. "Hey, Megan, do you remember the first time you said those words to me? The exact same words, I believe."

"Remind me."

"On top of Ayers Rock ..."

"Oh yes, now I do ... when you were gazing at Suzi's bum, as she bent down to tie her shoe laces. Yes ... I do remember."

"It's been quite a trip, hasn't it? I am just so glad I met the two of you. And Megan, I really can't thank you enough for coming over to Auckland to find me."

"Well, it wasn't just to find you. Sure, that was a big part of it, but I think Suzi and I also needed some space ... a bit of time away from each other. I also did want to see at least a bit of New Zealand before coming home ... even if only a tiny bit."

"Had you thought of doing a bit more, and staying out here longer? You could go down to the rotten eggs of Rotorua?"

"I don't know, BJ. I don't think I feel like too much more travel right now ... and not by myself. I am probably ready to head back home. I need to sort things out with James, and it will be nice to have a long summer. I also need to try to find somewhere to live in London. I think I start work a bit earlier than you and Suzi ... you both start in September, don't you?"

"Yeah, that's right."

"Well, I start in August ... not sure why."

"I am not really looking forward to London, or the job. I can't really see myself liking the big city ... far too many people; too claustrophobic."

"Hey BJ, we should try to find places to rent close to each other. I guess we'll be seeing a lot more of you."

"Well, I really do hope so ... but I guess we'll just have to take it step by step. I have never managed a long-term relationship before. In fact, I guess that the few weeks I have been with Suzi is now my longest ... and yet we were only together for about 3 days of it. Ironic isn't it?"

"If it's meant to be, then it's meant to be," said Megan. "And you two really suit each other. Of course, I am a bit jealous ... but I am sure I can learn to love you like a brother, and stop having dirty thoughts. It will be really great to have another bestie." She put her arms around me for a cuddle.

"Dirty thoughts, Megan? ... You? ... Never." We laughed. "Oh, that reminds me, you were going to tell me about your dreams."

"Oh ... no ... no way. You are going to laugh at me ... and ..."

"Come on, you wouldn't have mentioned it if you didn't want to tell me."

"Oh ... alright then. Here goes. Well BJ, you weren't the only one to have dreams after that bus ride," she began to explain.

"Do you mean the bus from Tennant Creek?"

"Yes ... that bus. You know, after we left you in Townsville, I got so angry with myself and so embarrassed about my behaviour. Well, kissing you was one thing ... but offering to give you a blow-job on the bus ... Oh my God BJ, I felt so ashamed afterwards. I am so sorry; I really don't know what you must have thought of me."

"But ..."

"No ... just let me finish. I really felt ashamed. So much so, that I insisted that Suzi and I went to the Whitsundays rather than wait for you in Cairns. Suzi really wanted us to remain in Cairns to see you again. Well, actually, so did I ... I really wanted to see you ... but I just felt so ashamed. So, Suzi agreed to go to the Whitsundays, but only on the promise that if we ever saw you again, I would allow her 'a free shot at you.'"

"Wow!"

"Shut up! ... I just need to get this off my chest. So, while I am over the moon that Suzi has got you now, it also hurts because I blew my chance ... and, well, it really does hurt."

A tear or two appeared in Megan's eyes, as she finished.

"Wow!" I said with a deep breath. "We are both somewhat fucked up about each other, aren't we?"

"Yes, I guess so. But I love Suzi to bits, and I would never do anything to hurt her ... so, I just have to let you go. We can only be friends now BJ ... but I really do want that."

"Oh Megan ... so do I." I gave Megan a big hug, as we stood looking back across the harbour. After a couple of minutes just holding each other in silence, I remembered something.

241

"Megan?"

"Yes."

"You didn't actually tell me about any dreams."

We both laughed.

"Oh blimey! You are right, I didn't, but I don't know whether I should now."

"Come on ... what harm could it do? And, it's fun to hear them. Look, how about if you share yours, then I will share another of mine. We could keep going like that until we run out."

"Well, OK then. Hmm ... which one first?"

"Are there many?"

"Mm-hmm ... a few," Megan replied. "OK. Well then, I'll tell you about a dream that I had in Melbourne. It was a daydream ... on the day that Suzi left to go to the cricket. I was sitting on a bench in one of the shopping malls near the station ... actually, it was shortly after I had bought the silver bullet. I had drifted off ... and I imagined myself at the cricket ground. I wasn't with Suzi, but I had followed her down there. I sat and watched the two of you from the other side of the ground. I had seen you meet each other, and after your first hugs and kisses, you both appeared on the big screen. You then got down on one knee, and took out a ring from your pocket, and proposed ..."

"Wow!"

"No, wait! There's more. ... So, there you are on one knee, and, before Suzi could answer, I had stripped off all my clothes and was rushing across the pitch like a streaker, screaming at you to marry me instead."

"And ... what did I say?"

"I don't know what you said ... at that point I was interrupted by a man sitting down next to me, asking me the time."

"Hmm, interesting. And was it just the once that you had this dream?"

"Well, no. Actually, I have had more or less the same one several times since ... but I always wake up at the same point. I had the same one only a couple of nights ago ... just after I had found you again."

"Fuck, that's a weird one. Perhaps I should make sure I never propose to Suzi at a cricket game ... although ... the thought of seeing you as a streaker ..."

"Oh ... stop it," Megan said, as she prodded me in the ribs. "OK BJ, now it's your turn again."

"Well, OK, but shall we try to catch the next ferry back? I'll tell you one of my kinky dreams with you in a boat."

♦ ♦ ♦

We started descending the hill to make our way back to catch the return ferry. As we did so, I described in some detail the visions which I had first had out in Kakadu, while floating along Yellow Water Billabong. I vividly described the crocodile-infested waters, the egrets, storks and weaver birds, and the tropical storm which washed all the colour from the beautiful green oasis, turning it grey. I also described how I imagined Suzi and Megan in black-pvc dominatrix outfits, wrestling to control a small crocodile which had jumped into their boat ... only for that crocodile to magically transform itself into me.

"Hmm ... that's another interesting one," said Megan. "Do you think Suzi has weird dreams like we do?"

"Doesn't she tell you?"

"Well, no, not really. Perhaps she doesn't have such a dirty imagination. Is it my turn again?"

"Yep," I replied.

We didn't have to wait long before we were on the ferry, and heading back towards the high-rise buildings of the downtown area. As we approached the other side, we had already exchanged a couple of milder dreams in the first bit of the crossing.

"Me again?" asked Megan.

"Uh-huh."

"OK, babe ... you'll like this one," she giggled. "It's a really dirty one."

"Oh, do tell, please?" I must have appeared like a small child waiting to be given candy.

"OK ... so, you see those tall office buildings in the downtown area?"

"Yes ... go on."

"Well, you know ... when we were in Brisbane, we saw a group of high-rise towers down by the river. You went to Brisbane BJ, didn't you? Did you go to the Waterfront area? I think that's what it was called."

"Yeah, I remember it well. I had a dream there too ..."

"OK, well, that's your next one sorted then. But anyway, in this group of buildings there was one particular one: the tallest one ... a black-glass tower."

"Yeah, I remember it."

"Well, Suzi and I were in the park opposite, sitting on a bench just eating an ice cream. Then my mind wandered ... I was high up in this black tower, and I was dressed in something kinky ... yeah, a bit like your black leather dominatrix outfit ... no kidding ... and I had tied both you and Neil up to a couple of desks, and I was whipping you." Megan could hardly contain her giggles as she spoke.

"And were Neil and I naked?"

"Naturally," giggled Megan.

"And, if you don't mind me asking ... which one of us had the bigger cucumber?"

"I don't think I saw your cock in the dream," she responded giggling. "But I do remember from Broome that Neil's was perfectly satisfactory."

We both found it difficult to keep a straight face as she finished her story ... but it was such a coincidence. I then told her about my visions of her and Suzi in the exact same tower. This was really quite incredible ... not only was Megan somebody who had a mind just as filthy as my own, but we even seemed to share components of each other's dreams.

"This is so weird BJ," said Megan, after listening to my story. "I can now understand even more why you were so embarrassed by my lingerie shopping yesterday. Blimey, you and I are like two peas in a pod ... it is so amazing to be with someone who shares my dirty thoughts. Suzi just thinks I am sex-obsessed these days ... and, she's probably right. I never used to be."

On reaching the downtown boat terminal, we set off for a spot of lunch in Parnell Village. Having had a great meal there before, I decided to take Megan to the small open-air restaurant which I had visited previously. We were both tempted by the seafood linguini, and began to wash it down with a tasty sauvignon blanc from the Marlborough region of South Island.

Still conversing about some of our dreams, we were fascinated by how similar our minds seemed to work. We had both dreamt about taking a sailing yacht or cruiser out on Sydney harbour. In my dream, I had been cavorting drunkenly on the open deck with Megan and Suzi. In Megan's dream, she was on a yacht with her boyfriend James, together with Neil and I ... and the two of us had thrown James over the side. When we both revisited the dreams that we'd had of the black tower in Brisbane, we had both imagined a similar type of open-plan office, high up, overlooking the river. It also had similar types of desks, and 'imaginary Megan' had worn comparable dominatrix costumes, and had even used similar types of chains and restraints.

It was truly remarkable ... our minds just seemed totally aligned on the same wavelength of filth. Perhaps less remarkable was that we also seemed to share similar tastes in food and music too!

♦ ♦ ♦

After enjoying a delicious seafood lunch, we pottered around Parnell Village, looking for one or two souvenirs amongst the craft shops. I bought a couple of small presents for Suzi, for Megan to take back with her. One was a six-inch cuddly kiwi, while the other was a T-shirt with a rather tacky cartoon featuring two moas trying to mate, and a caption alluding to how they became extinct.

Mid-afternoon, we began walking back in the direction of the Park Towers and the YHA hostel. Just a few blocks away, we came across a bar with an outside area and a big screen, where we decided to stop off for a drink. We both thought this might be a good venue in which to pass a few hours watching tomorrow's cricket final. Even Megan seemed to be quite keen to see some of the final, now that England would be playing in it.

We had walked a lot, talked a lot, and laughed a lot. We were quite tired when we arrived back at the Park Towers Hotel. It was only around 6:00pm, but we decided to call it a day, and go and crash out by ourselves. I agreed to call by at 9:30am, and then hugged Megan before leaving her in the lobby and making my own way back to the YHA hostel. I felt shattered.

On returning to the room, I found Carsten arranging his clean laundry.

"I'm off north to the Bay of Islands early in the morning. I've just got myself another car for the week."

"Well, for me, tomorrow is all about the cricket ... I can't miss the final."

It had been a long journey for me, and indeed for England over the last month. Tomorrow, just perhaps, England could become World Champions.

◆ ◆ ◆

Wednesday 25 March - Auckland

Today should be my last full day in New Zealand. Tomorrow evening I should be flying out to Honolulu, on my way to Vancouver. It feels like today is going to be a weird day ... but I am not sure why. Perhaps by the end of today, England will be World Cup Winners.

It was the World Cup Final, and perhaps England would finally win their first major tournament in one of 'our' sports since 1966. We did appear to have a great chance ... in the earlier part of the tournament, England had dominated their group game against Pakistan, only for rain to intervene to prevent an England victory.

A start time of 10:30 or 11:00am, Melbourne time, would give me a full morning to do something with Megan before settling in somewhere to watch the match. I doubted that Megan would really wish to watch the full game. I wasn't actually too sure whether I wanted to either ... when it gets to the crunch, with anything that really matters, I get nervous. And this game really mattered to me. Perhaps it shouldn't have done so ... it was just a game of cricket, but, for once in my life, there was actually a realistic chance that England would win something big.

After saying farewell to Carsten, and wishing him luck for the rest of his trip, I strolled over to the Park Towers Hotel. At just after 9:30am, I arrived in the lobby, expecting to see Megan. The lady at reception, who recognised me, asked whether I wanted to ring through. I agreed, and having made contact, Megan said I should come up to the room.

I knocked on the door, and was met by a rather sad and listless Megan, still in her night-shirt. She had not slept well, and felt as though she might have caught a bug or food poisoning.

"Why don't you go on out and do something by yourself? I just feel like staying in bed right now."

"Hey Megan, you do look a little pale. Can I get you anything? I feel bad to leave you like this. Would you prefer to be by yourself, or can I keep you company? I am more than happy to stay."

"But there must be better things for you to do than to spend your day here with me. Do you not want to go out and do something? Oh, and you have the cricket final later, don't you?"

"Yeah, but there's nothing I really had in mind this morning. I really wanted to spend today with you, as I won't have much time before flying out tomorrow. I am sure you'll feel better in a couple of hours, if you get some rest. Now, is there anything you need? Or anything you'd like to eat? ... I could pop down to Queen Street to get something."

"You're so sweet, BJ."

"Well, is there anything you need right now? Do you feel like more sleep? Or watch a bit on your TV? ... or ..."

"Well, it's not far off 10:00am now. I don't feel like breakfast, and I don't feel too much like being in bed just trying to sleep. It's going to be so boring for you if you want to stay here, but I do appreciate the company."

"Hey look, if you really aren't feeling up to much, I could always watch the cricket on your small TV here this afternoon ... I imagine the match will be on one of the main channels. Well, that is, if you don't mind the cricket ... and also if you don't mind me being a grumpy bastard if England do badly."

"Look BJ, let's see. Why don't I just take a shower, and see how I feel afterwards? Help yourself to a coffee or tea. Can you make me a peppermint tea? Maybe that will help. There are some bags next to the kettle."

"OK sure ... but take it easy, there's no reason to rush anywhere, and I am sure we can still find lots of stuff to talk about. You haven't told me yet about any of your kinky dreams from last night."

I thought this might raise a laugh, but Megan only managed half a smile before retreating to the bathroom.

"Hey Megan," (I knocked on the bathroom door) "could you fill up the kettle for me."

Thankfully I caught her before she had stepped into the shower, and I passed the kettle around the door. The thought of Megan naked on the other side of the door was somewhat arousing. *My God, just cut it out ... stop thinking of her in that way ... I'm with Suzi now, remember? And Suzi says that she loves me.* As Megan stretched her arm to pass the kettle back to me, I got a quick flash of boob. *Don't even look.*

"Thanks Megan, one peppermint tea coming right up."

I plugged in the kettle, switched it on, and then proceeded to find the appropriate tea bag and also a coffee sachet for me. After a few minutes, the sounds of the shower and kettle were competing with each other to drown out the noise of the TV channels that I had started to flick through. There were a few channels, both international and local, but I settled for one which looked to be one of New Zealand's main news channels. It appeared that there wasn't much reportable news, and despite New Zealand not having made it to the final themselves, the media's attention was directed towards the cricket.

After a few minutes, Megan emerged from the bathroom, wrapped only (I thought) in one of the hotel's signature bathrobes. She looked a little brighter. Her face was now radiating a broad smile ... *and she looked so hot. BJ, behave!* I leapt up to remove the tea bag from her tea. As I passed it to her, I had one of those stupid visions that I desperately didn't want to enter my head: the vision of Megan suddenly dispensing with her bathrobe, and revealing herself in all her glory.

My hand shook a little as I passed the tea.

"Are you OK babe? ... You're shaking."

"Yes, I'm fine ... it's just ..."

"... The thought of me naked under this bathrobe makes you nervous?" Megan finished the sentence.

"Fuck ... am I that transparent?"

"Hey, think nothing of it. I am sure I'd be the same if it were you. It's just hormones and all that."

"Maybe. But it's quite a distraction, and I should be thinking about Suzi."

"Look BJ, if you and Suzi are still together, or at least back together, by the time we are in London, then you'll have to get used to me wandering around our house without any clothes on. I like to walk around naked."

"Sorry?" I looked up quizzically, trying to prevent my mind straying.

"Hey, I'm just kidding BJ ... I don't really do that."

"Oh. OK."

"But I have thought about it ... don't you think it would be so liberating just wandering around naked."

"Well, perhaps for some ... but I am not so sure that the little soldier wouldn't stand to attention rather too much."

We both laughed, as Megan sipped her peppermint tea.

"You know, BJ, I think I am starting to feel a bit brighter. Thanks for sticking around ... you really know how to cheer me up."

"Really?"

"Uh-huh ... it's just something about you; I don't know what."

"I wish I knew."

"Well, you do make a great peppermint tea."

"Shall I put that on my CV?"

We both sipped our respective drinks.

"You know, everyone in London seems to drink way too much caffeine," Megan commented, changing direction.

"Really?"

"Yeah, they seem to. When I went down for interviews with several of the big law firms, every time I went, the people I met just seemed to be hyperactive. And also, every few minutes in the interviews, they'd be asking me if I wanted a refill."

"Well, I guess that some work environments are quite stressful. I'm not looking forward to London. The only thing that makes it appealing is the thought of you and Suzi living nearby ... even if I have to close my eyes when I visit."

"Have you thought much about which part of London you might live in?"

"Not really, I'm only really starting to get to terms with it. Perhaps I was secretly hoping to find a dream job out on my travels, and meet the dream girl, and never come back. But now with Suzi, I have met my dream girl ... no offence ..."

"None taken ..."

"... and now, well, Suzi really trumps any job opportunity ... unless ..."

"Unless what, BJ?"

"I was going to say ... unless someone was offering me a million quid. But, actually, I don't think at the moment any amount would keep me from wanting to go back to be with Suzi."

"Oh BJ, you're just saying that. I am sure all of us have a price. However, what you just said is another big tick I can report to Suzi."

"Are you reporting back to her then?"

"Naturally, BJ ... in the minutest detail. Every comment, every stray look ..."

I looked across into her smiling eyes.

"Just kidding, BJ ... I think you're a gem, and she's bloody lucky to have you. You even make peppermint tea for me, what more could a girl want?"

"Look, it's around 11 o'clock now ... do you feel like anything to eat yet?"

"Not right now. Why? Are you getting hungry?"

"No, I am just thinking of you."

"Well, perhaps we could order room service for lunch a little later ... but I am sure I won't feel like much."

♦ ♦ ♦

At about 2:00pm, we ordered room service. It was nothing fancy ... just a couple of panini sandwiches with smoked salmon and cream cheese, together with some orange juice. I was now sitting in the tub chair beside the bed, intently watching the small TV screen. Megan sat up in bed, half-heartedly watching the action, while also reading a local newspaper.

The World Cup Final was well underway in Melbourne, with a stadium crowd of just under 90,000, and so many millions watching around the world. By the time our lunch arrived, Pakistan had won the toss and had elected to bat. Pakistan's innings began poorly, losing two early wickets, both to Pringle. However, after that, with Imran Khan and Javed Miandad at the wicket, Pakistan settled, and began to build some momentum. They were not going to be bowled out for a low score, as had been the case when the two teams had met earlier in the competition. The third wicket didn't fall until the 40th over, when Javed was dismissed for 58 with the Pakistan score on 163. They were building a solid score.

The final ten overs saw Pakistan, with Imran, Inzamam, and then Wasim Akram, scoring heavily to take Pakistan up to a score of 249 for 6 from their 50 overs. Imran had top scored with 72, and the Pakistan total, although not unassailable, certainly seemed like a competitive score.

At the halfway point of the match, I was still optimistic, but felt it was a 50:50 game. If England batted well, there was no doubt they could win, but today Pakistan had a far more motivated bowling attack than was seen earlier in the tournament.

I had been relatively quiet throughout much of the first innings, during which time Megan fell asleep. At the change of innings, she woke up again, and we resumed our conversation about different parts of London.

"What do you think of Fulham or Putney?" asked Megan.

"I don't know either too well, although my brother is now living somewhere in Fulham ... I think he quite likes it there. But I think he enjoys the busy London life too, certainly far more than I expect to."

"Well, I am sure that you will enjoy it when you get there, so don't be so negative. I have heard that those areas are quite good ... fairly central, well connected, and not as pricey as Chelsea, Notting Hill or somewhere like that."

"Yeah, could be," I agreed. "I have also heard that parts such as Little Venice, Primrose Hill and St John's Wood are pleasant, but also quite pricey. North of the Thames would be more convenient for mainline trains back home: both up to Cambridge, and for Newcastle. St John's Wood would be great in the summer for cricket ... that's where Lords is."

Megan looked rather blank.

"You know? Lords ... the home of cricket ... no?"

"No, sorry BJ. Mostly, when I see sport on the TV or in the papers, my eyes just glaze over."

I looked over towards Megan with a 'you should know it' kind of smile on my face.

"Yes, maybe I should know more about sport, but sorry, I'm afraid I am not like Suzi."

"Hey, don't be daft ... you are great just as you are. You also look as though you're feeling somewhat better now; you have bit more colour in your cheeks."

"Yeah, I do feel quite a bit better now."

♦ ♦ ♦

Fairly soon, it was me that was not feeling so good. As England began their innings, they struggled against the opening bowlers, Wasim Akram and Aaqib Javed. In his second over, Akram picked up the wicket of Botham, and then just a couple of overs later, Aaqib accounted for Stewart. This left England in trouble at 21 for 2.

It was still early, but I sensed that England had already blown their chances. They were never such a strong side when batting second, having to chase runs under pressure. They were normally much better when batting first, setting a score, and then trying to defend it.

For a few overs Hick steadied the ship, while he and Gooch slowly picked off a few runs. But then with the score on 59, Hick was also dismissed, this time by Mushtaq. I now had my head in my hands.

"I am sorry BJ. I know this means a lot to you."

I sighed. "Yeah ... I had so wanted England to win this time ... and," (I laughed) "... it really had nothing to do with your MOT rules for me and Suzi."

"Mm-hmm ... oh yeah, that as well ... shame. But, remember BJ, the rules were never specific about a time limit. You have still earned yourself the M and O prizes ... even if you have to wait a few months for them."

"Hah-hah," I said, in a rather resigned tone. "I know I shouldn't say this, but I sure wish I had taken you up on your offer on the Tennant Creek bus." *Shit!... too late.* "No ... no ... Megan, I'm sorry, I apologize ... I really shouldn't have said that. I'm really sorry. It's no excuse ... but ... well ... it's just that I still don't know what it feels like."

"Well, neither do I, babe ... as I don't have a dick," replied Megan, sarcastically laughing at the obvious.

"I suppose not ... but ... well ... how about your equivalent? What does oral sex feel like for a girl?"

"Oh, BJ ... given that you are with Suzi, I am not so sure this is an appropriate conversation."

"No, sorry, you are totally right ... I apologize. It's just I really want to learn and, if Suzi and I ever do get down to it ... well ... I really want to know more about what I am doing."

"Well, I am not so sure I can give advice here anyway, but I can say that there was a world of difference between James and Neil."

"Uh-huh ..."

"Yes. I guess it was partly the novelty, the freshness of someone new ... and also because I knew I was doing something bad, i.e. being unfaithful. I regret it in some ways ... but I just felt I had to try someone new. So ... novelty is exciting." Megan had quickly discarded any sense of it being inappropriate conversation, and was now getting into the description, closing her eyes and concentrating while she articulated her thoughts. "And then there is the kissing and the touching ... there is just SO MUCH you can do with your fingers, lips and tongue. And also, to different areas ... lips, neck, earlobes, and then of course the nipples and down to the pussy ... and especially the clit. Oh, yes, it's down there that you really start to be blown away. Oh my gosh yes, the feeling of the right tongue down there exploring ... it can be so mind-blowing ... orgasmic is the right word." Megan opened her eyes again, and smiled. "So, there's such a world to explore ... and we haven't even got to the cock yet."

I was suddenly jolted out of this horny dreamworld.

"Oh fuck!" I said, having just seen Graham Gooch dismissed by Mushtaq. "Bollocks! ... Bollocks! ... Bollocks," I cursed, as, once again, I held my head in my hands. I stood up and walked over to the window. "Always the bridesmaid, never the bride ... that's England. I often feel it's the same for me too ... never quite good enough at sport, never quite top of the class, never quite get the girl I want."

"Well, until now ... you've really hit gold with Suzi."

"Yeah, I know ... but I won't get to see her until June."

"I know ... you poor deprived thing," said Megan, slightly mocking me. "But you know what, BJ? Life isn't always about coming first ... especially in the bedroom. Just you remember that."

I laughed ... "Yeah, but I am probably no good at that either."

"Well, you won't be if you are always so negative. You always need to have a positive vibe."

"Uh-huh. ... Oh, yeah ... and how about the vibe? ... So, how does the bullet make you feel? Do you think I should get one for Suzi?"

"Well, not just yet. You need to find your own intimacy first, then see what turns you both on. But, yeah ... it's good ... it is REALLY, REALLY good. ... Now, that'll be a hundred pounds for the advice!"

"Oh, I'm sorry ... I know I shouldn't be asking."

"No, no worries BJ ... I don't mind, but I am hardly accustomed to a great love life myself. And, anyway, the last boy that I tried to hit on actually turned me down. Mm-hmm, yeah ... and that was you BJ ... do you remember that?"

"Well, I didn't exactly turn you down, did I?"

"OK, well, no ... not really, I suppose ... but I do think we both missed something back then. Anyway, let's talk about something different."

"Any thoughts?"

"Look babe ... that was a good shot," said Megan, seeing Fairbrother hit the ball through the covers for 4.

While Fairbrother and Lamb were at the crease, England were still in the game, but when Lamb was bowled by Wasim Akram with the score on 141, the probability of an England win was between remote and none. And then, the very next ball, Akram dismissed Chris Lewis. It was now 141 for 6. England were doomed.

Although the last four England wickets didn't fall without a fight, England were never back in the match. Pakistan turned the screw tighter and tighter, and eventually the last England wicket fell to Imran in the final over. England were all out for 227, falling 22 runs short.

Imran, the Pakistan captain, was jubilant ... as indeed were his team, as they lifted the trophy to be crowned the new World Champions. For England, losers once again, it was back to the drawing board.

My mood had sunk during the last hour of the match. I hadn't noticed that this was in direct contrast to Megan, who was now feeling much better, and seemed to have regained her strength.

"I know what you need now BJ. Yep, you need a night on the town. Come on, let's go out and find a bar."

"Oh Megan, I don't know. Aren't you still feeling poorly?"

"Come on. I will limit my drink a little, but there's no need for you to. Come on, I am not taking no for an answer. Grab your jacket babe ... let's go and get drunk."

Thursday 26 March - Auckland and Out

04:37am. I lay on my side as I open my eyes and I look at the bright red lights of the alarm clock.

Wait ... that's not my alarm clock.

My head is throbbing; there is way too much alcohol in my system.

Hang on ... this isn't my room ... and ... wait ... this isn't my bed.

I need to go to the bathroom to relieve my bladder.

The clock flickers to 04:38.

I see the tub chair beside the bed. I turn onto my back, and open my eyes wider. I see that I'm in a double bed.

Fuck ... I'm in Megan's bed.

The other side of the bed is empty. The bathroom door is pulled shut, and I can see light under the door. I can hear soft whispered singing; it's unmistakably Megan's voice.

Fuck ... what happened last night?

I can't recall.

Did we misbehave? ... Fuck ... how far did we go?

I checked ... I still had my boxers on, but nothing else.

Why can't I remember anything? ... Fuck, what have I done? ... And, what about Suzi?'

I tried to recall memories from yesterday. I could remember that England had lost the World Cup Final. I could also recall seeing Imran's joyful face as his teammates ran to congratulate him after the final wicket ... and also my own feeling of gut-wrenching disappointment.

Then I could remember drinking and there was definitely dancing ... I didn't often dance. I could also recollect seeing Megan's face laughing, and trying to cheer me up. And, I could picture a dance floor, with strobe lights ... brilliant white, blue, then red.

Was this all the same place?

But then I remembered the lift ... and then ...

It was back to room 64 ... we walked past the bed ... we were removing clothes by the window ... I was ...

"Hey there, beautiful." Megan emerged from the bathroom, wearing a long t-shirt. She climbed back into bed beside me. "Sorry babe, did I wake you?"

"Oh ... um ... uh ... no ... I just woke up needing the bathroom."

"Well, it's all yours, babe. Quite some night huh?"

"Uh ... yeah ... quite some night."

I got out of bed and walked over to the bathroom. I closed the door quietly behind me.

Were there any clues there from Megan? ... Oh fuck, what did we do?

I stood at the toilet to relieve my bladder. I did have a slight boner ... but that was common for early morning, not necessarily any giveaway sign of having sex.

I had certainly drunk several pints last night, probably several shorts as well.

Yeah ... I can recollect ... we did drink whisky in the hotel bar.

As I stood at the toilet, there was a wonderful pressure release from my bladder.

The bin ... check the waste bin.

I did. Thankfully, there were no used condoms.

How about her washbag?

I checked very quietly. Again, I was relieved that the two packets of condoms I had seen there before were still unopened.

Fuck ... but what if we didn't use a condom? ... And, what if I get her pregnant? Oh my God ... why can't I remember?'

I flushed the toilet and waited for the noise to stop completely, before turning the light off and opening the bathroom door. The bedroom itself was quite light, the curtains were half open, dawn was starting to break, and the lights from surrounding buildings floodlit the room.

I walked carefully back to my side of the bed. I checked the pockets of my jeans for my wallet ... I hadn't used those condoms either.

Another good sign ... well, at least not a bad one.

"Babe, what are you looking for? Are you OK?"

"Uh-huh ... yeah ... I guess. A headache though."

"There's some paracetamol in my washbag if you want some."

"Thanks ... that'd be great."

"Help yourself babe."

I went back to the bathroom, took two pills and also drank a couple of glasses of water. I returned to sit on my side of the bed.

"Hey, come back to bed," said Megan softly. "You should try to get some sleep."

I lay down and rested my head on the pillow next to Megan. By the way Megan had acted, there was still no indication one way or the other.

Fuck ... did we do it, or not?

I could just about remember kissing Megan, and then also recall smelling her hair. And then there was the removing of clothes, the tasting of skin, the soft caress of feminine flesh ...

But was any of this actually last night? And was it actually Megan?

Was this just my imagination again, or the piecing together of parts which didn't fit? I knew the taste of Megan's lips, and the smell of her hair ... the bus from Tennant Creek had given me those memories. I had tasted tender female skin quite recently too ... not Megan, nor indeed Suzi, but Elaine on Magnetic Island. And then I also had memories of pleasuring Jeannie in the Brisbane cinema. Was I just remembering different things?

What the fuck did we do last night? And if Megan and I actually did make love ... well ... what then? That would destroy relationships with Suzi for both of us. Shit. Maybe whatever we did last night, it might be curtains for me now. Oh fuck, why am I such a moron? I love Suzi ... yeah ... I am sure I do. But fuck ... What if we ...? And, how do I feel about Megan? Good, I guess. And, what if she wants us to be together? ... Well, that'd be OK wouldn't it? She's a wonderful girl, and ...'

"Hey babe, can't you sleep?" whispered Megan. "Try to get some rest ... remember you need to fly out later today." Megan rolled onto her side, facing me, and caressed the side of my face. "Just shut your eyes babe, and get some rest."

Her hand felt so tender, so caring ... but she wasn't pulling me closer.

She might have done so, I suppose, if we had just been making love. Maybe we are OK. ... Maybe nothing did happen. ... Perhaps we did behave ourselves.

I loved Megan to bits, but I was in love with Suzi. I really didn't want to fuck everything up with either of them, but I just couldn't remember what had happened. I had to know ... and somehow, I was going to have to ask her.

To be continued ...

[Continue the journey in Diary of a Shy Backpacker: iii. No Looking Back]

Epilogue

My heart is beating faster this morning. I have just woken up, and I'm in bed with Megan. I cannot remember everything I got up to last night, but I guess that I'm about to find out. Megan is Suzi's best friend, and Suzi is my girlfriend ... yeah, it's complicated.

Yesterday England lost to Pakistan in the final of the Cricket World Cup, and I went out with Megan to drown my sorrows. I should have been spending last night with Suzi, but she is back in the UK now, with her dad in hospital. Suzi told me that she loves me, and I really think that I love her too. Fuck, I really pray that I didn't just blow it ... I so hope that me being here in Megan's bed has an innocent explanation.

The last month in New Zealand has been interesting, but also frustrating, and at times a bit lonely. After my first six weeks travelling in Australia, Suzi, a girl who I first met in Darwin at the beginning of my travels, stumbled across me watching West Indies vs. Pakistan at the Melbourne Cricket Ground. Suzi left me totally bowled over and lovestruck.

We only got to share a few days together, enjoying the cricket, some koalas and wombats, and the spectacular sights of the Great Ocean Road. Then we parted company, agreeing to meet again a month later in Auckland. While Suzi and Megan departed for Adelaide and then Western Australia, I flew out to Christchurch to explore New Zealand, with the intention of following England's progress in the Cricket World Cup. I was so desperate for England to claim the big prize at last.

Separated from my new-found love interest, I tried to find some alternative magic in the form of Christchurch's famous Wizard, before travelling to Kaikoura to see how close I could get to some of the world's largest off-shore wedding tackle ... sperm whales are pretty impressive beasts.

I marvelled at the scenery of the Southern Alps, before heading south to Dunedin and across to Queenstown. There, I went jetting up a creek without a paddle, and also discovered that it takes the balls of a whale to bungee jump from the bridge at Skippers Canyon ... certainly far bigger balls than I was endowed with.

In Franz Joseph I encountered ice ... lots of it. Not only the spectacular glacier that was beating its retreat up the valley, but also a stunning Norwegian roommate, who was undeniably lacking in warmth. While in geological timeframes, Franz Joseph Glacier was rapidly melting, the frosty veneer of Brigit most certainly wasn't.

I joined the barmy army of English cricket supporters to see defeat in Wellington, but discovered both Wellington and Nelson to be rather less distinguished than the historical British heroes they were named after. As for my thoughts on Rotorua ... well, it literally stunk the place out.

I reached Auckland with towering expectations for resuming my love match with Suzi, and also for the England team to lift the World Cup. Such hopes were sadly dashed, due to a combination of a badly timed heart attack and some inspired Pakistani bowling.

My own heart is under attack this morning. I have way too much alcohol in my blood and I still cannot remember what happened last night. I don't know how badly I behaved, but I'll soon find out. What I do know is that I should be flying out of Auckland tonight.

[The third book of the series is Diary of a Shy Backpacker: iii. No Looking Back]

Thanks and Citations ...

I wish to thank all those people who provided inspiration for writing this book; from those who provided the memories from my travels, to those who now allow me the freedom to write, and even encourage me to do so. Special thanks to Monica and Sheila.

Sound Track ...

Thanks to the following artists whose songs, referred to in this book, helped to provide inspiration for BJ's journey.

[1] I don't like cricket, I love it (dreadlock holiday) – 10CC
[2] Every breath you take – The Police
[3] Is this love - Whitesnake
[4] She's so modern – Boomtown Rats
[5] Romeo and Juliet – Dire Straits
[6] You're going to lose that girl - Beatles
[7] Wonderful life - Black
[8] Here I go again - Whitesnake
[9] I want to know what love is - Foreigner
[10] Waiting for a girl like you - Foreigner
[11] When tomorrow comes - Eurythmics
[12] So far away – Dire Straits
[13] You can't hurry love – Phil Collins

Printed in Great Britain
by Amazon